1 The Blue and Yellow Suite
2 The Balcony Room
3 The Buhl Guest Suite
4 The Chinese Dining Room
5 India Room
6 Prince Philip's Suite
7 The Queen's Suite
8 The Queen's Study
9 Page's Office
10 Corgis' Room
11 The Queen's Dining Room
12 Gift Room
13 The Audience Room
14 The Mall

PLAN OF THE PRINCIPAL
FLOOR (FIRST)

1 Household Bedroom
2 Lady-in-Waiting's Suite
3 The Duke of York's Suite
4 Princess Royal's Suite and Offices
5 Prince Edward's Suite
6 Lift
7 The Queen's Wardrobe
8 Miss Macdonald's Suite
9 Lift

PLAN OF THE BEDROOM
FLOOR (SECOND)

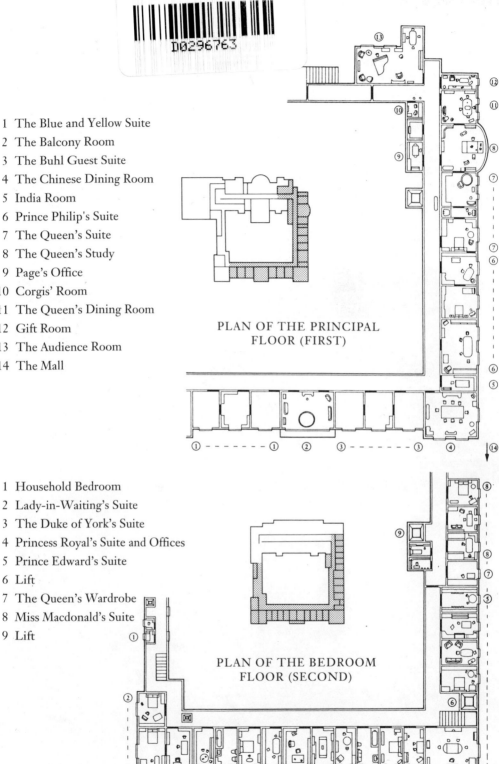

ALL THE QUEEN'S MEN

ALL THE QUEEN'S MEN

Inside the Royal Household

BRIAN HOEY

HarperCollins*Publishers*

HarperCollins*Publishers*,
77–85 Fulham Palace Road,
Hammersmith, London W6 8JB

Published by HarperCollins*Publishers* 1992

9 8 7 6 5 4 3 2 1

A catalogue record for this book is available
from the British Library

ISBN 0 246 13851 3

Photoset in Linotron Galliard by
Rowland Phototypesetting Ltd, Bury St Edmunds, Suffolk
Printed in Great Britain by
HarperCollinsManufacturing Glasgow

CONTENTS

LIST OF ILLUSTRATIONS   vi

THE QUEEN'S HOUSEHOLD   viii

THE MASTER OF THE HOUSEHOLD'S DEPARTMENT   x

THE ROYAL MEWS   xii

ACKNOWLEDGEMENTS   xiii

PHOTO CREDITS   xiv

PREFACE   xv

THE PRINCIPAL CHARACTERS   1

1   Headquarters   9

2   The Boss   24

3   The Great Officers of State   31

4   A Day in the Life of Buckingham Palace   36

5   The Lord Chamberlain   50

6   The Master of the Household   86

7   The Ladies-in-Waiting   107

8   The Keeper of the Privy Purse   113

9   The Private Secretary   133

10   The Press Office   149

11   The Crown Equerry   175

12   The Royal Collection   187

13   The Royalty Protection Department   200

14   Guards of Honour   206

Epilogue: The Values Unchanged   225

INDEX   232

ILLUSTRATIONS

Between pages 78 and 79

A coachman's livery costs over £1,000, while the preparation and decoration of The Queen's ceremonial horses takes several hours to complete.

The Earl of Westmorland, former Master of the Horse, leaving Buckingham Palace for The Queen's Birthday Parade.

Her Majesty's spiritual and temporal advisers – the Ecclesiastical and Medical Households.

The ten children of the Chapel Royal.

The Dean of Windsor, the Rt Rev Patrick Mitchell, with the Duke of York and Prince Edward following an Easter service.

Press Secretary Charles Anson with The Queen and Queen Elizabeth the Queen Mother in the Royal Box at the Derby.

Ian Thomas, one of the three designers who make the bulk of The Queen's wardrobe.

Clarence House, the London home of Queen Elizabeth the Queen Mother since 1952.

Cleaning the Royal silver.

Last-minute touches before the Royal party emerges from the Palace onto the rear terrace at a Buckingham Palace Garden Party.

A Garden Party at Buckingham Palace.

The Queen inspects her Yeomen of the Guard in the gardens at Buckingham Palace after presenting them with new colours.

The Queen inspects her Gentlemen at Arms.

The head of The Queen's Household, the Earl of Airlie, in his robes as a Knight of the Thistle.

One of the most colourful of all Royal occasions, the annual Garter Service held at Windsor Castle.

Between pages 142 and 143

Postilions getting dressed in their State uniforms prior to a rehearsal for the wedding of the Duke and Duchess of York.

The stables in the Royal Mews.

One of the five Rolls-Royce limousines in the Royal Mews being cleaned before being driven to collect The Queen.

A group from the Royalty Protection Department in formal morning clothes before leaving for Royal Ascot.

Lady Susan Hussey, one of The Queen's longest-serving
Ladies-in-Waiting, in an open landau with Sir Robert Fellowes,
Her Majesty's Private Secretary.

The Queen's racing manager, the Earl of Carnarvon, greets the
Princess Royal at Royal Ascot.

The Prince and Princess of Wales's office is one of the busiest in
Buckingham Palace.

The offices at Buckingham Palace receive more than 100,000 items
of mail every year from all over the world.

Felicity Murdo-Smith, the longest-serving member of the Palace Press
team.

One of the Master of the Household's staff makes sure the balcony is
in pristine condition before The Queen arrives with other members
of the Royal Family following the Sovereign's Birthday Parade.

Sir Kenneth Scott, The Queen's Deputy Private Secretary, and Sir
Paul Greening, the Master of the Household, on the balcony at
Buckingham Palace.

Sir Robert Fellowes, The Queen's Private Secretary, and Robin
Janvrin, the Assistant Private Secretary.

Philip Mackie, Press Adviser to the Prince of Wales, often
accompanies His Royal Highness on overseas visits.

Inspector Ken Wharf, the Princess of Wales's police officer.

The Hon. Mary Dugdale, The Queen's Ladies-in-Waiting.

THE LORD

THE PRIVATE SECRETARY'S OFFICE

Private Secretary to The Queen

Deputy Private Secretary

Assistant Private Secretary

Press Secretary

Deputy Press Secretary

2 Assistant Press Secretaries

Chief Clerk

Secretary to
the Private Secretary

Head of Information &
Correspondence Section

Clerks

Information Officers
Press Office

Clerks in Lady-in-Waiting's
Office

THE QUEEN'S ARCHIVES

Keeper of the Queen's Archives

Assistant Keeper

Registrar

Assistant Registrar

Curator of
the Photographic Section

THE PRIVY PURSE AND TREASURER'S OFFICE

Keeeper of the Privy Purse
& Treasurer to The Queen

Deputy Keeper of the Privy Purse
& Deputy Treasurer

Chief Accountant & Paymaster

Personnel Officer

Administrative Officer

Assistant Chief Accountant
and Paymaster

Assistant Personnel Officer

Superintendent of Public Enterprises

Accountants

Clerks

Clerk of Stationery

Land Agent, Sandringham

Resident Factor, Balmoral

ROYAL ALMONRY

Lord High Almoner

Hereditary Grand Almoner

Sub-Almoner

Secretary

Assistant Secretary

THE LORD CHAMBERLAIN'S OFFICE

Comptroller

Assistant Comptroller

Secretary

Assistant Secretary

State Invitations
Assistant

Registrar

Clerks

Permanent
Lords in Waiting

Lords in Waiting

Gentlemen Ushers

Extra Gentlemen Ushers

Gentleman Usher to
the Sword of State

Gentleman Usher
of the Black Rod

Serjeants at Arms

Marshal of
the Diplomatic Corps

Vice Marshal

Constable and Governor of
Windsor Castle

Keeper of the Jewel House
Tower of London

Master of the Queen's Music

Poet Laureate

Bargemaster

Keeper of the Swans

THE QUEEN'S HOUSEHOLD

CHAMBERLAIN

THE MASTER OF THE HOUSEHOLD'S DEPARTMENT	ROYAL MEWS DEPARTMENT	THE ROYAL COLLECTION DEPARTMENT
Master of the Household	Crown Equerry	Director of Royal Collection and Surveyor of The Queen's Works of Art
Deputy Master of the Household	Equerries	Surveyor of The Queen's Pictures
Assistants to the Master of the Household	Veterinary Surgeon	Librarian, The Royal Library, Windsor Castle
Chief Clerk	Superintendent Royal Mews	Deputy Surveyor of The Queen's Works of Art
Deputy to Assistant	Comptroller of Stores	Surveyor Emeritus of The Queen's Pictures
Senior Clerk	Chief Clerk	Advisor for The Queen's Works of Art
Clerks	Deputy Chief Clerk	Librarian Emeritus
Superintendent Windsor Castle	Office Keeperr	Curator of the Print Room
Assistant to Suprintendent		Registrar
Palace Steward		Assistant to Registrar
Chief Housekeeper		Assistants to Surveyor of The Queen's Pictures
		Inventory Assistant
		Clerks

Superintendent of the State Apartments, St. James's Palace

ASCOT OFFICE

Her Majest's Representative at Ascot

Secretary

ECCLESIASTICAL HOUSEHOLD

CHAPELS ROYAL

MEDICAL HOUSEHOLD

CENTRAL CHANCERY OF THE ORDERS OF KNIGHTHOOD

THE HONOURABLE CORPS OF GENTLEMEN AT ARMS

THE QUEEN'S BODYGUARD OF THE YEOMEN OF THE GUARD

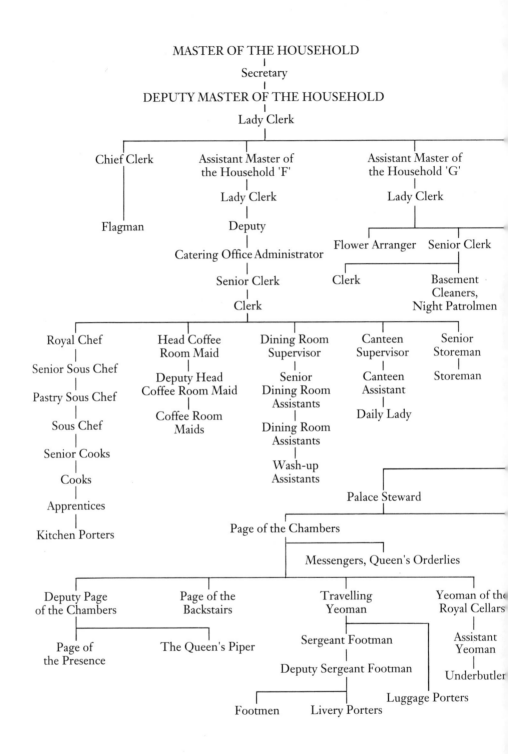

MASTER OF THE HOUSEHOLD
Secretary
DEPUTY MASTER OF THE HOUSEHOLD
Lady Clerk

Chief Clerk

Assistant Master of
the Household 'F'
Lady Clerk
Deputy
Catering Office Administrator
Senior Clerk
Clerk

Assistant Master of
the Household 'G'
Lady Clerk
Flower Arranger   Senior Clerk
Clerk   Basement
Cleaners,
Night Patrolmen

Flagman

Royal Chef
Senior Sous Chef
Pastry Sous Chef
Sous Chef
Senior Cooks
Cooks
Apprentices
Kitchen Porters

Head Coffee
Room Maid
Deputy Head
Coffee Room Maid
Coffee Room
Maids

Dining Room
Supervisor
Senior
Dining Room
Assistants
Dining Room
Assistants
Wash-up
Assistants

Canteen
Supervisor
Canteen
Assistant
Daily Lady

Senior
Storeman
Storeman

Palace Steward

Page of the Chambers

Messengers, Queen's Orderlies

Deputy Page
of the Chambers

Page of the
Backstairs

Travelling
Yeoman

Yeoman of the
Royal Cellars

Page of
the Presence

The Queen's Piper

Sergeant Footman

Deputy Sergeant Footman

Assistant
Yeoman

Underbutler

Footmen   Livery Porters

Luggage Porters

MASTER OF THE HOUSEHOLD'S DEPARTMENT

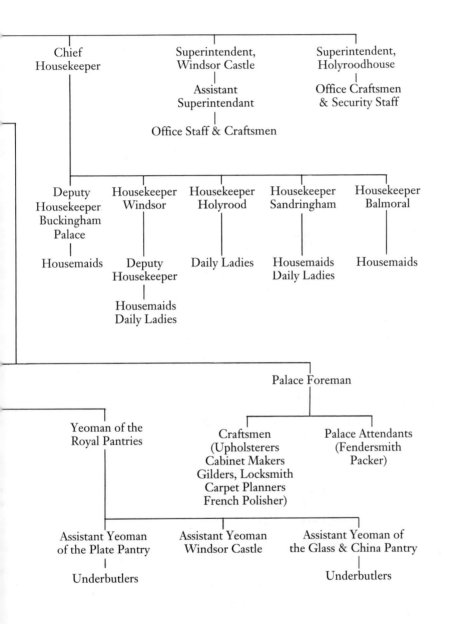

Chief Housekeeper

Superintendent, Windsor Castle
Assistant Superintendant
Office Staff & Craftsmen

Superintendent, Holyroodhouse
Office Craftsmen & Security Staff

Deputy Housekeeper Buckingham Palace
Housemaids

Housekeeper Windsor
Deputy Housekeeper
Housemaids Daily Ladies

Housekeeper Holyrood
Daily Ladies

Housekeeper Sandringham
Housemaids Daily Ladies

Housekeeper Balmoral
Housemaids

Palace Foreman

Yeoman of the Royal Pantries

Craftsmen
(Upholsterers Cabinet Makers Gilders, Locksmith Carpet Planners French Polisher)

Palace Attendants
(Fendersmith Packer)

Assistant Yeoman of the Plate Pantry
Underbutlers

Assistant Yeoman Windsor Castle

Assistant Yeoman of the Glass & China Pantry
Underbutlers

ROYAL MEWS DEPARTMENT

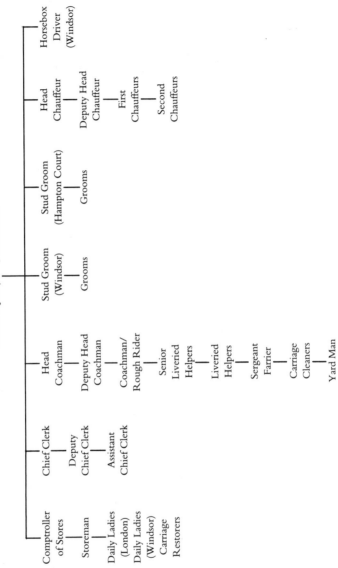

Crown Equerry / Superintendent

Comptroller of Stores
- Storeman
- Daily Ladies (London)
- Daily Ladies (Windsor)
- Carriage Restorers

Chief Clerk
- Deputy Chief Clerk
- Assistant Chief Clerk

Head Coachman
- Deputy Head Coachman
- Coachman / Rough Rider
- Senior Liveried Helpers
- Liveried Helpers
- Sergeant Farrier
- Carriage Cleaners
- Yard Man

Stud Groom (Windsor)
- Grooms

Stud Groom (Hampton Court)
- Grooms

Head Chauffeur
- Deputy Head Chauffeur
- First Chauffeurs
- Second Chauffeurs

Horsebox Driver (Windsor)

ACKNOWLEDGEMENTS

One of the strictest rules applied to members of the Royal Household is that they are never allowed to give interviews. Nor are they, either when they are employed by The Queen or subsequently, permitted to divulge information about the jobs they do or have done in the past.

Any author who intends to write about the Royal Family or the Royal Household is made aware of these rules, and he soon also becomes aware of the difficulties they impose on anyone who endeavours to portray the work of the Household in an authoritative and responsible manner.

Within the confines of these strictures, I have asked the Press Office at Buckingham Palace to check a number of facts relating to the Household, and these queries have been answered. This does not imply in any way that the Palace has approved my text or acted in any editorial capacity, simply that they were aware that I was writing this book.

I have also been able to call upon several present and past members of the Royal Household for guidance on a purely informal basis, and I am grateful for their help and assistance.

The figures quoted regarding staff numbers and the finances of the Royal Household are all matters of public record – the opinions, unless stated otherwise, are all mine.

PHOTO CREDITS

PREFACE

To attempt to write a precise description of The Queen's Household is a bit like trying to answer the age-old question, How long is a piece of string? For an organisation that has apparently remained almost constant for more than a century there appears to be a remarkable fluidity regarding the numbers of people involved and their precise duties day to day. To put it bluntly, Members of the Royal Household would be happiest if nothing were ever written about the way it works, and are reluctant – and that's an understatement – to reveal any but the most basic facts about their jobs.

For the purposes of this book I have tried to concentrate on Buckingham Palace, The Queen's London residence, where the Household, including administrative, clerical, manual and domestic staff, numbers just over three hundred. The other royal residences maintain skeleton staffs throughout the year, but when The Queen moves, the Court goes with her – in this Elizabeth II does not differ so very much from her ancestor Elizabeth I. This means that many of the jobs referred to in the text as relating to Buckingham Palace could just as easily be categorised under the headings of Balmoral, Windsor or the Palace of Holyroodhouse, although there are certain exceptions in Scotland. For instance, The Queen employs an Historiographer, a Painter and Limner and a Sculptor in Ordinary in the Royal Household in Scotland (all purely honorary posts), which she does not in any other part of the British Isles. But in the main when one writes about the work of key figures in her Household such as the Private Secretary, Master of the Household or the Keeper of the Privy Purse, one means The Queen's Household wherever it may be located – even on board the Royal Yacht.

Apart from Her Majesty herself, other members of the Royal Family maintain their own Households, several of them, including the Duke of Edinburgh, the Duke of York, Prince Edward and the

Princess Royal, inside Buckingham Palace. They are all officially listed as being part of the Royal Household, but for the purposes of this book I have, in the main, ignored their contributions and concentrated on the men and women whose daily task is to work directly for The Queen.

The domestic staff all serve under the umbrella of the Master of the Household's Department, while those who handle personnel matters, wages and salaries, pensions and Household expenses and pay Her Majesty's bills, work in the office of the Keeper of the Privy Purse. All aspects of the ceremonial side of the Monarchy are looked after by the Lord Chamberlain's Office while the Royal Mews provides transport for every occasion and the Private Secretary's office is responsible for every aspect of The Queen's work in political and public life. The newest department, and arguably the one with the biggest responsibility of all − certainly in terms of the value of the items for which they are accountable − is the Royal Collection Department, which, although it comes under the heading of The Queen's Household in Buckingham Palace, is actually based across the road in St James's Palace.

All these departments come under the overall supervision of the Lord Chamberlain, the Earl of Airlie, who doesn't involve himself in the daily routine of any of them. He just carries the can if anything goes wrong! Then there are the Great Officers of State such as the Lord Great Chamberlain, the Lord High Constable, the Earl Marshal and the Lord High Steward in addition to the political Officers of the Household: the Treasurer, Comptroller and Vice-Chamberlain. Strictly speaking, the Royalty Protection Department is a branch of London's Metropolitan Police, but their work in protecting the Royal Family is so vital and so much a part of every day and night within the palaces that it is included here. So too are The Queen's more decorative bodyguards: the colourful Yeomen of the Guard whose uniforms are so complex that they have to help each other to don them, dressing in pairs; the famous Yeomen Warders at the Tower and, in Scotland, the Royal Company of Archers and the High Constables of the Palace of Holyroodhouse.

Nowadays Buckingham Palace is run on a modern, almost commercial basis, with every department responsible for its own budget. This has led to a number of grumbles from within; as with any other large organisation, there will always be some people who resist change, but change there will be and eventually the modifications will be seen as improvements, even if somewhat reluctantly.

In the succeeding pages I have attempted to explain how the Royal Household works; who does what and why, and how much it all costs. I have dealt with the six departments that make up the Royal Household proper and also, briefly, with those who do not work full time but are nevertheless an integral part of the monarch's life: the Great Officers of State, including those who are appointed only for special occasions such as coronations, the ladies-in-waiting, perhaps the closest of all royal companions, and the policemen, some of whom spend more time with their royal charges than with their own families. Details of the Medical and Ecclesiastical Households are included, as are the Honourable Corps of Gentlemen at Arms and the Central Chancery of the Orders of Knighthood. The figures used in the chapter dealing with The Queen's finances are all from official sources and are the latest available at the time of writing.

A problem facing any author writing about the Royal Household is the lack of readily available information from official sources. I have been fortunate in being able to talk to a number of the Household on a non-attributable basis, and so I can reasonably claim that this version is as accurate an account of life inside the Royal Household as has yet been published.

BRIAN HOEY
Cowbridge 1991

THE PRINCIPAL
CHARACTERS

THE LORD CHAMBERLAIN

THE 13TH EARL OF AIRLIE, known as David to his family and close friends, was born in 1926 and succeeded his father in 1968. He has the classic background for a courtier; he was educated at Eton and served as a Lieutenant in the Scots Guards, seeing active service during the emergency in Malaya in 1948–9. Before joining the Royal Household he achieved distinction in the world of merchant banking, rising to become chairman of Schroder Wagg, a position he held from 1977 to 1984. He holds a number of other directorships including Scottish & Newcastle Breweries and the Royal Bank of Scotland. Most of his public offices are associated with his home country and he is President of the Scouts Association of Scotland and has been Lord Lieutenant of Angus since 1989.

It was in 1952 that he married Fortune Ryan, an American from Newport, Rhode Island, and they have six children, three sons and three daughters. The Countess of Airlie has been involved in Court life even longer than her husband. She has been a Lady of the Bedchamber to The Queen since 1973. She is also a Trustee of the Tate Gallery.

When Lord 'Chips' Maclean retired in 1984, Her Majesty invited the Earl of Airlie to replace him as Lord Chamberlain, at the same time making him a Privy Councillor and awarding him the GCVO. A year later he became a Knight of the Thistle, Scotland's senior Order of Chivalry. The Airlie family seat is at Cortachy Castle in the romantically named town of Kirriemuir, near Forfar in Tayside, which has been immortalised in the famous rugby song 'The Ball of Kirriemuir'.

1

THE PRIVATE SECRETARY TO THE QUEEN

The Queen has been served by six Private Secretaries since she came to the throne in 1952. The latest, who was appointed in 1990, is Sir Robert Fellowes KCVO, CB, PC who received his knighthood from Her Majesty in 1989 when he was her Assistant Private Secretary.

In becoming a KCVO Robert Fellowes followed his late father Sir William, who was The Queen's Land Agent at Sandringham, and it was while the family was living on the royal estates in Norfolk that Robert met his wife to be, Lady Jane Spencer, a sister of the now Princess of Wales. They were married in 1978 and have three children, a son and two daughters. Their home is a comfortable 'Grace and Favour' house at Kensington Palace, practically next door to the Prince and Princess of Wales.

Sir Robert's education and early life followed precisely the same pattern as that of the Lord Chamberlain, five years at Eton followed by a commission in the Scots Guards. He also then pursued a career in finance, becoming a successful discount broker with the leading City firm of Allen Harvey and Ross with whom he served as a director from 1968 to 1977.

He was recruited to the Royal Household by Sir Philip Moore, another former Private Secretary to The Queen, and his progress to the top of the Household ladder has been rapid. In fourteen years he has been promoted from an Assistant on probation, to his present position as The Queen's closest aide and easily the most influential person in the Household.

His manner is casual and he appears to be diffident, but his colleagues have found him to be a tough, uncompromising chief executive who knows exactly what he wants — and what he expects from them. When he is not on duty he likes to shoot and play golf, but he says his main pleasure these days is watching cricket, which is perhaps why one of his clubs is the MCC.

THE KEEPER OF THE PRIVY PURSE
AND TREASURER TO THE QUEEN

Perhaps the trickiest of all positions in the Royal Household is that of the man who has to balance the royal books. He also has to pay all the bills, sign the cheques and make sure the £7.9 million a year Civil List allowance is never overspent. An Irishman has this unenviable task, but as he has been doing it, first as Assistant Keeper and then in the top job, since 1975, he obviously does not find the chore too difficult.

Major Sir Shane Blewitt KCVO (he received his knighthood in 1989 after being made a Lieutenant of the Royal Victorian Order in 1981 and a Companion in 1987) has held his present post since 1988, during which time he has been involved in a management reorganisation within the Palace and has seen the accounting procedure used in the Royal Household streamlined to its present highly efficient system.

Born in 1935, Shane Blewitt was educated at the Roman Catholic public school of Ampleforth and at Christ Church, Oxford, where he obtained an Honours degree in Modern Languages before joining the Irish Guards in which he served for eight years, resigning his commission in 1974. He then began his career in finance with the firm of Antony Gibbs & Son but this lasted only until the following year when he was asked to become Assistant Keeper of the Privy Purse.

His wife Julia was a widow when they married in 1969 and there are four children: a son and daughter from this marriage, plus another son and daughter from Lady Blewitt's first marriage to the late Major John Morrogh-Bernard of the Irish Guards.

THE MASTER OF THE HOUSEHOLD

The present Master of the Household is a rarity among his colleagues in that he was not in any of the Guards regiments. The sole representative of the senior service, Rear-Admiral Sir Paul Greening KCVO comes from a naval family, his father being a distinguished and gallant Captain who won both the DSO and the DSC in the Second World War.

With such a background there was never any doubt about the direction the son's life would take, and after being educated at the nautical college at Pangbourne in Berkshire he entered the Royal Navy in 1946 at the age of eighteen. During his forty years' service he held a wide variety of commands, the two which equipped him best of all for his present post being perhaps Director of Officer Appointments and then, from 1981 until he retired from the navy in 1985, his command of *Britannia* as Flag Officer Royal Yachts. In that capacity he became friendly with all the members of the Royal Family and learned a great deal about their domestic requirements, which has of course stood him in good stead as Master of the Household.

Sir Paul has been married since 1951 and he and his wife Monica have two children, a son and daughter who enjoy staying with them at their elegant apartment in St James's Palace.

With some three hundred staff to look after and responsibility for all the royal residences, Sir Paul does not get a lot of free time, but when he does he likes to play tennis or work in his garden at his country home.

THE COMPTROLLER OF
THE LORD CHAMBERLAIN'S OFFICE

The ideal credentials for anyone wishing to work in the Lord Chamberlain's Office would be a military background, preferably in the Guards, plus a meticulous eye for detail and an enthusiasm for the ceremonial. All these requirements are fulfilled by Lieutenant-Colonel Malcolm Ross.

Born in 1943, he was educated at Eton and Sandhurst before joining the Scots Guards in 1964 and serving with them for twenty-three years. When he married in 1969, he could not have chosen a bride from a more military family. His wife Susie is the daughter of General Sir Michael Gow, who, when he retired from active service, had achieved the distinction of being the longest-serving soldier in the British Army.

When he was first appointed in December 1987 Colonel Ross, who is also a member of the Royal Company of Archers, The Queen's personal bodyguard in Scotland, had expected, in the normal course of events, to remain as Assistant Comptroller for some years as his immediate superior, George West, who assumed his appointment as Comptroller on the same date, is only a few years older. However, the sudden departure of Colonel West at th. beginning of 1991 meant rapid promotions within the department and Malcolm Ross found himself Comptroller responsible for all ceremonial aspects of The Queen's Household. He appears to be enjoying himself and, to use army vernacular, so far there have been 'no complaints'.

THE CROWN EQUERRY

The man charged with overall responsibility for The Queen's transport and with making sure all royal processions run to time is Lieutenant-Colonel Seymour Gilbart-Denham, who took over the Royal Mews in 1987. Born just after the Second World War broke out in 1939, he was only a year old when his father, a Colonel in the Irish Guards, was killed in action at Narvik in 1940.

When Seymour Gilbart-Denham was twenty years old he was commissioned into the Life Guards, the senior regiment of the British Army, and one of the two – the other is the Blues and Royals – which comprise the Household Cavalry. A successful military career, during which he saw service in Cyprus, Germany and the Far East, was crowned when he was appointed to command the Household Cavalry in March 1986, a post he held until July 1987. Like all senior officers in the Household Division, he came into contact with the Royal Family and, as Captain of the Sovereign's Escort, was the man who came closest to The Queen on ceremonial occasions.

Married with two daughters, Colonel Gilbart-Denham is a keen sportsman who is obviously, by the very nature of his job, at home in the saddle. He is also an excellent shot, expert angler and a more than competent skier.

THE DIRECTOR OF
THE ROYAL COLLECTION

When the Royal Collection was set up as a separate department within the Royal Household in 1988 there was only one obvious candidate for the job of being its first Director. Sir Geoffrey de Bellaigue KCVO had been Surveyor of The Queen's Works of Art since 1972 and his credentials were impeccable. Born in 1931, he was educated at Wellington College and Cambridge and, apart from a spell in merchant banking, has spent his entire working life in the world of fine arts. He spent some time with the National Trust and is now President of the French Porcelain Society and acknowledged as one of the world's experts on the subject. His books include the definitive work on Sèvres Porcelain in the Royal Collection, and to tour the State Apartments in his company is to view the treasures through another, and much more perceptive, pair of eyes.

Sir Geoffrey's wife Sheila is Registrar of The Queen's Archives at Windsor Castle and many authors working in the Round Tower to research their books have had cause to be grateful for her expertise and enthusiasm.

From this brief description it will be seen that all the Heads of Department in the Royal Household are men. In fact there has never been a female in charge of one of the main departments, either in this or any other reign. And while women have their place in the working Palace – indeed, it would be difficult to imagine it functioning without them – they have not figured largely in terms of holding positions of responsibility.

The Queen is known to prefer dealing with men on an official basis, and as a working monarch she has been surrounded and supported by men for more than forty years. It is a situation that is unlikely to change in the immediate future, as Her Majesty is an unrepentant traditionalist, and the thought of a woman becoming Private Secretary to The Queen is as improbable today as it would have been in Queen Victoria's time.

1

HEADQUARTERS

As the official London residence of The Queen, Buckingham Palace is the very symbol of British sovereignty. Yet it has been in the possession of the Royal Family for only a little over two hundred years. It is also the only official royal residence in the world which has kept a name bestowed on it by a nobleman – John Sheffield, Duke of Buckingham. Until the end of the eighteenth century, Buckingham House, which occupied the site on which the Palace now stands, was the London home of the Dukes of Buckingham. It was bought by King George III in 1762 for £28,000, and on 22 May of the same year, His Majesty and his eighteen-year-old consort, Queen Charlotte, moved in – the first royal couple to occupy the Palace. However, it was never intended to be the principal residence of the monarch. George III bought it as a suitable home for his wife if he should die before her.

When King George IV acceded to the throne he commissioned John Nash, the leading architect of the day, to design him 'a Palace fit for a King', and much of the structure, and even the decoration of Buckingham Palace as we see it today, are the work of Nash and his royal patron.

Buckingham Palace is unusual in that it is never open to the public, although on ceremonial occasions the State Apartments are accessible to a lucky few. Indeed, to really enjoy the Palace's true glories, one must be present at a State Banquet or official Reception, when all the State Apartments are in use. Servants in scarlet and gold livery, ladies in full-length ballgowns, complete with sparkling diamonds and glittering tiaras, and gentlemen in formal Court Dress, ceremonial uniforms or national costume, bedecked with decorations and sashes, all combine to bring to life the true brilliance of the Court.

But of course, Buckingham Palace, with its 19 state rooms, 52 bedrooms, 92 offices and 98 bathrooms, is far more than just the home of the Royal Family or a place of lavish entertainment. It is also the centre of an important administrative complex, where the affairs of State are handled by an efficient, modern and intensely loyal Household.

It is here also that The Queen receives foreign Heads of State, leaders of the Commonwealth and representatives of the Diplomatic Corps. And it is to Buckingham Palace that the crowds throng at times of national importance – victory in wartime, declarations of peace, royal weddings and funerals, and on the Sovereign's birthday. When a prime minister is asked to form a Government, it is here that he (or she) is given the formal request by The Queen.

Day in, day out, the business of a modern constitutional monarchy is conducted within its walls by a dedicated group of people devoted to their employer and her family. It is, quite simply, the most famous address in the world.

Visitors to Buckingham Palace, apart from those who are arriving as special guests of The Queen as part of a State Visit, usually enter the forecourt by the North Centre Gate. There, two police officers are permanently on duty to see that only those with business in the Palace are allowed in. As you wait while one of the policemen checks your identity and telephones from a tiny police box just inside the gates, you are aware of the curious scrutiny of the ever present onlookers from all over the world who crowd around the railings waiting for someone famous, preferably royal, to appear. Sometimes they are lucky, especially if Her Majesty is in residence, which you can tell by looking up at the roof. If she is there the Royal Standard will be flying; if not, then the flag-pole will be bare. During the time when The Queen is at Buckingham Palace, there is a good chance of seeing a well-known face. Even when she is not in residence, her daughter, the Princess Royal, pops in and out to work in her suite of offices on the second floor, and the Duchess of York also used the Palace as a headquarters during the working week.

Once your credentials have been approved you will be directed across the gravel forecourt to the Privy Purse Entrance – so called because at one time the doorway led directly to the office occupied by the Keeper of the Privy Purse, though now it's used by the Press Secretary. It's the entrance on the extreme right of the Palace as seen from The Mall, and as you walk the fifty yards or so you become acutely aware of the many eyes upon you as the onlookers detained beyond the Palace boundaries study your back. They are all wondering who you are, whether you are famous and why you have been given a privilege denied to them – access to The Queen's London home.

The five shallow steps leading to the Privy Purse Door are carpeted in red; not surprisingly rather shabby after years of wear and tear and being open to the elements. And, as you approach the door, it is opened by a liveried footman. At Buckingham Palace no one ever has to knock. The footman, one of thirteen employed in the Master of the Household's Department, who is clad in dark green frock-coat, black trousers, white shirt and striped waistcoat (unless a State Visit is in progress, when the dress will be a scarlet tail-coat), greets you by name and asks you to step into the waiting room.

The room is small and to the right of the Privy Purse door. It is furnished with gilt chairs covered in lime green silk, and there are two writing tables (but no paper or pens since visitors began taking items marked with the royal crest as souvenirs). There is an umbrella stand and a further small table on which are placed three newspapers, *The Times*, the *Daily Telegraph* and the *Daily Express* (the last once referred to by Prince Philip as 'that bloody awful paper'). No one seems to know why these should be the newspapers selected as required reading for royal guests, but they have been the choice for many years; and as such things rarely change at Buckingham Palace, it is likely that they will be in the waiting room for some time to come. The walls are adorned with three large paintings which are replaced from time to time, and on the marble mantelpiece is an ornate gilt clock which is usually a couple of minutes fast.

Until a few years ago anyone could enter the Palace simply by asking the police officers at the North Centre Gate for permission to sign the visitor's book. You would be directed into a tiny room alongside the main waiting room where you would be invited to sign your name with a pen provided for the occasion. Visitors to London often availed themselves of this opportunity, and were able to say afterwards that they had actually stepped inside The Queen's home. Unfortunately, because of the security risks involved, this practice was ended and nowadays the Palace is closed to all but official visitors. You can still ask to sign the book, but it's now kept in the police hut at the gate.

It is unusual for anyone to be left in the waiting room for longer than a couple of minutes because punctuality is a byword in the Royal Household, so shortly after you have arrived, and almost before you have had the opportunity to get your bearings, another footman will ask you to follow him.

As you walk into the Palace you can hardly fail to notice a number of furled umbrellas lying in serried ranks on an oak table in the entrance hall. These have been left by senior members of the Household. To many of the Private Secretaries and Assistants, former service officers (mostly from the Household Division of the Brigade of Guards), umbrellas are part of the 'off-duty' everyday uniform.

The Privy Purse entrance leads past an antiquated lift with wood panelling and mirrored walls. It was once slowed down on the personal orders of The Queen after Princess Anne, when she was very young, showed a tendency to try and frighten her older brother, Prince Charles, when they rode in the lift together to the schoolroom on the second floor.

Down the right hand side of the ground floor of the Palace lies a series of quiet dignified apartments whose doors, by long tradition, are rarely closed. As you pass you can occasionally pick up fascinating snippets of conversations conducted on the telephone: 'Yes, I think The Queen might like that,' or 'Her Majesty would love to accept but she is going to be in Nigeria at that time.' All tantalising to the curious visitor who is perhaps making his or her first visit to the Palace. This is where the most senior of The Queen's servants, her Private Secretaries, carry out the bulk of their daily duties. The corridor is lined with portraits of former Private Secretaries, each of whom has served the Sovereign with distinction and loyalty, and for most of whom the reward has been a peerage on retirement.

Sir Martin Charteris, now Lord Charteris of Amisfield, who served The Queen as Assistant and Private Secretary for many years before becoming Provost of Eton College (1977–91) is there. So too is Sir Philip Moore, a former member of RAF Bomber Command, prisoner-of-war in Germany and England rugby international, who was elevated to the peerage on his retirement in 1986 and now sits in the House of Lords as Lord Moore of Wolvercote. Also occupying a place of honour is Lord Adeane, whose family had served royalty for generations, until his son, Edward, resigned his post as Private Secretary to the Prince of Wales early in 1985 after six years' service. And the most famous Private Secretary of all, Lord Stamfordham, who served as Private Secretary to Queen Victoria and remained at Buckingham Palace for thirty years, completing his royal service in the reign of King George V.

The rooms occupied by the Private Secretaries and other confidential servants of The Queen are located immediately beneath her own apartments on the first floor, and while they are all comfortably furnished, by no stretch of the imagination could they be described as luxurious. Neither would any of the occupants wish them to be. They are functional and their main purpose is to provide working accommodation for the men whose sole task is to assist Her Majesty in the many duties associated with a constitutional monarchy.

If you arrive around 4.30 P.M. you may be invited to join members of the Household in the Equerries' Withdrawing Room overlooking the garden on the west side. Here they gather – all standing although there are plenty of chairs – to drink India or China tea out of bone china cups decorated with the royal cypher and munch biscuits as they chat informally. It is a daily ritual which has been carried out for as long as anyone can remember, and even though the men stay for only a few minutes, it makes a pleasant break in a working day, which for many in the Royal Household can last well into the late evening. It also gives them a chance to exchange news about the activities of each royal charge, rather as barristers, who enjoy a similar custom at the Inns of Court, might discuss the cases of the day.

In former times the Court was made up of gentlemen who all came from the aristocracy. They might seek preferment but had no need of a salary – and the Sovereign would never have dreamed of offering one. The actual business of monarchy, the writing of letters between the Sovereign and his subjects, was in the hands of learned men, almost all of them clerics, whose task was to conduct the royal correspondence without in any way offering advice or exercising any influence on their royal master. In the Middle Ages these were called Clerks and later Secretaries, becoming, by Elizabethan times, Secretaries of State. By this time too they had acquired power and influence, for they reported to Parliament, to which responsibility for government had moved. Today the great Offices of State – for Education, the Environment, etcetera – are political appointments made by the prime minister while the Queen's role in government has become largely, though not entirely, ceremonial.

Within her Household there are rigid divisions in the hierarchy, with three distinct categories of employee: Member, Official and Staff. Right at the top are the Members of the Royal Household: the Private Secretaries and Assistant Private Secretaries. These are the very cream of The Queen's servants, who come into daily contact with her and the other members of her family. They handle the royal diaries and accompany the family on duties in Britain and overseas. They are included in many social functions such as State Banquets and receptions and, from time to time, can be invited as guests of The Queen to Windsor, Sandringham or Balmoral. Most of them remain in royal service for many years and if they have not already received them by the time they retire, can usually rely on a knighthood or peerage at the end of a successful and loyal career. They live, rent free, in elegant 'Grace and Favour' houses and apartments loaned to them by The Queen, and their lifestyle is comfortable, in some cases luxurious, without in any way coming close to resembling that of their employer.

If they have reason to stay overnight at Buckingham Palace Members will be offered a pleasant room on the third floor; their bags will be unpacked by a servant and if they are attending a formal function in the evening a valet will press their clothes and lay out their outfits in perfect condition. If they wish, they may have breakfast, lunch and dinner in the beautiful Household dining room adjoining the 1855 room and alongside the Bow Room leading on to the terrace overlooking the Palace gardens, where they will be served by liveried footmen. If they feel like a whisky and soda in the early evening, another footman will oblige, again free of charge. Visits to the theatre are simplicity itself. Every London theatre keeps a small supply of tickets available to the Royal Household and similar arrangements are made with Wimbledon for the tennis champion-ships and every other major sporting event in the country. Two things, however, which are available to many other senior executives in leading commercial undertakings, are not granted to Members of the Royal Household: company cars and high salaries. The Private Secretaries, Assistant Private Secretaries and Comptrollers are paid Civil Service rates with the highest paid, The Queen's Private Secre-tary, earning around £60,000 a year; equivalent to a Permanent Secretary at the Home Office. Farther down the scale, salaries remain on the low side with very few members of staff earning more than £20,000 a year: not exactly paupers but by no means receiving what they could earn in banking or industry.

Expense accounts are practically non-existent, so whereas, in most commercial companies, executives expect to be able to make a small profit on their expenses, in the Royal Household there is no chance of that happening. The Keeper of the Privy Purse supervises all expen-diture and any costs incurred by Members when they are on The Queen's business are scrutinised in great detail to make sure nothing unnecessary has been added. This does not mean that Members of the Household have to stint themselves when they are abroad on reconnaissance trips prior to official visits. Far from it. They usually travel first class by air or, at the very least, business class, and the hotels they use are all in the five star category.

Similarly, at home they travel first class on British Rail and when they need transport around London for official occasions the Royal Mews will provide a chauffeur-driven car. But Members are never allowed the luxury of a car at the weekend or overnight, even if, for some reason, they happen to be working late. Legitimate expenses are allowed; but no extras.

So what are the advantages of working in the Royal Household and where do its members come from?

Clearly, the working conditions are very pleasant, but the main advantage of royal service is proximity to the Sovereign and her family. In royal terms power has always meant access to the monarch, and the closer one gets on a regular basis the more powerful one becomes. A former Crown Equerry, Sir John Miller, who retired in 1989 after more than a quarter of a century in royal service, reached a unique relationship with the Royal Family. He had taught most of them to ride at some time and because they spend so much time in the saddle (or in the Duke of Edinburgh's case on carriage driving) Sir John had developed a close relationship which went far beyond what is normal between the Royal Family and their servants. If he wanted to see The Queen he never had to go through the Lord Chamberlain's office or even the Private Secretary. He would simply telephone Her Majesty's Page and tell him he wanted to call in – and was never refused. During his long years at Buckingham Palace he was probably the only senior member of the Household with these privileges – and he exploited them unashamedly, taking great pleasure in by-passing the official channels of communication. This is just one example of the way in which power and influence at Court may be used.

There are three main reasons why a significant number of The Queen's senior advisers are former officers from the armed forces. In the first place, if they have served in the Household Division of the Brigade of Guards, they are likely to 'know the form' – which is considered quite important for those who will be in almost daily contact with The Queen. Then again, army officers are known for their attention to detail, and this is thought to be a prime qualification for anyone joining the Royal Household. The reason why every royal occasion goes so well is that nothing is left to chance; every tiny detail is checked and timed almost to the second in precisely the same way that military operations are planned. The final, and perhaps most practical reason why service officers are chosen, is that they are among the few people who can afford to take these jobs. To a man they are retired, but on a service pension; the salary from The Queen combined with rent-free accommodation at one of the best addresses in the country makes working at the Palace reasonably attractive. Very few other people of their seniority would be willing or able to subsidise the Royal Family in this way.

When Sir John Riddell became Private Secretary to the Prince of Wales in 1985, at a salary much higher than that paid to The Queen's Private Secretary, the money came from the Duchy of Cornwall not the Civil List. Even so, Sir John, who had been a very senior executive in a merchant bank, took a drastic cut in earnings to join Prince Charles's household. He didn't last very long in royal terms. For a number of reasons, one of which was said to be the attraction of his former career, he resigned after four and a half years and rejoined his bank at a salary believed to be at least four times what he was getting from the Prince of Wales.

The present Private Secretary to The Queen, Sir Robert Fellowes, was a highly successful discount broker in the City of London when he was approached to become Assistant Private Secretary. At that time his income was well over £30,000 a year – a substantial figure in the late nineteen seventies. When he joined the Royal Household, his salary dipped to around half that figure, but he was proud to be invited and delighted to forgo his former earning power.

For many years the Duke of Edinburgh employed Lord Rupert Neville as his Private Secretary at a salary of some £15,000 a year. When he died in 1982 his will revealed that he was worth over £30 million, so in his case the salary was completely irrelevant; but such courtiers are now few and far between. Britain is running out of landed gentry whose sons are encouraged to enter royal service purely for the privilege and prestige. The need today is for dedicated, intelligent and loyal servants who can attend to their duties with complete professionalism.

These then are the Members of the Household, those right at the very top. Next in order of descent come the Officials, the men and women who look after the day-to-day running of the various departments and without whom the Palace would cease to function. The Chief Clerk to the Master of the Household is an integral part of the team that organises the domestic side of the Royal Family's activities. Without his knowledge and experience of catering, book-keeping, supplies and industrial relations, Her Majesty's many social functions could never run as efficiently as they do. Similarly, the man who deputises for the Keeper of the Privy Purse is a qualified accountant with a formidable reputation for obtaining the best discounts when he authorises the payment of royal bills. In the Lord Chamberlain's office, the senior clerk, until recently, was John Titman, a man with over forty years in royal service and the last remaining person in the Household who had served in two reigns: those of The Queen and of her father King George VI. There was very little he didn't know about the ceremonial side of royal occasions and successive Comptrollers used his expertise to great effect at royal weddings, funerals, state visits and numerous other events on which an intimate knowledge of the protocol can mean the difference between triumph and disaster. When John Titman retired he was invited to a private audience of The Queen to make his farewells. As he entered Her Majesty's presence he received the biggest surprise of his life – The Queen knighted him on the spot as a mark of gratitude for his long years of service. He went in to say goodbye as plain Mr Titman; he came out as Sir John Titman KCVO.

Officials in the Royal Household are never promoted to become Members and to the outside world they remain largely unknown – which is how they like it. Anonymity is considered to be essential for Officials, and if they remain unsung heroes in the hierarchy of royal servants they are well satisfied. The Queen is all too aware of their value, as are their immediate superiors – and that's good enough for them.

At the bottom of the social scale come the Royal Household Staff. This is the umbrella term for all the domestic servants, junior clerical staff, manual labourers and ancillary workers, of whom around two hundred are employed. Life below stairs is a world of its own, and even here a strict pecking order is observed. The word of the Palace Steward, the senior of The Queen's domestic servants, is law among the Footmen, Butlers, Pages and Stewards who attend the Royal Family and the senior members of the Household.

One way of telling in which category of royal servant a person falls is to note how they are addressed. For example: Members address each other by their Christian names, no matter how senior in years or service they may be. The most junior Assistant Press Secretary, who might have joined the Royal Household only a few months before on secondment from one of the Commonwealth countries, would immediately call Sir Robert Fellowes, the most influential person in the Palace, Robert, and would be encouraged so to do. At this level there is an air of delightful informality between colleagues, even when they are furious with each other and in the midst of a blazing row.

Officials are never referred to by their Christian names. Surnames are always used, preceded by Mr, Mrs or Miss (there are no Ms's in the Royal Household) while they in turn refer to Members by their titles; as many of them are knights, it is a convenient and simple rule.

The Staff have it easiest of all; they call everybody above them Sir or Madam, while they, depending on age and length of service, will be addressed by their Christian name (at the junior end) or by their surname preceded by Mr, Mrs or Miss. The old practice of calling servants simply by surnames or job titles disappeared many years ago.

There are the odd exceptions to the rules, the most notable being Miss Margaret McDonald, The Queen's dresser. 'Bobo', as she is affectionately called by Her Majesty (but not by anyone else), has been the closest personal servant of The Queen for more than fifty years and occupies a position of considerable influence in the Royal Household. She is now nearly ninety and lives in a suite of rooms immediately above the private apartments of The Queen. Nowadays she does practically nothing by way of royal duties – yet she always appears to know everything that's going on, at Buckingham Palace and all the other royal residences, through a network of backstairs 'informers' who keep her up to date. She is not afraid to voice her opinion directly to Her Majesty if she feels that The Queen should hear it; and what she has to say is heard. As a dresser, a comparatively humble position, she is required to call all Members of the Household 'sir', and she complies with the order on every occasion – yet they all know that really she does not mean it. She is being correct, as custom demands, but even if she did not conform they would reprimand her at their peril!

There is only one exception to the accepted rules of address and that is the Lord Chamberlain, the Earl of Airlie. He is the titular head of The Queen's Household and though very senior Members who may have known him privately for many years will occasionally call him David, nearly everyone else addresses him as Lord Chamberlain at all times.

All the people who make up the Royal Household, the men and women who work full-time as servants to The Queen, come under the supervision of one of the six main departments: the Private Secretary's Office, the Keeper of the Privy Purse, the Lord Chamberlain's Office, the Crown Equerry, the Master of the Household and the Royal Collection. It is an amalgam of varying backgrounds and disparate talents, all working together to ensure the monarchy runs like a well-oiled machine. That is their only task; the reason for their very existence during their working lives. Each one is dedicated to the service of the Sovereign, and if one or two at the top of the tree like to regard themselves as more important than others farther down, it is all a matter of degree. In the eyes of The Queen they are all essential to her well-being and she is as appreciative of the efforts of a junior footman as of those of the Lord Chamberlain himself. He too recognises the importance of everyone knowing they belong to a team and goes out of his way to learn the names of all those men and women who rarely come into contact with any member of the Royal Family. The cleaners, gardeners and seamstresses in the Royal Mews are made to feel they are an integral part of the organisation, and this is a major part of the success of the largest household in the land.

If The Queen has described life at Buckingham Palace and Windsor Castle as like living in a village, it is not only because of the Household's size. It has its own community, gossip, rumours and counter-rumours – and its own hierarchy, which does not always coincide with the official order of precedence. Senior stewards and long-serving maids occupy positions of power and influence far beyond their official status and jealously guard any special privileges they enjoy, none more so than 'Bobo' McDonald with her unique relationship with The Queen.

The Household has its own football club and it has no difficulty in arranging fixtures with much more prestigious teams. After all, the secretaries enjoy receiving correspondence on Buckingham Palace headed writing paper. In their off duty hours the staff are entitled to wear the Royal Household Social Club tie which has navy blue, maroon and thin gold stripes.

The Royal Household is perhaps the most exclusive club in the world. You cannot apply to join – you have to be invited – and it maintains its air of exclusivity and its mystique, because, once inside, its members never discuss their jobs or conditions of employment – or talk publicly about their employer. It is a fascinating world that seems strangely anachronistic in this day and age. A world where liveried footmen wait on senior officials, where afternoon tea is still regarded as an integral part of the daily routine and where all the housekeepers, even those that are single, are addressed as 'Mrs'.

Some of the titles still in use seem incongruous in a modern organisation: Yeoman of the Glass and China Pantry; Page of the Backstairs and Pages of the Presence sound as if they have sprung from the pages of a history book, as indeed they have. Many of these titles originated in medieval times, but the men who hold them today play as vital a role in the organisation of The Queen's domestic life as ever in the past.

The Palace is a self-contained microcosm where it is possible to live and die without ever really finding out what life outside is like. It has its own bank and post office; there are cafeterias and social clubs. Rooms are provided for every member of staff who needs them. Houses and flats are given, rent-free, to married couples while they remain in royal service. If they have been loyal servants they can depend on a pension from The Queen and a 'Grace and Favour' home for life when they retire. Food and drink is provided free for staff on duty. It was once decided to charge the senior members of the Household for the spirits they consumed, when the Lord Chamberlain of the day felt the drain on The Queen's cellars was getting rather out of hand. But the experiment was short-lived. It cost so much to collect the money, they decided it wasn't worth the effort and the idea was abandoned.

No one ever seems to be in a hurry inside any royal residence. An air of quiet tranquillity prevails, rather like one of the older London clubs, and even though most of the departments have been modernised and computerised, there is still an atmosphere of dignified gentility; the idea of anyone running in the corridors is unthinkable.

One afternoon a Private Secretary to The Queen was leaving the Palace when he bumped into a visitor coming to see another of his colleagues. They chatted for a few minutes, neither, apparently, in much of a hurry, and then the Private Secretary excused himself with the words, 'I'm sorry if I appear to be in a bit of a rush, but I've just been told my house is on fire.' This was some years ago but such an occurrence could just as easily take place today; exquisite manners seem to be a prerequisite for all who serve The Queen.

By training and disposition the men and women who work in the Royal Household are reticent to what seems an almost extraordinary degree when it comes to personal publicity or talking about their job or their employer. They would far prefer it if no one ever wrote anything about them – favourable or otherwise – and if they share one quality above all others it is their loyalty to The Queen.

No matter what position they hold, whether they work directly for The Queen herself or for one of the other members of her family, all are guided by the same principle: is it good for Her Majesty? When the Duke of York, the Princess of Wales or the Princess Royal is considering an invitation, an engagement, a public function or overseas visit, each one asks the same question: 'How will this reflect on The Queen?' And if the answer is in doubt, their decision never is. Where there is doubt, there is no doubt. Any possibility that something might reflect badly on Her Majesty personally or on the monarchy as an institution and the reply is an immediate and definite 'No.'

Similarly, when the Private Secretaries meet to decide which of the thousands of invitations they will forward to their employers, even before they are discussed at royal level, the same criterion is applied. The entire operation at Buckingham Palace is geared to the well-being of The Queen, and no one is left in any doubt for a single instant that this is the case and indeed the sole reason for their existence.

Many articles have been written about the Royal Household, a number of them uninformed if well intentioned. So it comes as no surprise if its members are sometimes regarded as completely out of touch and lacking in contemporary experience. The truth is that they are all intelligent and cultured, capable and experienced, with wide-ranging knowledge of the outside world, some of which has been gathered at first hand while working in Commonwealth governments or British embassies abroad. The Household plays an important role in widening The Queen's already vast knowledge of the world, and if she were to rely, as has been suggested from time to time, only on the opinions of those who think as she does, and who tell her only what they believe she wants to hear, she would quickly realise the futility of their advice and dispense with their services equally rapidly. Today's Royal Household works with efficiency and economy, and while they still do not advertise, in the main, any of the more senior, personal posts, promotion within the Palace is based on a system of meritocracy rather than the nepotism that once prevailed.

There are few perks for those who spend their lives working in the Royal Household. The pay is not particularly good at any level and the hours can be very long. But housing and meals are provided by a grateful employer and it is pleasant for a young footman to be able to invite a friend to the Palace for a drink. Every member of the Royal Household, whether he or she comes from a family that has served royalty for generations or simply joined the domestic staff straight from the local jobcentre, finds a great deal of satisfaction in working for one of the best-run organisations in the world. Above all there is the knowledge that by helping to make life a little easier for The Queen, he or she is serving someone who fully appreciates what is done for her and who leads by dedicated personal example.

2

THE BOSS

THE ROYAL STANDARD, which flies above Buckingham Palace when The Queen is in residence, is the only flag in the country which is never flown at half-mast as a sign of mourning, even when the Sovereign dies. For in the eyes of royalty the monarchy never dies. Hence the cry on the death of a Sovereign: 'The King (or Queen) is dead: Long live the King.'

The words of Her Majesty Queen Elizabeth II in her Accession Speech delivered on 8 February 1952, just twenty-four hours after learning that her father King George VI had died in his sleep, were typically simple:

> By the sudden death of my dear father I am called to assume the duties and responsibility of sovereignty.

At twenty-five years of age, Elizabeth had become the forty-second sovereign of England since William the Conqueror, yet only its sixth Queen Regnant, monarch in her own right. At her coronation in Westminster Abbey on 2 June 1953, her full titles were revealed as: Elizabeth the Second, by the Grace of God, of the United Kingdom of Great Britain and Northern Ireland, and of her other Realms and Territories Queen, Head of the Commonwealth, Defender of the Faith.

Elizabeth Alexandra Mary, the first child of Prince Albert and Elizabeth, Duke and Duchess of York, was born on 21 April 1926, in a private house at 17 Bruton Street, the home of her maternal grandparents, in the heart of London's West End. Her father was the shy, introverted second son of King George V and Queen Mary (whom physically Elizabeth resembles more closely than her own mother). He had no expectation or desire to inherit the throne, and his elder brother David, the Prince of Wales (later Duke of Windsor) was confidently expected to marry and eventually provide heirs. So even though Elizabeth was third in line of succession at her birth, no one could foresee the events which ten years later would propel her from a place of comparative obscurity to the position of heir presumptive. For when King George V died in 1936 and his son David succeeded as Edward VIII, his reign lasted less than a year. He was never crowned and his love affair with a twice divorced American, Wallis Simpson, led to the Abdication and subsequent accession of his brother Bertie as King George VI.

From that moment Princess Elizabeth's training for her future role as Sovereign began. Her grandmother Queen Mary took it upon herself to help educate the young princess so far as the historical aspect of sovereignty was concerned. She insisted on dragging the reluctant princesses (The Queen's sister Princess Margaret Rose was born in 1930) around such historic London landmarks as the Tower, the Royal Mint and Hampton Court with rarely a thought about whether they were enjoying themselves – only that they were learning something of the background and traditions of the land over which one of them would one day reign. Neither princess went to school. They were educated privately by a succession of governesses and tutors; but this did not prevent The Queen, when the time came, from sending all four of her children away to boarding school.

Towards the end of the Second World War (1939–45) the nineteen-year-old Princess Elizabeth joined the ATS (Auxiliary Terri-torial Service). She was given the number 230873 – which she said she would remember for the rest of her life – and commissioned as a Second Lieutenant. She was taught how to drive and service heavy lorries, and driving, when time allows, has remained one of her pleasures.

The Princess's twenty-first birthday, celebrated in South Africa on 21 April 1947, was significant for the prophetic speech she made which was broadcast to the world. In it she dedicated her future life to the service of the people over whom she would shortly reign:

I declare that my whole life, whether it be long or short, shall be devoted to your service and the service of our great Imperial Commonwealth . . . But I shall not have strength enough to carry out this resolution unless you join in it with me . . .

It was in that same year, on 20 November 1947, that Princess Elizabeth was married to Lieutenant Philip Mountbatten, newly created Duke of Edinburgh. He had also been invested as a Knight of the Garter – but a week later than his wife in order to preserve her seniority.

Princess Elizabeth and her husband enjoyed only five short years of 'ordinary' married life before she became Queen. During those first five years two children were born: Prince Charles in 1948 and Princess Anne (now the Princess Royal) in 1950. Their 'second family' came ten years later with Prince Andrew (now Duke of York) born in 1960 and their youngest son Prince Edward arriving in 1964.

In the forty years that Queen Elizabeth has reigned she has become the most experienced Head of State in the world, and she is by far the most experienced political figure in Britain. She has been served by nine Prime Ministers, beginning with Sir Winston Churchill; the present Prime Minister, John Major, was just seven years old when she came to the throne. Her workload is prodigious. Every day, wherever she is in the world, the ubiquitous 'Red Boxes' containing communications (State Papers, telegrams and documents) from Ministers of the Crown are delivered to her desk. The contents are examined only by The Queen – she has one key and the minister who sent the box the other – and she reads every document. One of these is a report of the previous day's proceedings in Parliament which has been written for her by the Vice Chamberlain of the Household, a working MP and third in order of precedence of political appointments to the Royal Household.

The Vice Chamberlain also enjoyed the privilege of handing the Queen to and from her carriage. In the reign of William and Mary there was a Vice Chamberlain named Smith who took his duties very seriously. Queen Mary asked one of her ladies-in-waiting what a squeeze of the hand was supposed to indicate. 'Love' was the reply.

'Then,' said the Queen, 'my Vice Chamberlain must be violently in love with me because he always squeezes my hand.' Even today the Vice Chamberlain remains at Buckingham Palace during the State Opening of Parliament. He also carries communications between the Sovereign and Parliament. Official messages from the House of Commons, in the form of a 'Humble Address or Prayer', are taken to The Queen in audience, and her reply – always on the same day – is carried by the Vice Chamberlain who stands at the bar of the House immediately after prayers and announces to the Speaker: 'A Message from The Queen, Sir, in reply to a loyal and dutiful address from the House.' He then approaches the Table and reads the Message in full to the assembled Members. The Humble Address usually takes the form of a letter of congratulation after an important royal event such as The Queen's Silver Jubilee in 1977 or on Her Majesty's return from a particularly successful State Visit. The reply is the Sovereign's thanks for the Humble Address.

Arguably the most important achievement of The Queen's reign has been the development of her beloved 'Commonwealth family' as she herself calls it. One of the Commonwealth's elder statesmen, Kenneth Kaunda, former President of Zambia, says, 'She is loved not because she is Queen, but because of who she is first and foremost.' And Sir 'Sonny' Ramphal, former Secretary-General of the Commonwealth, is equally emphatic about the personal qualities of Her Majesty: 'There is no doubt in my mind, and the minds of all the leaders of the Commonwealth countries – and there are fifty today – that the Queen occupies a unique position which is unique because of who she is . . . She regards many of the Commonwealth leaders as personal friends and even those who have only recently taken over as leaders look to her for guidance and advice . . .'

The Queen has introduced a personal style to monarchy. She is by far the most widely travelled Sovereign in British history and has been seen by more of her people than all her predecessors combined. It was at her insistence that the 'royal walkabout' was first introduced. She wanted to meet more of the 'ordinary' people in informal surroundings, rather than the usual dignitaries who were always lined up to greet her on royal visits, both at home and overseas.

In 1969, Her Majesty allowed television cameras to film the Royal

Family for a year. The resulting programme brought the monarchy into people's homes and gave a fascinating insight into both the working life of the Sovereign and the private family life of the most famous woman in the world. The annual Christmas television messages broadcast by The Queen throughout the Commonwealth have become her own Christmas card to a family of nations which now numbers some nine hundred million.

Every year at least eighty functions are held at Buckingham Palace, ranging from the State Banquets and Garden Parties with thousands of guests to the monthly private luncheons given by The Queen for eight guests who come from all walks of life. These provide a unique opportunity for her to hear opinions from a wide variety of people, on any number of subjects from acting and the latest developments in television to the more pressing problems of the Third World.

In addition to all her public duties The Queen has the added responsibilities of the domestic arrangements in the royal residences. In short, she has to 'run the house' – something a male Sovereign would leave to his consort. The Queen is not only the nation's hostess, she is also mistress of the house; in fact several houses. She involves herself in practically every aspect of royal entertaining, giving a great deal of personal thought to the comfort of her guests.

She is aware of the need for servants to be supervised and although much of the day-to-day business of running the royal houses is of course left to her able Household she does not delegate this task entirely. Also, when new Members of the Household are being considered, each one is personally interviewed by The Queen before being offered a job. They will have been vetted by other senior courtiers but it is not unknown for The Queen to veto an appointment if she thinks the candidate unsuitable. For nearly all the top jobs, The Queen makes the same condition: 'Let's give it a try for a year. Then if we decide we can't stand each other we can let it go at that.' It is a convenient formula with a 'let-out' clause that applies to both parties. Farther down the scale, officials and most staff members are employed by the head of the department concerned. The Private Secretary, for example, chooses his own staff and that of the Press Office; the Keeper of the Privy Purse is responsible for the accounts personnel and the Master of the Household looks after the domestic staff. But when personal servants are engaged they are always interviewed by The Queen, and this comes as something of a surprise to a maid who expects to see only the housekeeper or perhaps the Master of the Household. The same system applies with other members of her family, when the Duke of Edinburgh, a Prince or Princess invariably conducts the interview. The Queen does not involve herself in any of these appointments. She is kept informed of all staff changes but leaves the choice strictly to her husband or children.

The largest Household outside that of The Queen is that of the Prince and Princess of Wales. Until 1989 their offices were located in a corner of Buckingham Palace's second floor but Prince Charles felt cramped as his staff expanded and asked his mother for permission to move to St James's Palace. To enable him to do so, the Lord Chamberlain's Office was transferred to Buckingham Palace, a move that was not received with any great enthusiasm by those who had previously enjoyed the best offices in the Royal Household. However, when one of The Queen's children wants something they usually get it and the change-over was made. The Prince of Wales wanted a separate establishment but he would be the first to deny that he has set up an independent Court. Others are not so sure. Members of The Queen's Household are convinced that by moving his centre of administration into what has for centuries been the seat of monarchy (foreign diplomats are still accredited to the Court of St James's) he has done precisely that, until the time when he becomes King.

In any case The Queen fully approved of the move and as we have seen has nothing to do with appointments made by either the Prince or the Princess. All the salaries and expenses, with the exception of the Waleses' Assistant Press Secretary, who works for The Queen, are paid by the Duchy of Cornwall which is the personal fiefdom of the heir to the throne.

Privately Her Majesty leads a very quiet life. She enjoys country pursuits: riding, walking and training gun-dogs. Her one passion in life is horse-racing on which she has become one of the most knowledgeable experts in the world. But she still has one unfulfilled ambition – to win the Derby; something achieved on two occasions by her great-grandfather King Edward VII. Her personality remains something of an enigma. She retains the shyness and reserve that characterised her early life, yet with close friends she relaxes into a warm, humorous, fun loving person. Her laugh is unaffected and spontaneous; the royal glare so glacial it can freeze a senior politician at ten paces – the only way The Queen ever shows disapproval in public. She is a loving mother and doting grandparent but the quality she possesses above all others is her devotion to duty. Nothing can interfere with the business of monarchy and hers is a job for life. When she was anointed at her Coronation she inherited a sacred trust, and as far as she is concerned it is a lifetime trust which cannot be broken.

Elizabeth II is the longest-reigning British monarch since Queen Victoria – the last Queen Regnant, who reigned for almost sixty-three years. Their predecessor Elizabeth I occupied the throne for forty-four. Today's Queen has adapted to the times but has refused to adopt any of the vulgarity of the latter part of the twentieth century. And throughout the world, though other female sovereigns may occupy similar positions, a reference to 'The Queen' leaves no doubt which one is meant. A headline about 'The Queen' refers to Elizabeth II.

3

THE GREAT OFFICERS
OF STATE

BEFORE LOOKING AT the Royal Household in detail it might be helpful to explain the difference between the officials who are commonly supposed to constitute the working Household and those whose titles single them out as the Great Officers of State but who are by no means occupied at the Palace from day to day.

In fact, although much has been written over the years about these Great Officers of State, the late Randolph Churchill was able to state categorically in his book *They Serve The Queen* that no such being exists because no Royal Warrant or Act of Parliament has ever called them into being. The true designation for what we commonly call the Great Officers of State should be Great Officers of the Realm. However, the official programme of the Coronation of Queen Elizabeth II, issued by the Earl Marshal, clearly indicates that there are Great Officers of State; and call them what you will, there are still eight:

The Lord Chancellor
The Lord President of the Council
The Lord Privy Seal
The Lord Great Chamberlain
The Lord High Constable
The Earl Marshal
The Lord High Steward
The Lord Chamberlain

Of these only five have any responsibilities in the Royal Household today and even these in certain cases are merely titular. The first three:

31

Lord Chancellor, Lord President of the Council and Lord Privy Seal, are held by active politicians with full-time jobs in Parliament, so theirs are government appointments with no contemporary royal duties; while the Lord Chamberlain, the last figure in the list, is the only one to retain day-to-day responsibilities in the Royal Household.

The Lord Great Chamberlain was originally head of the Sovereign's personal household and all royal palaces. The office dates back to the reign of Henry I, the youngest son of William the Conqueror and a popular king who reigned from 1100 to 1135. Since that date the Lord Great Chamberlain has always come from one of the same three families: the Cholmondeley family (who are the present holders of the office and who hold it every alternate reign) and the Ancasters and Carringtons, who each hold it every fourth reign. The family of the present Lord Carrington or his heir will assume responsibility on the death of Queen Elizabeth II.

The present-day duties of the Lord Great Chamberlain consist of attending the Sovereign's coronation. He stands on the immediate left of the monarch in Westminster Abbey, fastens the clasp of the Imperial Mantle after the Investiture and then arrays the newly-crowned monarch in purple robes before the procession out of the Abbey. He also makes some of the arrangements for the State Opening of Parliament as the Keeper of the Palace of Westminster, where he has a permanent office in the House of Lords, manned by a secretary, who is usually a very senior retired service officer, and a clerk.

Also originated in the reign of Henry I was the office of Earl Marshal, the premier Duke of England, which has been hereditary in the Norfolk family since 1672. The Earl Marshal is head of the College of Arms and, in conjunction with the Lord Chamberlain, has overall responsibility for the arrangements of the monarch's funeral and other State funerals. (The Queen decreed, for example, that the funeral of Sir Winston Churchill should be a State Occasion.) He also heads the committee which organises the coronation, though he no longer has the right to certain perks claimed by his ancestors: being allowed to keep the horses used to convey the Sovereign to and from Westminster Abbey, the tablecloth used at the banquet held in Westminster Hall and all the fines for offences committed on Coronation Day. From this short list it is obvious that the duties do not arise too frequently and otherwise the Earl Marshal has little connection with the everyday running of the Royal Household.

The Lord High Steward is among the most ancient of all Great Offices but his duties these days are purely ceremonial. Nobody knows precisely when the office was instituted but royal records show that it was certainly before the reign of Edward the Confessor (1042–66), when the Lord High Steward ranked as the first Great Officer under the Crown. The last permanent holder was the Duke of Clarence, son of Henry IV (1367–1413). Today it is a temporary appointment for a coronation, at which the Lord High Steward has the honour of carrying St Edward's Crown (the one used for the actual crowning as opposed to the Imperial State Crown which is worn before and after) and during the ceremony takes precedence over all other laymen in the procession. At The Queen's coronation the Lord High Steward was Admiral of the Fleet the Viscount Cunningham of Hyndhope.

The office of Lord Steward, the titular head of the Master of the Household's department, originated in the Middle Ages when the Royal Household was the centre of public business, and it was in control of Civil List expenditure until the late eighteenth century, when an Act of 1782 transferred to the Treasury the functions of the Board of Green Cloth, the Lord Steward's financial committee. Today the Lord Steward, who is always a peer – the present holder of the office is Viscount Ridley – is in attendance at Court on all important ceremonial occasions including State Visits where, at the Banquet, he presents guests to the Queen and the Duke of Edinburgh and to the visiting Head of State. During the State Opening of Parliament the Lord Steward can be seen walking backwards before The Queen as she processes from the Robing Room to the House of Lords. He no longer has to pay the Household accounts or look after any of the domestic arrangements in the royal palaces as in days gone by, but he does preside at the Board of Green Cloth, a committee of The Queen's Household charged with examining and passing all Household accounts. The name is derived from the green-covered table at which its transactions were originally conducted.

The Lord High Constable is a non-hereditary appointment and is made for only a limited period to cover the duration of a coronation. He receives the Royal Regalia from the Lord Chamberlain's Comptroller as it enters Westminster Abbey. For The Queen's coronation in 1953 Field-Marshal the Viscount Alanbrooke, one of Britain's most distinguished soldiers, was appointed Lord High Constable.

The Lord Chamberlain is head of The Queen's Household, and although in centuries past he was deputy to the Lord Great Chamberlain, today he is completely independent. As head of the Household he has responsibility for all six departments within the Palace, and his personal responsibilities involve all ceremonial aspects of the monarchy apart from the Sovereign's funeral and coronation. He acts as emissary between The Queen and the House of Lords (where he sits on the Cross Benches) but he has no department of his own within the Royal Household. Even the one which bears his name, the Lord Chamberlain's Office, is not, in practice, his personal kingdom. The Comptroller runs it with the Lord Chamberlain having very little to do with its day-to-day administration.

One other office which is not listed above but which ranks as a Great Officer of the Household is that of Master of the Horse, currently Lord Somerleyton. Once one of the most powerful and influential positions at Court, the Master of the Horse is responsible for The Queen's safety whenever she is mounted or in a carriage. To this end, he must be as close to The Queen as possible. At the Trooping of the Colour ceremony he rides immediately behind her, and when she attends the State Opening of Parliament, it is his duty to ride in the next carriage. When Queen Victoria was crowned she was unmarried, so the Master of the Horse rode with her and the Mistress of the Robes in the State Coach.

In the days when the Sovereign also constituted the seat of government in Britain, the Great Officers of State were not only members of the King or Queen's personal household but officers of Parliament as well. But as power devolved to the people and Parliament became independent of the Crown, so the duties of these former members of the Royal Household came to be taken over by the political administration of the day. Today we have politicians bearing titles such as: Lord Chancellor; Lord Privy Seal; Lord President of the Council;

the three White Staff Officers, who carry a white stave on certain ceremonial occasions, are the Treasurer, Comptroller and Vice Chamberlain of the Household; and the Captains of both Royal Bodyguards: the Honourable Corps of Gentlemen at Arms and the Yeomen of the Guard. All are political appointments made by the prime minister in power, and changed accordingly, and each one has important governmental duties which take precedence over their responsibilities to the monarch. The Treasurer of Her Majesty's Household is Deputy Chief Government Whip while his colleagues the Comptroller and Vice Chamberlain are also Whips who work full time in the House of Commons. The Captain of the Honourable Corps of Gentlemen at Arms is the Government Chief Whip in the House of Lords while his Deputy Chief Whip takes on the junior role of Captain of the Queen's Bodyguard of the Yeomen of the Guard. The Lord Chancellor is Speaker of the House of Lords and the senior legal authority in the country, while the Lord Privy Seal is Government Leader in the House of Lords and the Lord President of the Council is Leader of the Commons. These political appointees are all paid out of public funds according to their political duties and not as members of the Royal Household.

4

A DAY IN THE LIFE
OF BUCKINGHAM PALACE

THE TIME IS 6.45 A.M. It is still dark outside as a solitary light comes on in a room on the second floor of the North Front of Buckingham Palace. The Princess Royal is awake and ready to leave for the 100-mile drive down the M4 motorway to the stables in Gloucestershire where she rides out for her trainer David Nicholson. The Palace is silent as she walks along the corridor lined with portraits of long-dead ancestors, takes the lift to the ground floor and joins her police officer who is waiting there. There is a brief 'Good morning, Your Royal Highness' from him and no more talk. He knows from long experience that the Princess is not very chatty first thing in the morning.

The uniformed policeman on the gate recognises the Reliant Scimitar with its distinctive number plate 1420 H (a twenty-first birthday present from one of her regiments, the 14th/20th Hussars) and the Princess at the wheel. None of her policemen has ever been allowed to drive her anywhere, apart from a short period in 1990 when she lost her licence after a speeding offence. The man in charge of the gate talks softly into his radio set, informing his colleagues in the traffic department that her Royal Highness is setting off.

Back inside the Palace things are beginning to stir as a new day starts for the three hundred men and women who work in the Sovereign's London residence. For the single men and women, carefully segregated, each in a different part of the Palace, the day's routine starts with a rush for the bathrooms, while the married men who occupy flats in the Royal Mews walk to work through the underground passages to the main building of the Palace. Those who live

36

out – about a quarter of the total workforce – have to get up a lot earlier than their colleagues as their duties all commence at the same time.

The Palace Steward, Anthony Jarred, the senior domestic servant to The Queen, moves into his private kingdom on the ground floor. He checks that all those who should be awake and about their duties are on time. A junior footman serves the steward with his early morning tea in his sitting room just off the main kitchen. Mr Jarred has worked his way up through the ranks and knows every domestic job in the Palace backwards – and what to look for when his staff think they have managed to get away with something. He carries out on-the-spot inspections, never giving any notice of his intentions, and junior footmen, perhaps preparing the royal table for a State Banquet, find out that the legends are true. He really does carry a ruler with him to measure that each knife, fork and spoon is exactly the right distance from its neighbour.

The Head Chef Lionel Mann and his team have started to prepare the breakfast menus for the Royal Family and the staff. These were all agreed at the beginning of the week, when The Queen and the Master of the Household were offered a selection of menus and ticked the ones they preferred for the week ahead. The same system is employed in all the royal homes, the lady of the house, the Princess of Wales, Princess Margaret, the Queen Mother and so on deciding at 10 o'clock on Monday morning what they will eat for dinner on Thursday evening. It has been followed for generations and seems to work to everyone's satisfaction.

Anybody who works at the Palace is entitled to meals free of charge but those married servants who live in Grace and Favour apartments in the Royal Mews generally cook their own food. The single staff eat in cafeteria-style canteens below stairs. The food is plentiful, always fresh and beautifully prepared.

Nevertheless, at the side entrance in Buckingham Palace Road, a van from J. Lyons and Company is delivering fresh bread and rolls. The days when every slice of bread eaten at the Palace was home baked on the premises have long gone, as has the system of having two entirely separate kitchens – one for the Royal Family and one for everyone else. It was a former Master of the Household, Sir

Geoffrey Hardy-Roberts, who in the nineteen-sixties persuaded Her Majesty, without too much trouble, that it was a ridiculous waste of time and money to have two establishments doing almost the same work, simply because an ancient and outdated custom dictated that nothing served at the royal table should find its way into the mouths of commoners.

At 7.30 The Queen is woken by her maid who brings in the early morning tea – a special blend made solely for Her Majesty by R. Twining & Company of The Strand, London, who have the distinction of being London's oldest ratepayers, having occupied their premises continuously since 1706. The tea is served with milk but no sugar, as the maid draws the curtains in the first-floor bedroom overlooking Constitution Hill and prepares to draw The Queen's bath. Just along the corridor the Duke of Edinburgh is already up, drinking the first of several cups of coffee he will consume during the next hour or so.

Once The Queen and the Duke have bathed and dressed they meet in the breakfast room where they usually have the first meal of the day together at half past eight. Both occasionally enjoy a cooked breakfast of scrambled eggs, sausages and bacon, but just as often simply have fruit juice and toast with tea for Her Majesty and coffee for the Duke – he never drinks tea. The coffee too is a special blend, made just for the Royal Family by the Savoy Hotel Coffee Department. They had another important but non-royal customer during the Second World War, when General Eisenhower insisted on having a supply of their coffee delivered to him wherever he was throughout Europe.

On the ground floor the senior members of the Household have all arrived and taken their first glance at the day's newspapers and the morning mail. If anything particularly unusual or important has happened they will have been in touch with each other by telephone even earlier.

Throughout the Palace the heads of the various departments will be preparing for their daily meeting with colleagues. These always start at 9 A.M. and coffee is served. When Sir Philip Moore was The Queen's Private Secretary, he tried to make it a rule that all the other Private Secretaries and their Assistants turned up for a working meeting around the breakfast table. But some of those who lived nearby preferred to eat at home and the idea was quickly dropped. Sir Robert Fellowes, The Queen's Private Secretary, will have arrived on his bicycle from his home in Kensington Palace. He reckons he can do the journey in far less time than it would take if he drove a car, and it also helps to keep him fit. He is joined by the Deputy and Assistant Private Secretaries and the Press Secretary and together they go through the day's business. Elsewhere in the Palace, the Master of the Household, the Crown Equerry, the Comptroller of the Lord Chamberlain's Office and the Keeper of the Privy Purse are holding similar meetings with their own staff.

The meetings last no more than half an hour as The Queen is ready at her desk overlooking Green Park by 9.30 every morning. A digest of the day's news has been prepared for her by the Press Officer on duty who will have read all the national newspapers. Items of particular interest to The Queen will have been marked or cut out, and important articles will be filed for future reference.

If Parliament is sitting, Her Majesty also has before her a report on the previous day's proceedings at the Palace of Westminster. This is prepared for her by the Vice Chamberlain of the Household, but he no longer has to write it out himself, as was done until fairly recently. These days the report is produced on a word processor. It is part of the required reading of Her Majesty and a duty she does not shirk no matter how boring or repetitive it may seem. Both Lord Home and Lord Callaghan of Cardiff have recalled that The Queen referred to these reports on numerous occasions when they were prime minister, and heaven help either one of them if, at their regular Tuesday evening audience, they had not done their homework thoroughly and she caught them out.

The first duty of the three Private Secretaries to The Queen is to sort through the varied correspondence addressed to Her Majesty. With more than 100,000 letters a year being delivered to the Palace it's quite a job. There is a post office in the basement and every item of mail is scrutinised by a team of three men using a fluoroscope to make sure they contain no explosives. Letters from friends are recognised by the initials of the writer in the lower left-hand corner and are passed unopened to Her Majesty. (If she replies in her own hand the letters are either sent by registered post or hand delivered to avoid any possibility of their being retained by souvenir hunters.) Official letters may be passed to the appropriate Government department for action, and there are also many routine enquiries which the Private Secretaries can answer without consulting Her Majesty. Letters from children are given to one of the Ladies-in-Waiting for a reply.

Letters sent to The Queen range from the pathetic to the paranoiac: it might be a mother asking Her Majesty to intervene on behalf of a son who has been convicted of an offence; an eccentric demanding the influence of the royal prerogative over some invention he claims has been stolen by a large business concern; letters from lunatics offering marriage – and many other kinds of relationships – and petitions from the more responsible and obviously sane majority of the population for a variety of causes. Then there are those who write to every member of the Royal Family, knowing they will receive a reply even if it is only a two-line acknowledgement, simply for the thrill of receiving an answer on Buckingham Palace paper.

Almost all official papers arrive in leather-covered boxes, invariably referred to as Red Boxes though they are sometimes green or black. The majority of them are covered in scarlet or dull red morocco leather, with a brass handle for carrying and the words 'The Queen' engraved in gold.

Each Government department has its own collection of Red Boxes, some of them very ancient. They are used not only for despatches between Buckingham Palace and Whitehall but also, untitled, for carrying secret and highly confidential documents between various Government offices. They are delivered to The Queen wherever she is: London, Windsor, Sandringham or Scotland. Even when she is sailing on board *Britannia*, a helicopter will rendezvous every morning and deliver the mail for her attention. The Queen is the only person in the country, apart from the Prime Minister, who receives information from not just one or two but every Government department. And she is unique in that she also receives the same amount of intelligence from all the countries of the Commonwealth – which the British Prime Minister does not. Overnight telegrams from Commonwealth countries are delivered each morning, some of which will be digests prepared by the resident British High Commissioners, and others, which the diplomats will not be aware of, direct reports from the governments concerned. The Foreign Office also sends background briefings on some of the most important stories which have appeared in the press.

Another frequent duty of The Queen is the centenary telemessages which are sent when any subject reaches their one hundredth birthday. Around 2,000 of these are sent every year and Her Majesty likes to vary the content of the greeting. These telemessages are not sent automatically. Relatives or friends inform the Palace well in advance of the birthday date and a copy of the relevant birth certificate is required to verify the claim.

Besides the paperwork, The Queen will have a number of visitors to see. If an overseas tour is in the planning stage, one or more of her dressmakers will turn up to discuss the wardrobe. The designers themselves will arrive by the Privy Purse entrance, while their assistants, with bundles of materials, are admitted by the side entrance in Buckingham Palace Road. It's not snobbery; it's just that as with most large houses goods are not allowed through the front door. The Queen employs the services of a number of well-known designers and inside her wardrobe-room each is assigned his own space. So when, say, Ian Thomas arrives, the dresses of the other designers will be concealed behind large full-length mirror doors. Obviously they all know they do not enjoy exclusive rights to dressing The Queen but it is yet another example of Her Majesty's good manners and one which is greatly appreciated.

When The Queen is due to visit a town for an engagement the correspondence between the hosts and the Palace can run to dozens of letters and many more telephone calls. Will the Queen accept a bouquet of flowers from the Mayor's grand-daughter? Yes, but it must be small and unwired. (This is so that the flowers can be used again and to avoid any danger of the royal finger being pricked.) Can we offer a gift? Yes, but again it should be small and not too expensive or ostentatious. Details must be sent in advance to the Palace and approved. If a meal is included in the itinerary the menu must be submitted and approved. The Queen likes the plainest of food, no fancy sauces and definitely no shellfish. And no more than an hour for lunch. Neither Her Majesty nor the Duke of Edinburgh likes to dawdle over meals. What do we do about lavatories for the royal party? One should be set aside for the exclusive use of The Queen and her lady-in-waiting informed of its location. If a church service is to be included, is it permissible to offer the collection plate to The Queen? Yes, and if she is accompanied by Prince Philip, he will often agree to read the lesson. If a plaque is to be unveiled the precise wording must be agreed beforehand and the position of the cord to be pulled by Her Majesty carefully explained. A substitute will carry out several rehearsals before the big day anyway just to make sure the mechanism works perfectly.

Presumably for security reasons the names and dates of birth of all guests at the royal function must be notified to the police. But must ladies wear gloves if they are to be presented? It is left entirely to the person concerned; these days Her Majesty is very relaxed about things like that. If there is to be a reception, should a chair be provided for The Queen? No, Her Majesty can stand for hours without showing the slightest sign of fatigue. If The Queen is arriving by car, who opens the door? Her police officer who will be sitting alongside the chauffeur. All these detailed questions have been asked before, but every one receives a full and polite answer. That is why what is a routine occasion for the Royal Household always becomes for every-one else a memorable event.

At 10.30 there may be a meeting of the Privy Council. These take place once a month. There are around four hundred members of the Council but for normal business it is usual for only half a dozen or so to be present. Three Privy Counsellors form a quorum. The number and who they are depends on the business of the day. The nucleus of the Privy Council are men and women who hold, or have held, high government office, but archbishops and the most senior bishops of the Church of England are also included as well as a number of men and women who have achieved distinction in a variety of fields and who have been appointed as a personal honour. The Queen's Private Secretary is always made a Privy Counsellor in order that he can see confidential Cabinet papers. The Cabinet is the most important of all Privy Council committees and no one is allowed to sit in the Cabinet without first being 'sworn of the Council' and taking a solemn oath to 'preserve The Queen's secrets'. Members of the Cabinet 'advise' The Queen on the legislative action they propose and then, after enactment in the House of Commons and the House of Lords, their proposals must be authorised by The Queen in Council – which means that a quorum has to assemble in person before her so that she can agree. It might be anything from an increase in Value Added Tax to a declaration of war, but unless the Council physically meets and The Queen gives her approval in person it is not law.

There are occasions when The Queen is unable to be present in person – she may be on a State Visit overseas. When this happens, substitutes in the form of Counsellors of State act for her. They are all members of the Royal Family and by law are The Queen's husband, Queen Elizabeth the Queen Mother and the four adults next in line of succession to the throne: the Prince of Wales, the Duke of York, Prince Edward and the Princess Royal. If The Queen is not present, at least two Counsellors of State attend.

Membership of the Privy Council is for life but the only active working members are those who form part of the government of the day. Indeed Counsellors who are members of opposition parties are not permitted to attend the monthly business meetings. The only exception would be on the death of the Sovereign, when the full Council assembles; and after the Accession Council has legally declared the name of the person entitled to succeed, the full Council meets once more to take the oath of allegiance.

If The Queen is to announce the forthcoming marriage of one of her children, all the Counsellors will be invited as the only item on the Agenda will be non-governmental. At the Privy Council meeting to announce the engagement of the Prince of Wales in 1981 nearly three hundred turned up.

For a normal meeting, once the Agenda has been agreed by the Lord President of the Council, the Leader of the House of Commons, the ministers of the government departments concerned will be summoned by the Clerk of the Council in precisely the same way and using the identical wording that has been used for centuries:

> Let the Messenger acquaint the Lords and Others of Her
> Majesty's Most Honourable Privy Council that a Council
> is appointed to meet at the Court of Buckingham Palace
> on Tuesday [the date follows], at 10.30 of the Clock A.M.

As a courtesy a copy of the Summons is always sent to the Duke of Edinburgh to inform him that the meeting is taking place. The Agenda will have been delivered to The Queen in advance so that she is fully briefed on the business to be transacted, and Her Majesty always receives the Lord President of the Council before the meeting.

The office of Lord President of the Council is one of the most prestigious in the country, ranking ninth after the Sovereign in order of precedence. Only four commoners are higher placed: the Archbishop of Canterbury, the Lord Chancellor, the Archbishop of York and the Prime Minister. The Speaker of the House of Commons follows the Lord President in the list.

Once the Lord President and The Queen have concluded their meeting, the other Privy Counsellors are invited to enter the room in strict order of precedence, the Clerk of the Council bringing up the rear. Each approaches The Queen, bows, shakes hands and moves to his or her appointed place. It is a ritual that has been followed for hundreds of years and it never varies. The Queen stands at the head of a small round table with the Lord President of the Council on her right and the Clerk on her left. The meetings are held in the 1844 Room, named after the year Tsar Nicholas I of Russia stayed in it as a guest of Queen Victoria, and the entire meeting is conducted with everybody standing up. Her Majesty says just one word after each government proposal is placed before her: 'Approved' – without it the business of government would not function.

Although these days most Privy Councils are held during the working year at Buckingham Palace, Councils can be convened anywhere The Queen wishes. She has called for Privy Council meetings to be held at Balmoral, Windsor, Sandringham and even at private houses where she has been staying as a guest. Privy Councils have also been held on board the Royal Yacht *Britannia*; the most romantic of these occasions was in 1956 when, during a tour of the Scottish islands, a meeting was called to enable The Queen to give the Royal Consent to the marriage of Captain Alexander Ramsey, a great-great-grandson of Queen Victoria, to Miss Flora Fraser.

Normally a Privy Council lasts only about half an hour at the most, yet it is the oldest, and in many ways the most important part of the Sovereign's government, dating back to Norman times when the chief source of executive power was the Sovereign in Council. This form of government continued until the eighteenth century, when the system of Cabinet government developed, and it is from the Privy Council that even today all other forms of official administration originate.

About 10.30 one of the State carriages is despatched from the Royal Mews by the Crown Equerry, Lieutenant-Colonel Seymour Gilbart-Denham. He is responsible for all transport arrangements by road for the Royal Family: by car, carriage or on horseback. This particular morning a carriage is required to collect a new ambassador from his residence and bring him to Buckingham Palace where he will present his credentials to The Queen.

As the carriage enters the Forecourt of the Palace the Changing of the Guard is taking place, watched through the railings by hundreds of tourists who turn up rain or shine every morning in the summer and every other morning in the winter months. There is also a small select group who have been invited to view the ceremony from inside the Palace Forecourt. This morning they are from the Girl Guides of America Association and their invitation has been arranged through the office of the Keeper of the Privy Purse. It is not too difficult to organise a special treat such as this; you simply write to the Keeper, well in advance of the date you want, and if there is no other booking on that day, and you belong to a group considered worthy of the privilege, permission will be granted.

The incoming ambassador, accompanied by members of his entourage, all dressed in formal Court dress, tail-coat, knee breeches and black silk stockings with buckled shoes, or national costume, is met by the Master of the Household on the steps of the Grand Entrance inside the main Quadrangle and conducted into the royal presence. The Queen will have been briefed on the diplomat's background and once the formalities are over she chats for a few minutes with her guests, displaying, to their great pleasure, a remarkable knowledge of their country and themselves. Although St James's Palace is still officially the seat of monarchy in Britain and all members of the Diplomatic Corps are accredited to the Court of St James's, these days the business of monarchy is conducted entirely at Buckingham Palace during the working year, at Windsor Castle on other occasions and at the Palace of Holyroodhouse in Edinburgh for one week only, when the Court moves to Scotland early in July.

The meeting with the ambassador and his staff lasts only about half an hour, but it is an essential part of the routine of The Queen and one which she regards as being as important as any of the other tasks she is required to perform in her role as Head of State.

Elsewhere in the Palace the various department heads are carrying out their many duties. Sir Paul Greening, the Master of the Household, consults the Palace Steward and the royal chef about the menus for any of the eighty or so functions that are held in Buckingham Palace every year. There is a State Visit planned some months ahead and the advance party from overseas have arrived to check the arrangements. Sir Paul shows them the Belgian Suite where the Head of State will be accommodated and the rooms in which members of his entourage will stay. Later The Queen herself will inspect the accommodation. It's something she does before every visit even though she knows that the Master of the Household and his team will have made sure everything is as perfect as can be. As hostess for the nation The Queen takes extra pains to ensure that her guests want for nothing and by looking at the rooms and checking the floral arrangements and all other items herself, she shows her guests that she takes a personal interest in their welfare, and her own staff that she appreciates their efforts.

In his office on the ground floor of the North Wing, Lieutenant-Colonel Malcolm Ross, the Comptroller of the Lord Chamberlain's Office, is preparing for one of the fourteen Investitures which takes place every year, at each of which 150 men and women will be presented with their award for public service personally by The Queen. He writes to one recipient explaining as tactfully as he can why only two guests are allowed to accompany each person. The State Ballroom simply isn't big enough for everyone who would like to come. His department looks after all the ceremonial aspects of The Queen's work, and even though all the formal occasions are organised precisely as they have been for many years, so that the routine has been refined to a polished art, every official function is approached with as much care as if it were being prepared for the first time.

On the second floor Lieutenant-Colonel Peter Gibbs, the Princess

Royal's Private Secretary, is dealing with a flow of enquiries about a forthcoming visit to Africa. This is only the start of what will become a torrent once more details of the schedule are revealed. He also knows that when they return there will be a massive influx of mail to be answered. It always happens when the Princess visits a Third World country for the Save the Children Fund, of which she is President.

Elsewhere on the same floor the tiny staffs of the Duke of York and Prince Edward are dealing with a mountain of paperwork that never seems to diminish. The Duke's staff consists of a joint Private Secretary and Treasurer, a Comptroller and Assistant Private Secretary and a lady clerk. Prince Edward has a Private Secretary and Equerry. Invitations to open factories, attend events and make speeches continue to pour in, and every one receives careful and serious consideration – and a polite reply.

In the Press Office on the ground floor, the Press Secretary and his team are discussing the press, radio and television coverage of several events in the coming year. An important occasion in 1992 was the 40th anniversary of The Queen's Accession to the Throne on 6 February, with extensive coverage from all sections of the media. At the service in Westminster Abbey both the BBC and ITV asked for the best positions. Press Secretary Charles Anson had to balance the claims of both so that everyone was satisfied and, more importantly, ensure that The Queen was happy with the arrangements.

The computers in the Privy Purse office are humming away as the accounts department deals with the hundreds of invoices and statements that have to be checked and paid. The Palace prides itself on always paying on the dot – and on obtaining the best discounts.

The ladies who clean the Palace have been busy all morning, changing the beds, vacuuming the carpets, polishing and dusting. If a member of the Royal Family passes while they are working in one of the corridors, they will curtsey and reply to the greeting they always receive. Although only a tiny part of Buckingham Palace is used by the Royal Family itself, all 351 rooms are kept in immaculate condition throughout the year. It's a continuous process and at least one housekeeper has described it as 'like painting the Forth Bridge. When you finish at one end you start again at the other.'

At the end of a working morning at the Palace The Queen usually lunches alone, except on those days when she has invited guests. If a close member of the family is in the Palace they may well be asked to join her, but they do not drop in uninvited.

In the afternoon Her Majesty will often have an engagement in the London area. The royal chauffeur brings the Rolls-Royce Phantom limousine (one of five) around from the Mews where he parks at the garden side entrance – which cannot be seen from outside. Her Majesty's personal detective checks that all is as it should be and that a rug is ready to cover the royal knees.

Shortly before The Queen is due to leave, several of the most senior members of her Household will gather to see her off. It happens every time, an old custom which no one can remember starting; and they will appear again when she returns.

Late in the afternoon the Lord Chamberlain, the Earl of Airlie, Sir Angus Ogilvy's elder brother, and brother-in-law of The Queen's cousin Princess Alexandra, may come to call. He is titular Head of the Royal Household, but there is no question of his simply popping his head around the door. He has to make an appointment like everyone else, by telephoning Her Majesty's Page, a senior domestic servant who is stationed throughout the day in an ante-room adjacent to The Queen's sitting-room, to see if she is free. The Page then informs Sir Robert Fellowes' office in keeping with the rule that no one sees Her Majesty without her Private Secretary's knowledge.

Of course all the senior members of the Royal Household know one another, and if they need information frequently speak on the internal telephone. But there is a curious formality about life at Buckingham Palace and many of the communications between the various departments are conducted in writing. All the offices have an extensive filing system and one of the golden rules seems to be 'let's refer back to the files'. When Sir John Riddell was Private Secretary to the Prince of Wales he earned a reputation for never once answering a direct question; he always preferred to 'refer back'.

One age-old custom that has survived at Buckingham Palace is that of afternoon tea. The Queen enjoys the daily ritual of cucumber sandwiches, Dundee cake and tea which she pours herself; replenishing the hot water from a kettle mounted on a special swivel stand designed for her by Prince Philip.

Towards the end of the day there is always another pile of documents to be read, initialled and acted upon; but if there is no official function to attend the evening will be free. The Private Secretary and his staff leave around seven and the Press Secretary goes home shortly after. But someone from the Press Office is permanently on call, and there are not many nights without a telephone call from the other side of the world about some aspect of the Royal Family's life and work.

The Queen likes a quiet supper, sometimes served on a tray as she sits in front of the television set. The Duke of Edinburgh is often out at night attending a service dinner or giving a speech to one of the many organisations for which he works.

As darkness settles over Buckingham Palace, the gates are closed until morning, the security men and dogs patrol the gardens and when The Queen retires, a uniformed police sergeant takes his place on a chair outside her bedroom where he will sit all night. He wears slippers instead of heavy regulation shoes, the only concession to the informality of night.

Downstairs the police office is manned throughout the night and often the last light to be seen in Buckingham Palace is The Queen's as she works on her papers. The business of monarchy never stops.

5

THE LORD
CHAMBERLAIN

THE LORD CHAMBERLAIN is titular head of the Royal Household with overall responsibility for all its departments. In theory at least he is in charge of everything.

Since The Queen came to the Throne in 1952 she has been served by five Lord Chamberlains: the Earl of Clarendon (who was Lord Chamberlain to King George VI for fourteen years, and who remained with The Queen for the first eight months of her reign, until the new Household was established), the Earl of Scarbrough, Lord Cobbold, Lord Maclean and the present holder of this distinguished office, the Earl of Airlie.

The one characteristic shared by these latter four appointments is that each was made personally by Her Majesty. She might have consulted with a number of people: senior members of her Household or leading politicians such as former Prime Ministers Lords Callaghan and Wilson, and, perhaps the most important of all, her husband the Duke of Edinburgh. But the final decision rested with The Queen herself, and when a new Lord Chamberlain is chosen he can be sure that it is because Her Majesty wants him and not just because she has been advised that he might be 'suitable'.

It wasn't until the first Labour Government was formed by Ramsay MacDonald in 1923 that the Sovereign was given the right to make this choice. Until then, the Lord Chamberlain had been appointed by the prime minister and a new Lord Chamberlain took office upon the formation of each new government. But Ramsay MacDonald did not feel that, as the head of Britain's first Labour

Government, he could recommend anyone who would both perform the role to the satisfaction of King George V and at the same time be acceptable to his socialist colleagues in Parliament. So in true political style a compromise was reached. The King found someone he wanted; he told the Prime Minister, who in turn formally submitted the name back to him.

Since that time the appointment of the Lord Chamberlain has remained in the personal gift of the Sovereign. The first non-political appointment was Lord Cromer, who accepted the post in 1923 and occupied it until 1938, including the brief spell when Edward VIII was on the throne in 1936. He was succeeded by Lord Clarendon, who remained, as we have seen, throughout the reign of King George VI and until The Queen had settled in at Buckingham Palace and chosen her own Household in the latter part of 1952.

Her first choice was Lord Scarbrough, who, even though this was a 'non-political' appointment, had a wealth of experience in political matters as he had served in the House of Commons for ten years, first as Member of Parliament for Hull and later as Member for York. He had also been Governor of Bombay and put his knowledge of India to good use when he became Under-Secretary of State for India.

When Lord Cobbold became Lord Chamberlain he was able to utilise the vast financial knowledge he had acquired as Governor of the Bank of England to compile a masterly report on the finances of the monarchy. This was presented to Parliament in 1971 at a time when a major inquiry into the cost of the monarchy was under way and there was some danger that, without such an illuminating and carefully prepared document, the exercise might have proved a humiliating experience for The Queen and her family.

The present Lord Chamberlain, Lord Airlie, is also putting his years of experience as Chairman of merchant bankers Schroder Wagg to good use on behalf of Her Majesty. The recent review of all Household expenses and the decision to invite a firm of management consultants to look into the way the Royal Palaces are run were both taken under his leadership and are discussed further in the chapter on the Privy Purse.

In the days when the office of Lord Chamberlain was still a political appointment it was not always the safest of positions, in fact on at least one occasion it was extremely dangerous. In the fifteenth century a Lord Chamberlain named Sir William Stanley, the younger brother of the first Earl of Derby, was beheaded in the Tower of London for his part in a rising against Henry VII. His high position at Court was no defence. There was no appeal. The King's word was final.

Nowadays the office requires a great knowledge of ceremonial and social behaviour but no great practical knowledge of day-to-day life at Buckingham Palace and the other royal residences and nearly all the Lord Chamberlains, recognising the truth of this, have been 'part-timers', coming into the office only two or three times a week or when their presence was required for a State Occasion. The exception was Lord Maclean who served from 1971 to 1984. He was a full-time Lord Chamberlain and lived 'over the shop' in an attractive Grace and Favour apartment on the corner of St James's Palace. This was because, unlike his predecessors, he had no other job: no great estate to manage or business to run. Until he was approached by Lord Cobbold, who was about to retire and was assisting The Queen in finding a replacement, Sir Charles Maclean (as he then was) had been Chief Scout of the Commonwealth. His appointment came as a complete surprise to most of the senior members of the Royal Household; he had simply failed to come into the reckoning owing to the fact that he was not a peer, a minor omission immediately corrected by The Queen when she offered him the position and conferred a Life Peerage on her new Lord Chamberlain. Lord Maclean was to become one of the most popular of all Lord Chamberlains, with both the Royal Family and his colleagues, but his continual presence was sometimes slightly wearing, especially to senior members of the Household who were not used to having to look over their shoulders in case the 'boss' was around.

As head of The Queen's Household, the Lord Chamberlain's responsibilities range from Court Ceremonial and Court Mourning, royal weddings and funerals (except those of the Sovereign which are the responsibility of the Earl Marshal), to the cleaning of the Crown Jewels and the care of the 5,000 pictures in the Royal Collection. In between come the State Visits by overseas Heads of State (there are usually two or three every year), the three annual Garden Parties at

Buckingham Palace and the one at the Palace of Holyroodhouse, to each of which some nine thousand invitations are hand written; making sure all the right flags are flying at all the royal residences and, after consultation with Her Majesty, making all appointments to the Royal Household. For within his department come officials with distinguished and, in many cases, ancient titles; and each position is filled with as much dedication and taken just as seriously today as they were centuries ago.

There is a Marshal of the Diplomatic Corps, whose tricky task is to keep all the members of London's many embassies and high commissions happy in their dealings with the Palace, and there is a Constable of Windsor Castle, who is not a policeman but a retired very senior service officer who lives in a grand house surrounded by the largest inhabited fortress in Europe and whose duties are to supervise the running of the Castle. Within the Ecclesiastical Household are a Clerk of the Closet, three Priests in Ordinary and someone who rejoices in the title of Organist, Choirmaster and Composer, though he is not called upon to do a great deal of the last. The Medical Household contains Apothecaries at Buckingham Palace, Windsor Castle and Sandringham and a Coroner to the Queen's Household, whose royal role cannot be too demanding as there has been only one death in suspicious circumstances in the past twenty years. This was a case of a young maid committing suicide over a love affair with a footman who turned out to be homosexual. But the Coroner's post is mainly honorary in that he is a doctor with an outside practice who can be called on when required.

Until 1968, an important part of the Lord Chamberlain's duties was to act as official censor for all plays which were to be performed publicly in Britain. For centuries, playwrights and theatre managers brought their scripts to the Lord Chamberlain's Office where, for a fee that was two guineas in the 1960s, they were scrutinised by 'readers' specially brought in for the task. It was their job to see that nothing 'unsuitable or blasphemous' was licensed for public performance: hence the old description of the 'legitimate' theatre, meaning that the play had been passed, or licensed, by the Lord Chamberlain. The Theatres Act of 1968 ended this role of censor and the part played by the Lord Chamberlain in the theatrical life of the country.

Sir John Johnston, a former Comptroller, says that when he first came into the Lord Chamberlain's Office he was told that theatrical producers sometimes brought their latest female starlets along when trying to influence the Lord Chamberlain's staff, and legend had it that at one time there was a 'casting couch' in St James's Palace; but no one would admit to ever having seen it, let alone used it. If in fact it ever happened, it wasn't in Sir John's day. Perhaps it was just another good showbusiness story.

The passing of the Theatres Act brought to an end another 'perk'. It had been the practice for many years for those who worked in the department to visit the theatres where plays licensed by the Lord Chamberlain were performed. In theory they were there to see that no extra lines had been inserted after the licence had been granted, but what it really meant was that the Lord Chamberlain's staff enjoyed free seats to any show in town. They had only to telephone the theatre manager and let him know they intended to see the show and he provided the best seats in the house, drinks in the interval and occasionally supper afterwards. It was an innocent 'bribe' that did no one any harm as all the shows had been passed long before, but as salaries in the Royal Household have never been of the highest it meant a night out that few could have afforded otherwise. All this ended in 1968.

As Head of The Queen's Household, the Lord Chamberlain acts as Chairman of The Lord Chamberlain's Committee, consisting of the Heads of Departments of the Household and meeting once a month. He is also Chairman of the Committee of Royal Warrants of Appointments, the body which awards Warrants and the right to display the royal coat of arms to certain individuals and companies who have supplied goods or services to The Queen, the Queen Mother, the Duke of Edinburgh or the Prince of Wales for a minimum of three years. Other responsibilities (all exercised through the Comptroller) include the Lords and Grooms-in-Waiting (with the exception of the six political appointments mentioned in the chapter on Great Officers of State), the Ecclesiastical and Medical Households, the Gentleman Usher of the Sword of State, the Gentlemen at Arms, the Yeomen of the Guard, the Royal Company of Archers (The Queen's Bodyguard in Scotland), the Gentlemen Ushers, the

Serjeants at Arms, the Central Chancery of the Orders of Knighthood, the Master of The Queen's Music, the Poet Laureate, the Royal Library, the Royal Palaces, Her Majesty's Bargemaster and Watermen and, one of the most colourful titles in the entire Household, Keeper of The Queen's Swans.

As the man responsible to The Queen for all the ceremonial surrounding the Royal Family, even in these days when his position is regarded as non-executive, the Lord Chamberlain is very much the person in command. No decisions regarding the Royal Household are taken without his agreement, and in the final analysis it is he who has to answer to The Queen. It is a job that requires the utmost tact and diplomacy. For example, the Lord Chamberlain (through the Marshal of the Diplomatic Corps) supervises the arrangements for incoming foreign diplomats to present their credentials to The Queen, and occasionally ambassadors and ministers from certain countries may not be aware of the protocol involved. Then it's up to the Lord Chamberlain and his staff to explain, as delicately as possible, what is required.

The procedure never varies when an incoming High Commissioner or Ambassador is received in audience by The Queen in order to present his Letters of Credence. No matter the size and status of the country the diplomat represents, the Crown makes no distinction; all are treated with equal courtesy.

On the morning of the audience the Marshal of the Diplomatic Corps, in full Court dress, travels to the diplomat's residence in a State landau from the Royal Mews. There he collects his honoured guest to bring him to Buckingham Palace. The diplomat is usually accompanied by senior members of his staff, all of whom ride behind the State landau in other carriages provided by the Palace. The timing will be perfect, for a carriage will have covered the same route before with a coachman, stopwatch in hand, checking the time taken and assessing the amount of traffic at that particular time of day.

Waiting to greet them at the Grand Entrance to the Palace are the Vice-Marshal of the Diplomatic Corps and the Equerry-in-Waiting to The Queen. They conduct the party to the top of the shallow steps where the Comptroller of the Lord Chancellor's Office is introduced, along with the Permanent Under-Secretary at the Foreign and

Commonwealth Office. They then proceed to the Bow Room on the ground floor (the room best known to members of the public, as they have to pass through it to get to the rear terrace at Garden Parties) and from there to the 1844 Room next door. Here The Queen is waiting for them and, as they approach, with the Marshal of the Diplomatic Corps on one side of the diplomat and the Comptroller of the Lord Chamberlain's Office on the other, they take one pace forward, bow from the neck, another pace and another bow. At this point the Marshal of the Diplomatic Corps formally announces the diplomat and then he and the Comptroller withdraw, leaving The Queen and her guest alone. He walks towards her, bows once more and shakes the hand that is offered. He then presents his Letters of Credence and his predecessor's Letters of Recall. Once these little formalities have been completed The Queen will chat for a few minutes. She will have been briefed about the diplomat and if he happens to have come from one of the Commonwealth countries she will have visited it and probably knows it well. Not all the conversations are conducted in English. If French is the mother tongue of her visitor Her Majesty pays him the compliment of using that language, which she speaks fluently.

After five minutes or so The Queen will invite her guest to present his entourage who have been waiting just outside the door and who enter one by one. The Marshal of the Diplomatic Corps then brings the wife of the diplomat into the room to be formally presented. She usually curtseys before Her Majesty although during the years of the Cold War some women from the eastern European republics felt such a salutation might be frowned upon. The Queen did not insist; she is very relaxed about such formalities from those for whom they are not the accepted custom. At one time however there was very nearly an international incident when the American Ambassador refused to wear Court dress to be presented to Queen Mary. Court dress consisted of a black tail-coat, starched white shirt and tie, sash and decorations, black velvet breeches buckled below the knee, black silk stockings and patent leather pumps. In 1929 Mr Charles Dawes took up his post as Ambassador to the Court of St James's and immediately announced his refusal to wear knee breeches and silk stockings 'at Court or anywhere else'. King George V was furious, particularly as, due to the King's illness, the presentation was to be before Queen Mary alone, for the King felt that the breach with custom would be seen as an insult to her. What at first appeared only a minor domestic hiccup escalated into a major row involving the Foreign Office, the Lord Chamberlain and even the Prince of Wales who was a personal friend of the Ambassador. It was all to no avail. When the time for the presentation arrived the Ambassador advanced towards the throne wearing full evening dress – but no knee breeches or silk stockings. When the ceremony was over The Queen was heard to murmur: 'What a pity such a distinguished man should be so difficult.'

These days, however, The Queen is not so concerned about such matters, and when she and her guests have enjoyed a few minutes' conversation the audience is brought to a close. The diplomat and his entourage walk to the door of the 1844 Room (they no longer have to back away from the Sovereign as in days past) where they turn and bow for the final time (with great sighs of relief if it has all gone well). They are then escorted to the Grand Entrance and the procession of State landaus carries them back to the diplomatic residence.

Palace diplomacy is a delicate art and one that needs to be learned over a long period. Lady Airlie tries to ease the path of some of the wives of incoming diplomats by holding informal coffee mornings which turn into unscheduled but highly informative lessons in royal protocol. She also uses the occasion to enlighten her guests about some of the delights of London: the best places to shop – and where to pick up bargains.

Another of the Lord Chamberlain's responsibilities, but one which these days does not require quite the same amount of diplomacy, is advising The Queen on who should be invited to Court – and, more importantly, who not. Queen Victoria would not allow anybody who had been involved in a divorce to attend Court whether the 'innocent' or the 'guilty' party. This state of affairs continued until well into the twentieth century and in the early years of our present Queen's reign only 'innocent' parties were admitted. The first 'guilty' parties allowed to attend Court functions were politicians, but Ministers of the Crown were admitted to Court only in their 'official capacity'. All this has of course now changed. The custom was ended in the latter part of the sixties. If The Queen were to discriminate between divorced and non-divorced people in the 1990s the guest lists at royal functions would look very sparse indeed as several members of her own family and a number of the Royal Household fall into this category. The Lord Chamberlain still advises The Queen on such matters, but nowadays the criteria are much more whether or not the intended guest has a serious criminal record or is currently involved in some major scandal.

Perhaps one of the most intriguing departments within the Lord Chamberlain's office is the Garden Party Office which comes under the supervision of the State Invitations Assistant, Major J. C. Leech who is a Household Official. This is a position in which there are surely more opportunities for corruption than any other in the Royal Household, for thousands of people will do almost anything to be invited to a royal function. But as it happens the men who have held this post have all been models of propriety.

The Garden Party Office is staffed by eight or nine ladies who in spring and early summer write out in longhand some 31,000 invitations to the four Garden Parties which The Queen holds every year. The ladies are called 'Temporary Lady Clerks' although some of these 'temps' have been doing the job for more than twenty years, and they all come from similar backgrounds – from families who could expect to receive invitations themselves to any number of royal entertainments.

When someone is being considered as a guest at a royal function, his or her name is processed through the Lord Chamberlain's vetting machine. Quite a large number never make it. The reasons are many and varied. For instance, if someone applies for an invitation to a Garden Party or lobbies through a third person they are barred – and nothing will remove their name from the list. Every potential name is filed and indexed and a great deal of attention is paid to titles, decorations and professional qualifications. So if a lady claims that she is the Hon. Mrs . . . and, on checking, it is discovered that she has no right to such a prefix, it is recorded in the files. There are hundreds of such false claims in the five 'Black List' cabinets.

In the early days of The Queen's reign, when the qualifications for royal invitations were much stricter than they are today, the slightest brush with the law would mean instant banishment. There are cases in the files of prominent Members of Parliament being refused because many years earlier, while at university, they were fined two pounds for being drunk. Even a minor motoring offence could make the difference between acceptance at Court and being refused admittance.

One particularly unpleasant file, which is kept permanently locked, contains the anonymous letters. So much jealousy surrounds admission to Court that some will go to extreme lengths not only to promote their own ambitions but to thwart those of others. There are many letters which start: 'Your Majesty has seen fit to receive ... at Court. I feel it is only right that you should know ...' Then follows a string of allegations, and even though the letters are unsigned, the Lord Chamberlain's office takes note and investigates, taking considerable trouble, not only to make sure that The Queen does not receive unsuitable people but also that innocent parties are not victimised.

Because the rules governing the admission of divorcees have been relaxed, there is no longer the need to check allegations of this sort. But there are still documents in the filing cabinets relating to scandalous divorce cases of many years ago.

As guardian of the 'Black List' the State Invitations Assistant is responsible for secrets for which the tabloid press would pay a fortune to obtain just a glimpse. A former courtier who once held this post discovered that of the nine ladies working in his department writing out the invitations, the parents of eight were on the Black List – and they never knew. Though perhaps they sometimes wondered why they were not asked to any of the eighty or so functions held at Buckingham Palace every year.

Another, somewhat unusual talent that has to be learned by every new Lord Chamberlain is the ability to walk backwards. At all State Banquets at Buckingham Palace and Windsor Castle, the Lord Chamberlain and the Lord Steward precede The Queen and her guests into the Banqueting Hall – and they have to do so while facing Her Majesty at all times. A couple of secrets are passed on from Lord Chamberlain to Lord Chamberlain to make sure they do not deviate from a straight path: at Buckingham Palace they follow the seam on the carpet in the State Ballroom where all State Banquets are held; but at Windsor it is a little more difficult as the Lord Chamberlain and the Lord Steward are separated on either side of the long dining table, so they have to make sure one does not go faster than the other. The Queen herself will sometimes indicate with her eyes if one is straying too far. The late Lord Maclean used to tell the story of one particular State Banquet at Windsor when he was walking too fast. The Queen whispered the information that he was 'leading by a short head'.

Although nominally head of The Queen's Household, the Lord Chamberlain does not see Her Majesty every day. If there is something he needs to discuss with her he has to make an appointment through her Page. The only Member of the Household who has an audience regularly every morning is The Queen's Private Secretary.

The Lord Chamberlain is on duty at every State Occasion, usually in a position close to The Queen – with one exception. At the State Opening of Parliament he remains at Buckingham Palace as a 'hostage' for the Sovereign's safe return. This custom is a throwback to the days when the Lord Chamberlain was a political appointment and relations between Parliament and Crown were not always as friendly as they are today. So just in case the politicians decided to hold on to the Sovereign, the Lord Chamberlain was not released until the Monarch's safe return. Today the Lord Chamberlain and the Vice Chamberlain of the Household (who is a Member of Parliament) sit drinking coffee until the royal procession arrives back. Prince Philip always greets them with the same words: 'I hope you've looked after the shop while we've been away.'

One of the most ancient functions involving the Lord Chamberlain is that of 'Swan Upping'. This is a centuries-old custom whereby all mute swans on a stretch of the River Thames, between Sunbury and Pangbourne, are marked as being either the property of The Queen or of one of the two Livery Companies of the City of London, to whom the swans on the River Thames belong. This custom dates from the time when people could own swans only with the permission of the Sovereign, and the Worshipful Company of Vintners and the Worshipful Company of Dyers were granted privileges to claim ownership of some of the swans on the Thames. Nobody knows why these two organisations were singled out for royal preference, and it was not only an honour but a profitable privilege as swans were regarded as a delicacy in the winter months from October to January when fresh food was difficult to obtain. The Dyers have exercised their right since 1483 in the reign of Richard III, and the Vintners since 1510 when Henry VIII was on the throne.

Swan Upping takes place every July when the swans which were hatched out in May are marked. Her Majesty's Swan Keeper, accompanied by the Swan Marker of the Vintners' Company and the Swan Master of the Dyers' Company, set out in six rowing boats called Thames skiffs. The boats have special flags: The Queen's have a white flag with the royal crown superimposed on the Royal Cypher, while the Vintners' flags have a swan on a red background and the Dyers' flags are blue with a swan and the Company's badge in one corner.

All those taking part wear special uniforms. The Queen's Swan Keeper has a scarlet jacket with brass buttons and white trousers and a white peaked cap with the royal crown as a badge. On his left arm is a badge with a swan and the words 'Her Majesty's Swan Keeper'. The Queen's Swan Uppers are dressed in scarlet jerseys and white duck trousers. The Vintners' uniform is a green coat with silver braid and buttons for the Marker while the Uppers are all in white. The Dyers' Swan Master wears a blue coat with gold braid and brass buttons and his Uppers are in blue jerseys and white trousers.

Whenever a cob or hen with a group of cygnets is sighted, the cry 'Up, Up, Up' is heard and the group is herded into the bank of the river where the birds are inspected to see to whom they belong by examining their beaks. Those belonging to The Queen are not marked, while the Vintners' swans will have two little nicks, one on each side of the beak. The Dyers' birds have one nick on the right side of the beak. The cygnets are then marked in the same way.

The office of Keeper of The Queen's Swans has resided in the Turk family of watermen for generations and they are rightly proud of their royal connections. The present Keeper, Mr F. J. Turk, who lives at Bourne End on the banks of the Thames, has held the office for thirty years and has been awarded the MVO for his services, while his father held the post before him. The Turk family have been boatbuilders with yards along the Thames for 250 years and they still earn their living from the river.

The Uppers – the men who actually catch and mark the young swans – are very fit, experienced boatmen who spend their lives working on the river, inspecting the banks for wear and tear and running pleasure craft in the summer months. They row alongside the official motor launch containing the Lord Chamberlain's party and always invite the Lord Chamberlain to join them in their boat for a while. Most Lord Chamberlains are wise to this ploy, however and, knowing the boatmen only want to see them make fools of themselves, remain firmly in the comfort of the larger motor launch.

But Lord Maclean, who had made something of a name for himself at school as an oarsman, accepted the challenge – and soon found himself out of his depth, in more ways than one. He could not match the expertise of the Turk family and they have a unique photograph of the Lord Chamberlain in a most undignified pose, legs in the air and flat on his back as he 'caught a crab'. The Queen is said to have been highly amused when she heard about this 'lovely day out on the river' and demanded to see the evidence. Since that day the head of The Queen's Household has contented himself with watching from a safe distance as the experts carry out The Queen's work.

In the days when the riverside Palaces of Greenwich, Westminster, Sheen and the Tower of London were all royal residences, a barge provided the quickest and safest way to travel and from time immemorial there has been a Royal Bargemaster. Until 1919 each British Sovereign had his own Royal Barge and appointed a Bargemaster and Watermen. These days the appointment is purely ceremonial and the occasions when they are on duty are few. Before the State Opening of Parliament the Bargemaster and four Watermen accompany the Crown as it is taken from Buckingham Palace to Westminster as a symbolic offering to the past. The Bargemaster will also usually accompany The Queen to any functions associated with the River Thames. All the Watermen are actively connected with the river and they consider their royal appointment to be the highest honour even though they receive very little money for their duties to the Crown.

A further annual duty of the Lord Chamberlain, but one in which he always takes a spectacular role, is the cleaning of the Crown Jewels.

Garrard's of London are the Crown jewellers, and every January an eight-strong team of polishers descends on the Jewel House in the Tower of London to give the priceless regalia its yearly brush-up. Every one of the crowns, swords of State, tiaras, brooches and chalices is painstakingly checked by the very experienced men (there are no women) who wear leather aprons as they work to catch any precious stone that might pop out.

Bill Summers, who heads the team and who first worked on the Crown Jewels when The Queen came to the Throne in 1952, says he takes no chances, even though 'We've not lost any – yet.' There are tens of thousands of gems. The Imperial State Crown alone, which Her Majesty wears at the State Opening of Parliament, contains 3,538 diamonds, seventeen sapphires, eight emeralds, five rubies and 165 pearls, so there is every possibility of one accidentally going astray. The most valuable single piece is the crown of Queen Elizabeth the Queen Mother, containing almost 6,000 precious stones including the legendary Koh-i-noor diamond, presented to Queen Victoria by the Honourable East India Company in 1851 and weighing 106 carats.

The Deputy Governor of the Tower of London has day-to-day responsibility for the Jewel House and he remains with the team every minute they are in the Tower. The Crown Jewels may not be removed from their secure exhibition areas, protected behind electronic beams and steel shutters, even though it would be more convenient for the cleaning to take place at Garrard's own premises in Regent Street. And the reason why the jewel collection has never been seen in a television programme is that the Lord Chamberlain refuses to allow them to be taken from their display cases for the benefit of the cameras, and it would be difficult if not impossible to light them effectively behind glass.

With all the sophisticated security equipment that surrounds the Crown Jewels it would be reasonable to assume that their cleaning is undertaken by equally up-to-date methods. But in fact the system has not changed in generations. The men erect their oak work-benches in the Jewel House and set to with cotton buds, bought in any chemists' shop, soft detergent, sterilised water and specially impregnated polishing cloths. Everything is done by hand; no machinery of any description is used. At one time jeweller's rouge and whiting were employed but it was discovered that these were slightly abrasive and marked some of the surfaces. So now it's back to good old 'spit and polish'.

Bill Summers supervises the overall, month-long operation and impresses on his team that they cannot be too careful. 'Even with a fairly modern crown like Queen Mary's [made for the Coronation of 1911 with interchangeable diamonds in the centre of the Maltese Cross at the front], diamonds pop out however careful you are,' he says. 'You just make jolly certain you find them again.' Security is always tight at the Jewel House, and it does not relax just because the general public isn't present. Armed guards patrol inside while the cleaning is taking place and the regalia is checked every night before the workers from Garrard's leave. It is not because they are not trusted. It is simply to see that nothing has accidentally fallen into a trouser turn-up or odd pocket. There is one other reason: because the Crown Jewels are literally priceless and could not be replaced, they are all uninsured.

Cleaning the Crown Jewels is an expensive annual task, costing thousands of pounds, but for the men concerned it is surely a labour of love, while some of the items in the Royal Regalia are now so very old that they require even more specialised treatment. A department of the British Museum has taken over their maintenance and also provides the annual cleaning for these rare and delicate pieces.

THE LORDS-IN-WAITING

Within the Lord Chamberlain's Office there are courtiers whose royal duties are comparatively few but who nevertheless remain an important part of the Royal Household.

THE PERMANENT LORDS-IN-WAITING, who rarely number more than two, are appointed personally by the Sovereign in order to secure the continuance in royal service of senior Members of the Household who have retired from full-time duty. They are always

Peers and conform to the Household convention regarding political activity, which means that they sit on the Cross-Benches in the House of Lords and do not speak or vote against the Government of the day. Their royal duties include representing The Queen at funeral or memorial services (usually Her Majesty attends only the funeral services of her immediate family and close personal friends) and meeting important visitors on their arrival and departure to and from the United Kingdom. They also accompany Her Majesty on occasions which are considered too important for an Equerry to handle on his own.

THE LORDS OR BARONESSES-IN-WAITING, who perform similar duties, are appointed by the Sovereign partly on the recommendation of the Prime Minister. Three are Junior Ministers in the House of Lords which means that their terms of office can vary considerably. A further three are appointed by the Sovereign personally.

THE GENTLEMEN USHERS have been in existence since the reign of King Edward IV (1461–83), and their duties at Court have barely changed in five hundred years. They still carry out the tasks their title implies: marshalling the Sovereign's guests at social functions and making sure visitors to Court are comfortable and at ease. They are often retired Members of the Household who receive a small honorarium, but one qualification has now been relaxed in that they no longer have to live in London. At one time the Ushers worked to a monthly rota and for this reason had to live in or near the capital, but now they are called upon when required and no particular place of residence is specified.

These days one of the most distinguished and easily recognisable of the Gentlemen Ushers is Sir Julian Paget, who is on duty at nearly every Investiture directing the recipients towards the State Ballroom and explaining the procedure to the other guests. As a former Lieutenant-Colonel in the Brigade of Guards he wears a black frock tunic on all ceremonial occasions, and as the official historian of the Yeomen of the Guard, no one knows better than he the significance and protocol of life at Court.

There are ten Gentlemen Ushers and approximately fifteen Extra

Gentlemen Ushers, some of whom are appointed from Common-wealth Missions in London.

One of the highest functionaries of the Court is the Gentleman Usher of the Black Rod, whose symbol of office is an ebony stick surmounted with a gold lion. The office has been in existence since 1348 when the Order of the Garter was founded and Black Rod is still Usher to the Order and also the principal usher in the land. He bears all messages from the House of Lords to the Commons, the most regular of which is when he summons Members of Parliament to the bar of the Lords to hear The Queen's speech at the State Opening of Parliament. Since 1642, when King Charles I attempted to arrest five members of the House of Commons, the door has always been slammed shut in the face of Black Rod as he approaches. He then knocks three times with his staff of office and announces his identity before he is admitted.

Another senior functionary, the Gentleman Usher of the Sword of State, has duties only at a Coronation, where he carries the large two-handed sword with its scabbard of crimson velvet decorated with gold plates of the Royal Badge. One side of the guard is fashioned as a lion and the other as a unicorn. The Gentleman Usher, always a peer, carries this Sword of State into Westminster Abbey in the royal procession and delivers it to the Lord Great Chamberlain who deposits it in the traverse in St Edward's Chapel. A smaller Sword of State (there are five altogether: State, Mercy, Spiritual Justice, Temporal Justice and the Jewelled Sword) is then placed in the Sovereign's hands while the Archbishop of Canterbury says: 'Receive this Kingly sword brought now from the altar of God . . .' The Sovereign then places the sword back on the altar and the Gentleman Usher offers the price of one hundred shillings to redeem it. He then draws the sword from its scabbard and carries it unsheathed before the Sovereign during the remainder of the ceremony.

THE SERJEANTS AT ARMS

As one of the oldest armed bodies in existence, the origin of this group goes back to the twelfth century, when King Richard I formed a bodyguard of Serjeants at Arms during the Third Crusade. They were composed of twenty-four Knights and Gentlemen of high degree and provided a small armed force that remained in a state of readiness at a time when there was otherwise no standing army. In times of peace they were used mainly to arrest noblemen with whom the ordinary courts were unable to deal. Over the years the mace carried by the Serjeants became not only their distinctive weapon but also their badge of office and symbol of authority. A number of the Sovereign's high officers of State had Serjeants at Arms attached to them and their successors survive in both Houses of Parliament.

Within the modern Royal Household there are three Serjeants at Arms whose nominal function remains to guard the Sovereign but whose duties nowadays are purely ceremonial. Two attend the Sovereign at the State Opening of Parliament while one is held in reserve. They carry their maces in the procession at the Palace of Westminster.

The Serjeants at Arms are no longer knights and nowadays the appointment is invariably bestowed on a senior Official (never a Member) of the Household in recognition of long and meritorious service.

THE CENTRAL CHANCERY OF
THE ORDERS OF KNIGHTHOOD

If attention to detail is a byword in the Royal Household, it is the cardinal rule in the department of the Lord Chamberlain's Office which looks after the award of decorations. The office of the Central Chancery of the Orders of Knighthood is located in Stable Yard, St James's Palace and it has the responsibility for procuring the Insignia for the Orders of Chivalry in the United Kingdom and certain Commonwealth countries. It also summons recipients to Investitures at Buckingham Palace and maintains the list of the thousands of names recorded in the archives of the various Orders. The name of every single man and woman, whether living or dead, who has ever received an honour, is kept indefinitely.

Eleven staff man the Central Chancery, headed by one of The Queen's most senior Household Members, the Assistant Comptroller of the Lord Chamberlain's Office, who acts as Secretary to the Central Chancery. He is an officer of each of the five Great Orders of Chivalry, the Garter, St Michael and St George, the Bath, the British Empire and the Royal Victorian, and also the Registrar of the Imperial Service Order which is awarded to senior members of the Civil Services.

As the senior official with responsibility for the day-to-day running of the office the Assistant Secretary handles all personnel matters. He also arranges for the publication of honours in the *London Gazette* (in conjunction with his opposite number in the prime minister's office). This is done regularly twice a year, on New Year's Day and for the Queen's Official Birthday in June, but extra lists of honours may also be published at other times during the year, as, for example, at the end of the Gulf War in 1991.

The Insignia Clerk is another senior official. His job is to both order and issue the decorations and medals that are awarded. Meanwhile the Clerk of the Records is responsible for the issue of all Warrants of Appointment and for despatching British Empire Medals and Imperial Service Medals to recipients, for those awarded the BEM or ISM, which is the Medal of the Imperial Service Order, do not qualify for investiture by The Queen but are presented with their awards on Her Majesty's behalf, together with an accompanying letter or certificate. The Clerk of the Records also sends any medals and decorations that are required overseas and, as his name implies, looks after the records of all recipients past and present.

The rest of the office staff is made up of: a Clerk for the Orders of St Michael and St George and the Royal Victorian Order, two Clerks for the Orders of the Bath and the British Empire, two Clerks for Investitures and two Messengers.

The Orders

The Orders of Chivalry and the various decorations dealt with by the Central Chancery are as follows:

THE MOST NOBLE ORDER OF THE GARTER is awarded in conjunction with the College of Arms, who advise on the coats of arms and mottoes of those who are appointed. A church service, held once a year in June, in St George's Chapel, Windsor Castle, is organised jointly by the Central Chancery and the College of Arms.

Founded in 1348 by King Edward III, who wanted a body of elite knights who would swear personal allegiance to him, the Garter is the senior Order of Chivalry in both years and order of precedence. Legend has it that at a ball held to celebrate a great victory at Calais in 1347, Joan, the Fair Maid of Kent, who was married to the Earl of Salisbury, let her garter fall from her leg. This act was usually associated with a woman of loose morals and many of those present laughed at the poor woman's obvious discomfort. Whereupon the King retrieved the garter himself, tied it around his own leg and uttered the immortal words: 'Honi Soit Qui Mal Y Pense,' which is usually translated as: 'Evil be to him who evil thinks.' Since that time the words have been adopted as the motto of the Order and the emblem is a dark blue velvet garter edged with gold.

The 'exclusivity' of the Order is maintained by the fact that its numbers are restricted to twenty-four, plus the Royal Knights: the Duke of Edinburgh (1947), the Prince of Wales (1958) and the Duke of Kent (1985). There is also one Lady of the Garter, Queen Elizabeth the Queen Mother, who was admitted to the Order in 1936, while a number of extra Knights and Ladies include Princess Juliana of the Netherlands, the Queen of Denmark, the King of the Belgians, the Grand Duke of Luxemburg, the King of Sweden, the King of Spain and the Queen of the Netherlands, who was admitted in 1989. Among the twenty-four Knights are two former prime ministers, Lords Wilson and Callaghan, and a former Lord Chancellor, Lord Hailsham. The Queen is Sovereign of the Order of the Garter as she is of most of the Orders of Chivalry.

If a new Knight is to be installed the ceremony is conducted in private in the Throne Room at Windsor Castle, when The Queen fastens the Garter just below the left knee of the recipient. Later all the Knights walk in procession to St George's Chapel where each has his own stall with his personal crest above it. The Military Knights of Windsor lead the procession, followed by the Heralds and Pursuivants from the College of Arms. Then come the Knights of the Garter in their dark blue robes, in front of the Queen Mother and the royal princes, and finally The Queen's Procession which includes the Duke of Edinburgh, while the Yeomen of the Guard bring up the rear. A short service lasting about half an hour marks the founding of the Order and then they all return to the Robing Room to put away their finery for another year.

THE MOST ANCIENT AND MOST NOBLE ORDER OF THE THISTLE is Scotland's premier Order of Chivalry. Its motto is: 'No one provokes me with impunity.' The number of Knights is limited to sixteen, all of them prominent Scottish noblemen. The former prime minister Lord Home of the Hirsel was admitted in 1962 and today he is the Order's Chancellor. The Queen Mother became the only Lady of the Thistle in 1937, and the Royal Knights are the Duke of Edinburgh, who was appointed in 1952 on The Queen's succession, and the Prince of Wales (1977) who is known in Scotland as the Duke of Rothesay.

Lord Lyon King of Arms is Secretary of the Order and arranges their services in St Giles Cathedral in Edinburgh when the Court is in residence at the Palace of Holyroodhouse.

THE MOST HONOURABLE ORDER OF THE BATH was founded in 1725 and remodelled in 1815. The robes worn by the Knights of the Bath are crimson, and their motto is 'Three joined in one'. The Order is divided into several civil and military divisions, ranging from Knight (or Dame) Grand Cross to Companion, and women became eligible for the Order in 1971. The Queen's Private Secretary Sir Robert Fellowes is a member. A service is held once every four years in Westminster Abbey.

THE ORDER OF MERIT was founded in 1902 by Edward VII as a reward for 'savants and soldiers'. Originally intended to comprise sixty, its numbers are now limited to twenty-four, plus some foreign members, to maintain exclusivity. Since its inception the Order has remained in the personal gift of the Sovereign, although Edward VII agreed to consider any names put to him by his prime minister. Ostensibly it was to be awarded regardless of sex, but in the first five years of its existence only one woman managed to penetrate this all-male club. She was Florence Nightingale who was admitted at the age of eighty-seven, and even at that late date King Edward was reluctant to make the award, arguing that such an honour was more appropriate to men.

Many eminent political figures have been awarded the Order of Merit, but never for purely political services; at least that is the intention. However, by an extraordinary coincidence, of the first thirteen men on whom the honour was conferred, no fewer than five were Privy Counsellors or former Cabinet Ministers. In theory all recipients are admitted for their contributions to literature, science or the arts, including the former prime minister Margaret Thatcher, who was given the Order by The Queen in 1991.

THE MOST DISTINGUISHED ORDER OF ST MICHAEL AND ST GEORGE is given these days almost exclusively to members of the diplomatic corps, but there was one notable exception in 1991 when Charles Powell, Margaret Thatcher's press adviser, was awarded the KCMG in her resignation honours list. The Order was founded in 1818 and they hold an annual memorial service in St Paul's Cathedral. Their motto, optimistic and appropriate to the work of diplomats, is 'Token of a better age'.

THE ROYAL VICTORIAN ORDER, the Sovereign's personal Order of Chivalry, was founded in 1896 by, as the name implies, Queen Victoria. The recipients have all performed a service for the Sovereign or her immediate family and the honour ranges from Knight Commander to Royal Victorian Medal, which might be awarded to a domestic servant for long and loyal service. A member of the Royalty Protection Department who had served for ten years could expect to receive the MVO. A service for this order is generally held once every four years, the most recent being in 1991. However, as the Order's centenary falls in 1996, it has been decided by the Lord Chamberlain, after consultation with The Queen, to hold the next service on 21 April 1996, which happens also to be Her Majesty's seventieth birthday.

THE MOST EXCELLENT ORDER OF THE BRITISH EMPIRE. By far the largest of the Orders of Chivalry, this Order was founded in 1917 'in recognition of the manifold services, voluntary and otherwise, that have been rendered both by British subjects and their Allies in connection with the war'. In 1918 it was reorganised into two divisions: military and civil, and by 1919 no fewer than 22,000 men and women, from dukes to dustmen, had become recipients. By 1969 the figure had grown to some 90,000.

The lower grades of OBE and MBE are said to 'come up with the rations': in other words, if one serves in a particular job or rank in the services for a certain length of time, one of these medals is pretty sure to come – but there may be strings. A well-known broadcaster, who also supplemented his income by regularly acting as chairman at official seminars for various government departments, was pleasantly surprised to receive a letter offering an OBE. He accepted and later it was gently hinted that in future perhaps his services would be given free.

The Lord Mayor of a city in Wales was once so confident of being knighted during a forthcoming visit by The Queen that he ordered new personal stationery, complete with title, in advance. To his disappointment he received nothing during the visit but, his obvious dismay noted, a consolation offer of a CBE was made later that year. He accepted and two years later did get his KBE, proving, perhaps, that it may pay to anticipate.

Quite often the chief executives of local authorities and Lords Lieutenant of each county will canvass for suitable names for an award. As a result, a lady who has spent thirty years sticking down envelopes for her local political party may be delighted to receive a letter saying that '. . . the Prime Minister is considering recommending to Her Majesty that you should be offered an honour in the Birthday Honours List'. It is done this way so that there is no embarrassment if the honour is declined, for no definite offer has been made.

Generally about fourteen Investitures are held at Buckingham

72

Palace every year, with every few years an additional one at Holyrood-house while The Queen is in residence. In 1977 an Investiture was held at Hillsborough Castle in Northern Ireland. At a Buckingham Palace Investiture in 1980 an elderly Court official was carrying the tray on which the insignia are displayed when he tripped, sending the medals flying. As he made valiant attempts to retrieve them Her Majesty, growing more and more impatient, finally said, in a stage whisper heard throughout the State Ballroom, 'Give me something, for goodness sake. I can't let these poor people stand here all morning.' In the confusion that followed one or two highly delighted men and women were given CBEs instead of OBEs, while some were less pleased as they received the lower order by mistake. Outside the State Ballroom officials corrected the errors and eventually all the recipients went home with the appropriate decoration, their brief moment of glory over.

THE ORDER OF THE COMPANIONS OF HONOUR, also instituted in 1917, was devised by George V to reward men and women who had given outstanding service to the nation during the First World War. Most of the early recipients represented branches of industry which had contributed to the war effort or were leaders in their own field: the nursing profession, agriculture and the owners of factories making arms and munitions, many of whom had amassed considerable fortunes during the hostilities. It was to be many years before the Companion of Honour could be compared in prestige with the Order of Merit, and of those early recipients only one, the South African General Jan Smuts, remains in the public memory. Even today The Queen is not Sovereign of this Order, and at the time of writing only one woman is listed in its membership, which is limited to sixty-five. She is Dame Ninette de Valois, founder of the Sadler's Wells Ballet. Other Companions include the actor Sir John Gielgud, Mr Denis Healey, the Labour politician, and Pierre Trudeau, the former prime minister of Canada.

THE DISTINGUISHED SERVICE ORDER was created in 1886 in order to recognise special service in action of commissioned officers in the armed services and (since 1942) the Merchant Marine.

THE IMPERIAL SERVICE ORDER was introduced in 1902 and appointment as Companion of this Order is open only to those civil servants who have reached the highest grade, i.e. Permanent or Assistant Secretary. The number is limited to 1,700 of which 1,100 may come from the Home Civil Service and 600 from overseas Civil Services. The awards are given purely on reaching the correct grade as an indication of outstanding public service.

The Classes and Insignia:

THE GARTER – one class of Knights or Ladies Companion.

THE THISTLE – one class of Knights or Ladies.

THE BATH – three classes in both military and civil divisions with quite different insignia:

    GCB – Knight or Dame Grand Cross
    KCB – Knight Commander ⎤
    DCB – Dame Commander ⎦
    CB   – Companion

THE ORDER OF MERIT – one class (OM) in two divisions. The military badge has crossed swords and the civil one a design of oak leaves.

THE ST MICHAEL AND ST GEORGE – three classes:

    GCMG – Knight or Dame Grand Cross
    KCMG – Knight Commander ⎤
    DCMG – Dame Commander ⎦
    CMG   – Companion

THE ROYAL VICTORIAN ORDER – five classes and three grades of medal:

    GCVO – Knight or Dame Grand Cross
    KCVO – Knight Commander ⎤
    DCVO – Dame Commander ⎦
    CVO   – Commander
    LVO   – Lieutenant
    MVO   – Member

Plus the Royal Victorian Medal (RVM) which is awarded in gold, silver or bronze.

THE ORDER OF THE BRITISH EMPIRE – five classes in military or civil divisions but in a single grade of medal.

GBE – Knight or Dame Grand Cross
KBE – Knight Commander ⎱
DBE – Dame Commander ⎰
CBE – Commander
OBE – Officer
MBE – Member

Plus the British Empire Medal (BEM) in military or civil divisions.

THE COMPANIONS OF HONOUR – one class:
CH – Companion

THE DISTINGUISHED SERVICE ORDER – one class.
DSO – Companion

THE IMPERIAL SERVICE ORDER – one class.
ISO – Companion

Plus the Imperial Service Medal (ISM).

In addition the Central Chancery provides the insignia for the George Cross (GC) and The Queen's Gallantry Medal (QGM), and for The Queen's Commendations for Brave Conduct and for Valuable Service in the Air. For these conspicuous acts of bravery may well be brought to the Sovereign's attention by an outside organisation. For example, Valuable Service in the Air could be awarded to a civil pilot who averted a major accident. This would be made known to the Palace by the Civil Aviation Authority, and the award itself would be given by The Queen.

Although solid gold is no longer used, as it once was for important decorations presented to members of the Royal Family, the insignia of the various Orders remain very expensive. They are purchased from several suppliers, including the Royal Mint, Garrard's, Spink & Son Ltd, Collingwood Ltd and Toye, Kenning & Spencer Ltd. The insignia for knighthoods are made either from silver or from silver gilt. The more modest MBE is made of cupro-nickle which has been rhodium plated to give it that extra shiny look. The insignia for the comparatively modest Member of the Royal Victorian Order (MVO) cost around £450, while some of the collars (rather like a mayoral chain) given with the highest grades such as Knights or Dames Grand Cross are worth between £12,000 and £15,000. Because they are so expensive, they have to be returned on the death of the holder, as must the insignia of a lower grade when an individual is promoted to a higher grade within that order. For example, if an MBE is promoted to an OBE, the MBE medal must be returned for reissue. The only exception is promotion within an order, but to a different division. If the MBE had been in the military division and a civil OBE was subsequently awarded, then both badges may be worn on a medal bar.

For the most important of all military honours, the Victoria Cross (VC) – the only medal awarded regardless of rank – the insignia are provided by the Ministry of Defence who also provide the Military Cross (MC), Distinguished Flying Cross (DFC) and the Air Force Cross (AFC). The insignia of military honours are kept by the recipients or their families and sometimes, tragically, have to be sold for personal financial reasons.

The rarest of all honours bestowed personally by The Queen is the Royal Victorian Chain. It is in a category of its own and is not listed among the five classes of the Royal Victorian Order. Most of those who have received it are royalty themselves but Her Majesty has also on occasion conferred the honour on one of her Household who has given her exceptional service. This happened when Lord Maclean retired as Lord Chamberlain after thirteen years. He was given no notice of what was to take place, and as he said goodbye to The Queen and Prince Philip at his farewell audience, Her Majesty suddenly produced the exquisite chain and made the presentation there and then. The chains are numbered and extremely valuable. Lord Maclean's was insured for £60,000, and on his death his family returned it to the Central Chancery as custom demanded.

Because many of the insignia are so costly and are worn on very few occasions, some of the holders leave them at St James's Palace for safe-keeping until they are required. Lord Wilson of Rievaulx, the former Prime Minister, is one who does not care to have such an important item under his own roof, so once a year, as the date for the Garter ceremony approaches, he arrives in Stable Yard with a plastic carrier bag from Marks & Spencer – much to the amusement of the Household – and collects his insignia before driving down to Windsor. After the service he returns it until the following year, saving a considerable amount in insurance premiums.

The Department of the Environment, which looks after the maintenance of the Royal Palaces, employs a uniformed security guard throughout the night whose sole responsibility is to watch the strong room where the insignia are kept. The joke in Palace circles is that even if a fire broke out in the room next door, the security guard would not raise the alarm if it meant he had to leave his post. Those little items of precious metal are all that he cares about and nothing and nobody is going to divert him from his appointed task!

THE ECCLESIASTICAL HOUSEHOLDS

Although the Lord Chamberlain has overall control of all appointments to the Royal Household, there is one department in which he invariably accepts the recommendation of the departmental head. Her Majesty's Ecclesiastical Household contains three forms of Chaplain: Chaplains to The Queen (i.e. the College of Chaplains), Domestic Chaplains, and Chaplains of the Chapels Royal.

The College of Chaplains consists of a Clerk of the Closet, who is always a senior bishop of the Church of England, a Deputy Clerk, usually a Canon, and thirty-six Chaplains.

Clerk of the Closet is a very old office, dating back at least to the thirteenth century, but there is no record of there ever having been a description of what the post entails. In ancient times the position was influential in that the Clerk recommends to the Sovereign who is to be appointed as a Chaplain, but today the Chaplaincies are honorary and the duties involve no more than an occasional stint of preaching at the Chapel Royal or The Queen's Chapel in St James's Palace according to a Rota of Waits. A fee is paid for preaching at each service but since the Chaplains do not receive a stipend there is not much pecuniary advantage in being appointed to the College. In olden days, however, their very proximity to the Throne made them men of some influence and some of the Chaplains became rich as a result of the personal favours they were able to perform for wealthy patrons at Court.

The Clerk of the Closet is also required to introduce new bishops into the Royal Presence when they come to pay homage to The Queen. It is a simple ceremony, conducted with all due solemnity, as both the Clerk of the Closet and the newly appointed bishop, fully robed, are ushered into Her Majesty's presence by the Master of the Household. They are joined by the Home Secretary who reads the words of the Homage, which are repeated by the Bishop as he kneels before the seated Queen. He says:

> I acknowledge that I hold the said bishopric, as well the spiritualities as the temporalities thereof, only of Your Majesty and for these temporalities I presently give my Homage to Your Majesty.

As he is making this pledge, both his hands are placed between those of The Queen as a sign of loyalty. The ceremony lasts only a few minutes but without it the bishop would not legally hold his bishopric and would not be entitled to the income from the living.

Another duty of the Clerk of the Closet is to vet any theological books authors may wish to present to The Queen. This dates back to the days when the Sovereign exerted considerable political power and influence and one way for someone otherwise barred from personal contact to make his views known to the Sovereign was to include them in a book to be presented as a gift. Even today the Clerk of the Closet carefully reads every theological book or article that is submitted to make sure that nothing 'unsuitable' is accepted and that no gift is offered in order to gain publicity for the author.

The Queen has a private Chapel at Buckingham Palace and another at Windsor Castle (its full title is The Royal Chapel of All Saints and it is in Windsor Great Park). Each of these has a Domestic Chaplain and the services in these private chapels are never open to the public. The chaplain at Buckingham Palace is the Sub-Dean of the Chapels Royal (the Dean is the Bishop of London) and he also acts as Deputy Clerk of the Closet. At Windsor, the Domestic Chaplain is the Dean

1 A coachman's livery costs over £1,000, while the preparation and decoration of The Queen's ceremonial horses takes several hours to complete. This picture shows why the final result is worth all the effort

2 The Master of the Horse is titular head of the Royal Mews and by tradition escorts the sovereign on ceremonial occasions. The Earl of Westmorland, former Master of the Horse, is seen leaving Buckingham Palace for The Queen's Birthday Parade

3 *Opposite:* Her Majesty's spiritual and temporal advisers – the combined bodies of the Ecclesiasttical and Medical Households pictured for the first time together after attending a joint choral evensong in the Chapel Royal at St James's Palace. The only lady in the group was the then Nursing Sister to the Royal Mews

4 *Above:* The ten children of the Chapel Royal are all Queen's Scholars, educated at Her Majesty's expense at the City of London School from where they come to the Chapel Royal at St James's Palace twice a week for rehearsals and to sing at all Sunday services and on other Royal occasions

5 *Right:* A sense of humour is a prerequisite for all members of the Royal Household. Here the Dean of Windsor, the Rt Rev Patrick Mitchell, obviously sees the joke as he stands outside the Deanery with the Duke of York and Prince Edward, following an Easter service

6 *Opposite above:* A Press Secretary's life is not all duty. Charles Anson with Her Majesty and Queen Elizabeth the Queen Mother, in the Royal Box at the Derby

7 *Opposite below:* One of the three designers who make the bulk of The Queen's wardrobe, Ian Thomas is also the youngest and newest member of this exclusive group and has been credited with responsibility for many of Her Majesty's more fashionable outfits

8 *Above:* Clarence House has been the London home of Queen Elizabeth the Queen Mother since 1952. Inside it bears the unmistakable stamp of her personality, and her staff are among the longest-serving and most loyal in the Royal Household

9 *Right:* Members of staff describe cleaning the Royal silver as like painting the Forth Bridge. It never stops; once you have finished one lot, you start all over again

10 Last-minute touches before the Royal party emerges from the Palace onto the rear terrace at a Buckingham Palace Garden Party. The presence of a Yeoman of the Guard indicates that The Queen is about to make an appearance

11 Three Garden Parties are held at Buckingham Palace every July with another taking place at the Palace of Holyroodhouse in Edinburgh. Old hands arrive early to secure the best tables and chairs near the refreshment marquees

12 The Queen inspects her Yeomen of the Guard in the gardens at Buckingham Palace after presenting them with new colours. The Yeomen are all volunteers and are ex-Army, Marines or Royal Air Force, but not Royal Navy. By tradition ex-sailors are not permitted to join the ranks of the oldest bodyguard in the world

13 The Queen inspects her 'Nearest Guard'. Formed in 1509 by Henry VIII, the Honourable Corps of Gentlemen at Arms remains the sovereign's most exclusive bodyguard, with a complement of only five officers and twenty-seven Gentlemen

14 *Left:* The Head of The Queen's Household, the Earl of Airlie in his robes as a Knight of the Thistle. Lord Airlie is the elder brother of Sir Angus Ogilvy, while his wife is a Lady-in-Waiting to The Queen

15 *Below:* One of the most colourful of all Royal occasions, the annual Garter Service held at Windsor Castle. Leading the Royal procession are the Military Knights of Windsor, followed by the heralds in their multi-coloured tunics, while the Garter Knights bring up the rear. Lining the route are dismounted troopers of the Household Cavalry – all The Queen's men

of Windsor. When the Royal Family is at Sandringham The Queen worships at the parish church of St Mary Magdalene, whose Rector usually holds the post of Domestic Chaplain at Sandringham.

Although it is a common belief that every royal residence has its own Chapel Royal, there are in practice only three: at St James's Palace, Hampton Court Palace – whose last royal resident was George II and where Cardinal Wolsey's original chapel was enriched by Henry VIII who added the vaulted ceiling where pendant gold cherubs play musical instruments – and at the Tower of London, where the Norman Chapel of St John the Evangelist lies within the walls of the White Tower.

In the past, however, a Chapel Royal could be created wherever the Sovereign chose to worship, and the chapel in the Savoy in London became a Chapel Royal in 1773. It was the last building in England in which it was possible for fugitives from justice to claim sanctuary. Services in the Chapels Royal are open to the public from time to time.

The Sub-Dean of the Chapels Royal is also the Chaplain at St James's Palace where he is assisted by three Priests in Ordinary and two Deputy Priests in Ordinary. Each of the other two Chapels Royal has its own Chaplain who is also a Deputy Priest in Ordinary.

All Chaplains in the Ecclesiastical Household have the privilege of wearing scarlet cassocks, as do former Chaplains of the College. Domestic Chaplains and Chaplains of the College also wear a distinctive silver gilt Chaplain's Badge and Priests and Deputy Priests a silver Priest's Badge.

At two of the churches most closely associated with the Royal Family, Westminster Abbey (or, to give it its correct title – the Collegiate Church of St Peter in Westminster) and St George's Chapel, Windsor (The Sovereign's Free Chapel of St George in The Sovereign's Castle of Windsor), the clergy are not part of the Ecclesiastical Household. These churches are Royal Peculiars, a name given to churches directly linked with the Sovereign which means that they owe their allegiance not to the Bishop of their Diocese but to The Queen herself. Even the Archbishop of Canterbury has no right of entry to Westminster Abbey unless invited by The Queen, but oddly St George's Chapel at Windsor, although within the precincts of

Windsor Castle itself, does not belong to the Crown. The freehold is held in perpetuity by the Dean of Windsor whose stewardship exists while he holds office. The Deanery alongside St George's Chapel holds one further and unique link with royalty. In the Dean's study is a table on which the decapitated body of Charles I was laid after his execution in 1649, in order that the head could be sewn back on before burial.

The Queen is a deeply religious woman who attends church every Sunday – out of choice rather than a sense of duty. Her main spiritual adviser is of course the Archbishop of Canterbury, but until recently both she and the Duke of Edinburgh often turned also to the former Dean of Windsor, the Very Reverend Michael Mann who retired from royal service in 1991. Michael Mann came into the church comparatively late in life, having served for many years as a regular officer in one of the most fashionable cavalry regiments in the British army – 1st The Queen's Dragoon Guards, Captain Mark Phillips' regiment. Michael Mann retired from military life shortly after his son, also an army officer, was killed while on secondment in the Middle East. Entering the Church, he served in a number of parishes before being invited to join the Royal Household as Dean of Windsor. During his term of office he became a particularly close friend of the Duke of Edinburgh and part of their correspondence has been published in book form. Over the years he has been involved in a great many discussions with the Royal Family, and his spiritual guidance and no-nonsense approach to ecclesiastical matters has endeared him to not only The Queen herself but to all her family.

Within the Ecclesiastical Household there is an Organist, Choirmaster and Composer and also an Organist and Choirmaster at Hampton Court, and among the most colourful and tuneful ingredients of many royal religious services are the Children of the Choirs of the Chapels Royal which they supervise. The youngsters are all boys and they wear scarlet tunics faced with gold and black braid, lace collar and bands, scarlet knee-breeches and black shoes and stockings. They take part in Sunday services in the Chapel Royal at St James's Palace and at many other functions including royal christenings, the Maundy Service on the Thursday before Easter, and the Annual Remembrance Day Service at the Cenotaph in Whitehall when The

Queen places a wreath in memory of the dead of the two World Wars.

The boys of the choir are in frequent demand at Household functions and at weddings held in the Chapel Royal by permission of The Queen – and from which they usually do very well financially as the bride's father is expected to tip them generously. They are very popular and their repertoire extends far beyond the list of sacred and solemn music usually associated with such occasions. In fact they like nothing better than to be asked to let down their collective hair and give their own versions of some of the hit songs from popular musicals of the day.

A small Ecclesiastical Household in Scotland consists of a Dean of the Chapel Royal and ten Chaplains to The Queen in Scotland. Each of these is appointed by Her Majesty on the recommendation of the Dean and they serve until the age of seventy when they are appointed to be Extra Chaplains.

When the Royal Family is in residence at Balmoral Castle, The Queen worships every Sunday at the tiny Crathie Church, the estate's parish church located just outside the castle's gates. The Minister of Crathie is appointed a Domestic Chaplain. Although The Queen is head of the Church of England, all the members of her Ecclesiastical Household north of the border are Church of Scotland as is the church at which she worships.

THE MEDICAL HOUSEHOLDS

There are twenty-two members of The Queen's Medical Household in England and Scotland of whom one, Sir George Pinker, was in his time easily the best known. The reason is that as The Queen's Surgeon Gynaecologist, he was the man who attended the Princess of Wales at the birth of both her sons and the Duchess of York when she gave birth to her two daughters. Until recently Sir George ran his own clinic at St Mary's Hospital in London where the royal babies were born in the private Lindo Wing, and he was knighted in 1989 by The Queen for his services to the Royal Family.

He was never, however, the head of the Medical Household. That distinction belongs to Dr Anthony Dawson, a Fellow of the Royal College of Physicians who is the senior Physician to The Queen. Dr Dawson occupies a position of considerable influence in the medical profession as it is on his recommendation alone that the Lord Chamberlain appoints other eminent medical practitioners. The Queen actually has three physicians, the senior is Head of the Medical Household and one is usually a Homeopathist as Her Majesty and other members of the Royal Family have long had faith in this form of treatment.

There is also a Sergeant Surgeon, the senior surgeon to The Queen, an appointment at Court that dates from the thirteenth century when one Henry de Fardy became Sergeant Surgeon to Henry III. The original duty of the Sergeant Surgeon was to attend the Sovereign as he went into battle. He never left his master's side. There were Sergeant Surgeons at the Battle of Crécy in 1349 when John of Arderne accompanied Edward III and again in 1415, when Thomas Morstead attended Henry V at Agincourt. Within the Royal Archives at Windsor Castle the account books of the Royal Household in the fifteenth century record that Thomas Morstead was paid the sum of £10 a quarter and 10d (4p) subsistence daily. He also had the right to take prisoners and plunder, but if the value of the plunder was more than £20, he had to surrender one-third to the King.

There was a period in English history when the Surgeon to the Sovereign enjoyed far greater prominence than he does today. At one time he ranked twelfth after the Sovereign in the order of precedence at Court. In other European kingdoms, the surgeon was considered to be even closer to the Sovereign. There is one instance of a surgeon being beheaded on the death of his Sovereign so as to be buried with the royal remains. Whether this was at his own request or not has not been recorded.

The Company of Barber Surgeons was first incorporated in the fifteenth century with one William Hobbes appointed as Sergeant Surgeon. His salary was 40 marks a year and he also had the right to draw two butts of sack annually from the Royal Cellars. Another dubious honour was the right to retain all napkins and other fine linen used in dressing the wounds of the King. Surgeons of the period would often sell the bloodstained bandages to gullible members of the public who believed that anything that had been touched by royalty conveyed special powers. Unscrupulous surgeons were known to sell any old piece of cloth, stained with the blood of domestic animals, with the guarantee that it had come from the body of the Sovereign.

Until the twelfth century the only practitioners of medicine and surgery were members of religious orders. The men who assisted them were barbers, who not only cut hair but also performed other grooming tasks such as scaling teeth. It was when they helped the monks and priests who were practising medicine that they became known as Barber Surgeons. However, at the Council of Tours in 1163, the Pope decreed that no one in Holy Orders should engage in any activity that involved the shedding of blood. This meant that from then on the assistants or Barber Surgeons were in sole charge of all surgery. The present holder of the title Sergeant Surgeon to The Queen, Mr John Leonard Dawson, a distinguished liver surgeon and the younger brother of the Senior Physician to The Queen, holds a position that can be traced directly back to Henry de Fardy in 1253.

In the present Medical Household there is also an Apothecary to The Queen (who is not a chemist but a General Practitioner) and the following positions:
One Surgeon to the Household and one Surgeon-Oculist to the Household; one Surgeon-Gynaecologist, one Surgeon-Dentist, one Orthopaedic Surgeon and one Surgeon-Oculist; one Apothecary to the Household in London (this is usually the person who holds the position of Apothecary to The Queen) plus another at Windsor and one also at Sandringham; and one Medical Officer to The Queen abroad (usually a serving or former Royal Navy Surgeon though The Queen always takes her own physician with her whenever she travels away from the United Kingdom).
In Scotland there are: two Physicians and two Surgeons. There are also one Apothecary to the Household at the Palace of Holyroodhouse and one at Balmoral, plus two Extra Surgeons.

The only members of the Medical Household who receive an annual salary are the Apothecaries in London and Windsor, where daily surgeries are held for members of the Household and staff at Buckingham Palace and Windsor Castle. So many staff are employed at Buckingham Palace that two daily surgeries are required: one in the Royal Mews and the other in a small room on the ground floor of the main Palace building. And as so many of the Household spend much of their time abroad, either on 'recce' trips or official visits with various members of the Royal Family, the Household doctors hold all the records for the vaccinations they need. If a member of the Household needs attention he or she visits the surgery; if it is a member of the Royal Family who requires a consultation the doctor visits them in their own apartments. The remaining Apothecaries in the Medical Household are not paid an annual salary, but they do receive an honorarium which, as one said, is measured in hundreds rather than thousands of pounds.

To be appointed a member of the Medical Household is a unique honour and one which brings many practical benefits as well as the prestige of attending the Royal Family. Surgeons and physicians who are known to be associated with royalty can command large fees from private patients all over the world, and senior members of the Medical Household can expect knighthoods after a few years of loyal service. There is also one other practical benefit to the less well off members of the public. Nearly every one of the consultants and specialists in the Household devotes at least one working day every week to the treatment of patients under the National Health Service. The doctors are able and willing to undertake this work because of the fees paid by others who can afford them. Hundreds of people in Britain have cause to thank members of the Medical Household, and as one grateful patient once remarked, 'This morning Sir George was treating the Princess of Wales, now he is working on me. It can't be bad.'

When the late Lord Maclean was invited to succeed Lord Cobbold as Lord Chamberlain, he asked for a job description. 'There is no such thing,' he was told. 'The job is whatever you care to make of it.'

Each Lord Chamberlain has made his own contribution to the orderly running of The Queen's Household. Some have been conspicuous by their absence – with no apparent loss of efficiency. A few have combined the position with organising large commercial companies or running vast country estates. Only one has been in any way a full-time Lord Chamberlain, and that was because he had no other outside interests and was able to devote all his energies to that role. It did not mean that he was any more successful than the others; it was just that his way of doing things was different from what was expected.

What they have all had in common though is an extraordinary ability both to cope with the complicated protocol which surrounds life at Court and to apparently do the most demanding job with a minimum of effort. Nobody has ever seen Lord Airlie run or even appear to be in a hurry. And that is the secret of his, and their, success. All are masters of organisation and delegation. It was Lord Cobbold who said, 'If I'm doing my job right, there is no need for me to be here at all. What I've tried to do is organise myself out of a job.'

As a token of his office the Lord Chamberlain is presented with a long white wand by The Queen on his appointment. Again this is a tradition which had practical origins several hundred years ago. In the sixteenth and seventeenth centuries life at Court occasionally became quite lively and the Lord Chamberlain used his wand to restore order. If the Lord Chamberlain raised his wand and pointed it at someone, that person had either to acknowledge his transgression or be forcibly ejected from the royal presence. There is a story of one Lord Chamberlain during the reign of Charles I breaking his wand across the shoulders of a courtier who became too exuberant in the presence of the Sovereign. Records in the royal archives reveal that the Lord Chamberlain broke his staff over the shoulders of May the poet 'for being out of his place in a masque at Court'. These days the wand, like so many other former weapons – the pikes of the Yeomen of the Guard and the swords carried by equerries in dress uniform – has only a symbolic significance.

When a Sovereign dies the Lord Chamberlain's wand is formally broken over the royal grave; the last time this happened was when Lord Clarendon did so in 1952 on the death of King George VI. If the Lord Chamberlain retires the wand of office is returned to the Sovereign and in the case of all her former Lord Chamberlains, Her Majesty has always given the wand back as a memento. It is a thoughtful and generous gesture and those slender white staves bring back hundreds of happy memories to the men who have occupied the highest position in The Queen's Household.

6

THE MASTER
OF THE HOUSEHOLD

THE THREE HUNDRED men and women who make up the
domestic Household of The Queen all come under the jurisdiction
of the Master of the Household or, to give him and his office their
full style and title: the Master of the Household's Department, Board
of Green Cloth. In spite of its ancient sounding description which
might almost be a throwback to medieval times, the position of
Master of the Household is a comparatively recent one at Court. The
present Master of the Household owes his job, or at least the fact
that there is such a position, to the reforming zeal of Prince Albert,
Consort to Queen Victoria.

When Albert came to live at Buckingham Palace with his Teutonic
attitude to a well-ordered lifestyle he was appalled by the utter confusion he found within the Royal Household. There were so many
'mini-empires', each one jealously guarded by a head of department
who steadfastly refused to relinquish any tiny part of his responsibilities, that even the minor domestic chores became a cause for much
exasperation.

Until 1844, all the rooms at Buckingham Palace from the ground
floor up came under the Lord Chamberlain's Office. The basement
area, containing kitchens, sculleries and pantries, were the responsibility of the Lord Steward, while the Office of Woods and Forests took
charge of the gardens and everything else outside the building. The
result was a ludicrous division of labour. In those days before central
heating, when open fires were used throughout the Palace, if a fire
was needed in any one of the rooms, the Office of Woods and Forests

had to be contacted to provide the fuel: coal, paper and firewood, which they were allowed to bring only as far as the back door. There they would hand over to a member of the 'indoors-staff', who would have been given his orders by the Lord Steward's department. Then the Lord Chamberlain's Office provided one man to carry the fuel upstairs and another to lay and light the fire. If the fires to be lighted were in the kitchen area then the Lord Steward's department would take over once again as he would not allow staff from the Lord Chamberlain's Office to encroach on his territory. Five people could be involved in the simple process of lighting a fire in Queen Victoria's sitting room. And as this pantomime was repeated day after day, the sheer waste of manpower hours was horrendous. No one person had overall responsibility for actually running the Palace, and the various departments liaised with one another by means of handwritten notes, carried at a leisurely pace by footmen unused to hurrying. Prince Albert had grown up in European palaces where there was always a major-domo to look after every domestic detail, and was horrified by the wastage and inefficiency, so he brought his orderly mind to bear on the problem.

The obvious answer was to appoint a Master of the Household with total command of all the domestic staff, of whom there were some five hundred at the time, and eventually the Prince Consort managed to persuade Queen Victoria, who, although she disliked change in any form, could refuse her husband nothing, to create the position.

The office of the Master of the Household in Buckingham Palace is situated on the first floor of the Buckingham Gate side, directly opposite The Queen's private apartments but separated by the expanse of the Inner Quadrangle. In direct line, but one floor below, are the kitchens and pantries which form such an important part of his empire and which take up much of his time. The room Sir Paul Greening, the present Master, occupies has gained no small amount of notoriety in Palace circles because of the fact that it was through a window here that Michael Fagan gained entry in 1982, after scaling the outer railings and climbing a drainpipe. He then managed, with little apparent difficulty, to find his way to The Queen's bedroom, walked in and was eventually overpowered by a footman after he had

sat on the bed talking to Her Majesty for some time. Sir Paul was
not the Master of the Household at the time.

His is an awesome task for he has responsibility for all the Palace's
351 rooms (429 if you count bathrooms and lavatories), as well as
the hundreds of rooms in all the other royal residences and the staff
who look after them. There is no aspect of the domestic life of the
Palace that does not involve his department, from the menus for up
to six hundred meals every day, to ordering new sheets for the beds
in the servants' wing. He supervises the maintenance and reordering
of the vast stocks of wine and spirits in the royal cellars, the buying
of flowers (£37,000 worth a year) to decorate the tables at State
Banquets and other functions and even the allocation of seats when
members of the Royal Household are travelling by air.

This last duty is not so simple and straightforward as it may sound.
When Sir Paul and his team are working out a seating plan which
might involve a large number of staff they have to be quite sure that
they do not transgress the unwritten code by which a junior footman
may not be given a better place than a Page of the Presence. The
Palace Steward, the senior of all Her Majesty's domestic servants,
would never sit next to a housemaid, and the dignity of the Royal
Chef must be maintained at all times, so his own staff must be placed
in seats that are less favourable than his own. There is as strict an
order of precedence in the Royal Household as in the family they
serve, and the Master of the Household must recognise the subtleties
and little differences that can make or break a successful team.

A Royal Garden Party can cost nearly £50,000 – and it is the
Master of the Household who orders the 30,000 sandwiches, 18,000
pastries and 2,000 gallons of iced coffee that are consumed on each
occasion. He also hires the marquees and portable lavatories, makes
sure the cloakroom attendants are on duty and checks with the Royal
Chef that The Queen's favourite tea and cakes are ready for her in
the Royal Tent. (J. Lyons caters for all Garden Parties in London,
but everything The Queen eats and drinks is prepared in the royal
kitchens by her own chef.)

The Master of the Household has been variously described as the
most exalted major-domo in the world, the country's most important
housekeeper, manager of the most exclusive hotel, and The Queen's

head butler. All these descriptions are true in part, but none wholly describes the unique role he plays in the domestic life of The Queen and her family, for his department touches every other office in the Royal Household in a way that no other does.

The Queen's Private Secretary is her closest aide and is privy to more confidential information than anyone else in the Palace, yet he rarely involves himself in any of the domestic arrangements of the Royal Family. Similarly, the Crown Equerry, responsible for all personal matters within his own kingdom in the Royal Mews, plays no part in the decisions surrounding functions such as State Banquets, formal receptions or the arrangements made to accommodate The Queen's official guests. He provides the transport but his duties end once the guests enter the Palace itself. He does, however, have one responsibility at Garden Parties and that is to see that the lawns are mown and the gardens in perfect condition. The Keeper of the Privy Purse, for his part, pays all the bills once they have been approved by the department head concerned. But he is not in any other way involved in internal matters concerning any 'below stairs' staff in the royal residence.

The Master of the Household, though, spreads tentacles into all the other departments. When the Director of the Royal Collection arranges for paintings from among Her Majesty's 5,000 pictures to be loaned to Members to decorate their offices or homes, he chooses the pictures but the Master of the Household provides the men who hang them.

In many ways this seems a curious sort of job for a man who has had no previous experience of catering or running a large business, and perhaps even more so when one recalls that most of those who have held the position this century reached very senior rank in one of the armed forces before joining the Royal Household. Both the present holder of the post and his immediate predecessor, Sir Peter Ashmore, were Admirals in the Royal Navy, responsible for the safety and well-being of thousands of men and women under their command, as well as ships and equipment worth tens of millions of pounds.

Sir Paul Greening was Captain of the Royal Yacht *Britannia* (the only ship in the world of which the Captain is an Admiral) before he was appointed to his present position. So clearly he knew a great deal about the requirements of The Queen and her family when they were on board. Yet to move from a purely naval establishment with its rigid codes of discipline and behaviour, and where orders are obeyed without question, to a job where every command is made to sound like the most reasonable request and the prime objective is to look after The Queen's entertaining, takes a very special talent. Sir Paul obviously has that talent in abundance.

The men and women who work in the Master of the Household's department are divided into three distinct categories which are listed under the letters: F,G,H (Food, General and Housekeeping). The first of these, F, includes all those who work in the royal kitchens: chefs, under-chefs, pastry cooks, vegetable cooks, kitchen porters and dish-washers – in all around fifty men and women. Category G covers all the liveried staff and those who look after the furniture and fittings in the Palace. This section would include footmen, stewards and Pages, together with upholsterers, seamstresses and those who work in the royal cellars. The workforce of this section numbers eighty, but that number includes thirty men who are employed by the Department of the Environment, which has responsibility for maintaining the structure of the Palace, but take their orders from Sir Paul. In the third category, Housekeeping, are the fifty housemaids and cleaners at Buckingham Palace together with small staffs kept at Windsor and Holyroodhouse.

It is not all that difficult to get a job in the Royal Household. In fact there are usually several vacancies among the domestic staff even though The Queen, unlike many other would-be employers, does not find it hard to attract people into domestic service. Recently, after consultation with Her Majesty, The Master of the Household carried out a recruiting campaign for servants in a number of areas of high unemployment, thinking this would be a practical way in which the Royal Household could help to alleviate the problems experienced in places such as Liverpool, the North-East and parts of rural Cornwall. The local jobcentres were involved and also a number of reputable agencies who had been successful in the past in finding suitable staff. No previous experience was required (except for cooks, when a professional qualification was needed) and there was a lot of interest

– and jobs were offered to a number of young people, including school-leavers.

The youngest recruits – some of whom became trainee footmen – were given a starting salary of a little over £100 a week all found, which means a single room (they no longer have to live in dormitories) and all meals and livery provided. All staff training is carried out 'on the job', and although there is no career structure as such, all promotion comes from within. The men and women who occupy the senior posts in the domestic Household have all 'risen through the ranks'. Even Anthony Jarred, the Palace Steward, the most senior of all servants, started life as a junior footman more than thirty years ago.

The Royal Household operates a non-contributory pension scheme for all its staff, and while nobody comes to work at the Palace for the money alone, a number of the younger men regard the pension as a useful 'element of deferred income'. They intend to remain in royal service for only a few years and then move on to more lucrative employment in the commercial sector or in wealthy private homes abroad. A reference written on Buckingham Palace headed writing paper works wonders when applying for a job elsewhere! Americans in particular can be very impressed.

Life for those who work inside Buckingham Palace runs to a routine that rarely varies, even though the individual daily duties of, for example, the footmen, may change within a set rota. The day normally begins around 7.15 in the morning when alarm clocks start ringing on the top floor where the domestic live-in staff have their rooms. At one time a boy was employed to wake the staff, but these days each one uses his own clock. The staff bedrooms are comfortable with simple but sturdy furniture. Everybody gets exactly the same: a single bed (there are no double rooms for staff; married couples are given flats), a chest of drawers, a large wardrobe in which is hung the ceremonial livery and everyday uniforms, and an easy chair. Most of the rooms have small fireplaces, none of which are working as the whole of the Palace is now centrally heated. There is a wash-basin with constant hot water but no private bathroom. These are located at the end of each corridor.

With promotion comes a move up the scale in the type of accommodation allocated. For example, the Duke of Edinburgh's two valets, Barrie Lovell and David Berwick, both of whom have been with Prince Philip for over ten years, occupy pleasant suites of rooms overlooking Constitution Hill and the Palace gardens. The suites consist of a large bedroom, a sitting room, a work-room and two wardrobe rooms, all provided rent free and cleaned daily by one of the housemaids.

Each footman has several sets of uniform, each to be worn on particular occasions. When would-be footmen are being interviewed, the Palace Steward will often call one of the existing men to come and stand back-to-back with the new man to see if any of the livery available in the Palace Livery Room will fit him. The everyday uniform of dark-green tail-coat (or scarlet when a State Visit is taking place), stiff white shirt with wing collar and white bow tie and black trousers is simple enough, but when it comes to the livery worn at State Banquets with its yards of gold braid it's a different matter. Each outfit costs around £1,000, so the liveries are not replaced whenever a new man joins the staff. Some of the State outfits are well over fifty years old, a few nearer a hundred, and one of the main requirements for footmen who attend State Occasions is that they should be of perfectly average size, around 5 feet 9 inches tall with a thirty-eight-inch chest.

Another item of clothing that is given, or rather lent, to each member of staff is a black tail-coat to be worn during Court mourning. And there is a further uniform, one that the public rarely sees: a scarlet coat with a military collar that buttons down the side and blue breeches. This special outfit is worn by domestic staff when on duty on board the Royal Yacht.

Breakfast is served at Buckingham Palace from 7.30 A.M. There are three dining rooms: one for Members, one for Officials and one for Staff. The one used by the footmen is close to the kitchens, and to get to it from their rooms on the top floor they use the same lift that brings The Queen's food up to her dining room on a heated trolley, so they are forbidden to use it between one and two o'clock in the afternoon when Her Majesty's lunch is in transit. If they want to go up to their rooms at these times they have to climb several flights of stairs.

Although slightly over three hundred servants work in the Palace today, the Servants' Hall dates from grander times when almost double that figure were employed, so the present complement can be accommodated with ease. It functions like a self-service cafeteria with hot and cold food being served at every meal. Most of the staff opt for a full English cooked breakfast and even though some have their favourite seats, there is no 'pecking order' in the dining room. The tables are set for six and anyone can sit wherever he chooses. It's all quite democratic, but the older men tend to stick together and most of the noise comes from those tables where the youngest footmen are to be found. Some of the very youngest servants wanted piped music to be played in the cafeteria, but the old hands would have none of it and breakfast is eaten without any musical accompaniment. The only place in Buckingham Palace where music is played at breakfast time is on the terrace below The Queen's window where, every morning, a lone piper marches up and down playing Her Majesty's favourite Scottish tunes for half an hour.

Footmen who stay in royal service for many years can expect to be promoted to one of the more senior ranks of Page. There are three sets of Pages: Pages of the Chambers, Pages of the Presence and Pages of the Backstairs.

Two Pages of the Backstairs serve as The Queen's personal Pages, positions very close to Her Majesty, and the men chosen are very senior servants indeed. They take it in turn to wait on Her Majesty at her private apartments, and when a member of the Household wishes to see The Queen he will first of all telephone the Page to find out whether this is convenient. Two more Pages of the Backstairs perform similar duties for the Duke of Edinburgh.

Once breakfast is over, the footmen go to their allotted tasks which vary according to a rota worked out by the Sergeant Footman – the man who acts as foreman. Each man is assigned a different number, corresponding to a particular duty for that day.

Footman number one has the task of assisting the Pages of the Backstairs – helping to serve The Queen's meals, exercising the corgis and delivering the messages throughout the Palace. His first task in the morning is to carry up from the kitchens the Duke of Edinburgh's 'calling tray' with his early morning coffee and biscuits. The tray is delivered to whichever of the Duke's valets is on duty, outside the Duke's bedroom door, and the valet carries it into the bedroom.

Footmen numbers two and four look after The Queen's Household. Any Member of the Household – and that's Member with a capital M, denoting Assistant Private Secretaries and above – can eat in the Household Dining Room, which is on the ground floor at the rear of the Palace next to the 1855 room, but these days lunch is the only meal served on a normal working day. The footmen do not have to set the table. This is done by staff who work for the Yeoman of the Glass and China Pantry, who also clear away after the meal. Lines of demarcation are strictly observed at Buckingham Palace. They do, however, bring the food to the dining room on heated trays. It is a very informal meal. All the Members serve themselves, and nowadays only beer and soft drinks are available.

The name of the 1855 room commemorates a visit to London by Napoleon III and Empress Eugénie of France in that year. The room was used for a discussion with Queen Victoria and Prince Albert about the Crimean War in which Britain and France were allies. These days the room is used as a Household drawing room.

The job of being footman number three is rather unpopular because of the tedium. Number three is required to be at The King's Door, in the middle of the west side of Buckingham Palace, in the Inner Quadrangle, whenever a member of the Royal Family is due to come or go. You cannot see this door from outside the Palace and it is used by Prince Philip and the Princess Royal and also by the Prime Minister when he is admitted for his weekly audience. The door is close to the Equerry's Room and the office of The Queen's Private Secretary. The footman used to sit in a small ante-room opposite the office of The Keeper of the Privy Purse (formerly the study of King Edward VIII), but in the reorganisation of the Palace in 1989 his room was allocated to the Assistant Comptroller of the Lord Chamberlain's Office. He has a time-table listing the times when members of the Royal Family or other privileged visitors are due, so he is also available for certain other duties such as delivering papers from the Private Secretaries' offices to The Queen's Pages on the floor above.

Number three's responsibilities also include finding out how many of the Household will be in for lunch and making sure that the drinks tray is placed in the Equerry's Room every morning. This is a large apartment looking out onto the side garden in which the Equerry-in-Waiting works at a desk set against one of the walls, sometimes battling against the noise of several other people talking and drinking. A previous Lord Chamberlain once asked the Equerry-in-Waiting of the day if he would prefer a quieter room. He was politely told not to interfere as an intelligent Equerry can pick up all sorts of useful information if he keeps his ears open when others are gathered in his room. Afternoon tea is also available in the Equerry's Room and the number three footman has the job of carrying the trays for this meal.

Footman number five acts as valet to the Equerry and any other Member who stays in the Palace overnight. Quite often Members will find it convenient to remain in the Palace after a very late engagement or if there is to be a particularly early call the next day. They are given the use of a pleasant room and footman number five will lay out their clothes, clean their shoes and perform any other tasks that might be required.

The Equerry-in-Waiting no longer has to live in at Buckingham Palace. He is given the use of a flat in St James's Palace for the duration of his three-year appointment so that he is available immediately if he is required. In the days when he did live in the routine for waking him up in the morning was exacting and inflexible. The footman entered the room quietly carrying the calling tray (tea or coffee and biscuits). However, before he was allowed to put the tray down on the bedside table he had to draw back the curtains and turn on the radio. It was always tuned in to the 'Today' programme on BBC Radio 4. The footman did not speak to the Equerry unless the noise of the radio had not woken him. Some Equerries after only a short time at Buckingham Palace become afflicted with what the servants call 'red carpet fever' – in other words, become 'more royal than the Royals', very much aware of their privileged position and using it accordingly. They fail to realise that so far as The Queen herself is concerned, there is no difference between them and any other member of her Household. In her eyes they are all equal – and all servants! However, not all Equerries have been the same. Some were friendly to the staff and very easy to get on with, but just to be on the safe side the footmen always carried out the usual routine until they knew the sort of man they were dealing with.

Once the Equerry was fully awake and drinking his tea or coffee, the footman would remove his previous day's clothes and lay out a fresh set, having found out from his colleague at The King's Door whether Her Majesty was giving audiences or conducting an investiture. If so the Equerry's full dress uniform would be worn. If not, his normal number one uniform was laid out with gold braid worn over the right shoulder. The Equerry's bedroom was on the second floor, not very far from the Princess Royal's office. Her staff have seen many Equerries come and go and the ladies in the office are quietly amused at the changes they see in the manner of the Equerries once they have found their feet.

If the footman finds he has been allocated number six in the list of daily duties he knows that someone important must be arriving. For number six guards the Grand Entrance to the Palace within the main quadrangle by which a newly appointed ambassador or other visiting dignitary will arrive. The footman opens the car doors and works under the supervision of one of the Pages of the Presence who look after both this entrance and also the Privy Purse Door, the side entrance used by most visitors and at which the Government boxes containing State papers are delivered several times a day.

Pages of the Presence are the servants of The Queen who come into contact with members of the public most frequently and they are chosen for their discretion, tact and diplomacy. They work closely with the suites of visiting Heads of State who are staying at the Palace, so a knowledge of foreign languages can be useful. One long-serving Page was asked what he considered the most important attributes for his job. 'Good feet, hollow legs and a highly developed sense of the ridiculous,' he replied. A more mundane task performed by the Page of the Presence is to see that a fresh supply of stationery is placed on the desks of the Private Secretaries every day.

When a foreign ambassador is being given an audience with The Queen or an investiture is taking place, the arrangements within Buckingham Palace are the responsibility of the Page of the Chambers, who is also the Deputy Palace Steward. If an ambassador is calling to present his Letters of Credence the Page of the Chambers will arrange for two footmen to ride on the carriage conveying him. It is a popular job which is normally offered to off-duty footmen who are given further time off in lieu, and as the official appointments are rarely early in the morning they also get a lie-in. The duty takes only a couple of hours so the rest of the day is free.

At an Investiture the 150 men and women being honoured are each allowed to bring two guests and the Page of the Chambers makes sure the necessary number of footmen, cloakroom attendants and nurses in the first-aid room are on duty.

As lunch for the Royal Family and the Household is at one o'clock, footmen usually eat much earlier, around 11.30. The Servants' Hall is very busy at this time but most people manage to get through the meal in no more than twenty minutes.

Once the lunches have been served there is a quiet period except for staff on duty at the Privy Purse Door, which is always busy. Some of the footmen, stewards and catering staff retire to their own rooms, others go into the large recreation room beside the kitchens where there are tables, chairs, a small kitchenette for making tea or coffee and a television set. There is also a notice board giving details of social outings which is used as well for advertising anything anyone wants to buy or sell.

The Palace comes briefly back to life at tea-time, especially if several members of the Royal Family are at home. The Princess Royal enjoys afternoon tea, served in her sitting room on the second floor with a selection of sandwiches, gâteaux and pastries, and woe betide the footman who forgets to check that all her favourites are on the tray before he carries it up. Once he has placed it in her room, however, he can leave. Her Royal Highness serves herself and any guests who might be present.

Unless there is a function on in the Palace, the evenings tend to be rather quiet. The Queen's Page will check which of the Royal Family will be at home and also whether they plan to dine with The Queen or with guests of their own. If Her Majesty knows that one of her children is going to be in the Palace and alone she will usually invite him or her to join her, but they have to wait for an invitation. Without that telephone call no one, not even her only daughter, would dream of inviting themselves. Those who eat with The Queen are waited on by her footman. If, however, members of the Royal Family are dining in their own rooms, the number two or number four footman on duty will be allocated.

Dinner, even for the Royal Family, is an informal affair for which neither The Queen nor Prince Philip puts on evening dress. It is a far cry from the days of King George V and Queen Mary, when His Majesty invariably wore a frock coat and the Order of the Garter at dinner and The Queen a diamond tiara and a full-length formal evening gown – even when they dined alone. Today the only members of the Royal Family who usually dress for dinner are Queen Elizabeth the Queen Mother and Princess Margaret.

Once dinner is finished the footmen are free. They can leave the Palace, using a side entrance, or they can invite friends to join them for a drink inside Buckingham Palace itself. The rule is that all staff should apply in advance for permission to bring outsiders in but the Master of the Household takes a very relaxed attitude to these age-old regulations (when security allows), and if someone brings a friend without getting the necessary permission, there is rarely any fuss, so long as no undue noise is made. However, all visitors have to leave by 10 P.M. and overnight guests are definitely forbidden.

Buckingham Palace is surrounded by forty-five acres of the finest private gardens in London, but staff are never allowed to use them – even when the Royal Family is not in residence. The rules governing the use of the swimming pool in the south-west corner are slightly different, but apply only to senior Members of the Household. Domestic staff are never permitted to swim there. The Members may use the pool in the early morning, subject to one or two minor conditions. If, when they arrive, a member of the Royal Family is swimming, they do not enter the water unless invited to do so. If they are already swimming when one of the Royals turns up, they immediately get out – again unless invited to remain. The most regular user is the Princess of Wales, who likes the pool to herself, so the Household have got to know her times and avoid the pool when she is due.

Footmen do not work regular hours and because of this anti-social aspect of their jobs it is not too difficult for a suitable young man to get appointed. The requirements are intelligence and a capacity for hard work, and the easiest method of joining the Royal Household in this role is to apply direct to the Master of the Household. The money is not great but there is one perk. Other members of the extensive Royal Family who do not employ a large staff themselves often look for trained footmen to help out when they are giving a formal reception or dinner party. The pay is good, and The Queen – who knows full well what is going on – happily turns a blind eye to this 'moonlighting'. There have been many occasions when The Queen or her children have attended a private party only to find themselves waited upon by their own servants. The footmen and kitchen staff also occasionally work for other non-royal employers in the London area, where the money is even better. The staff have a 'fixer' who arranges all the extra duties and all the major party-givers know who to approach if they want to use Buckingham Palace staff in their spare time.

When members of the Royal Family visit friends in their country houses, either an Equerry or Lady-in-Waiting will tip the hosts' staff on their behalf – £10 for each person is the usual amount. However, royal servants are expressly forbidden from accepting gratuities from any of The Queen's guests. During the reign of George V The King felt it necessary to advise guests that the practice was forbidden, and ladies and gentlemen arriving at Windsor found the following note in their rooms:

> The Master of the Household presents his compliments and begs to ask the Guests of the King and Queen to refrain from offering presents of money to the Servants of Their Majesties' Establishment.
> The Servants do not expect presents of any kind and the Master of the Household would greatly appreciate assistance on the part of Their Majesties' Guests in maintaining the observance of this regulation.

The rule was welcomed by many of the guests as they often arrived without any cash and this may well be the reason why it was instituted, to spare guests any possible embarrassment rather than to deprive the servants of the extra money.

The same rules apply today but from time to time some guests ignore it and footmen have been given large gifts of money, especially when the guest has been the ruler of one of the Middle-East countries where generosity is considered an indispensable common courtesy.

There is also the chance of some foreign travel. The Travelling Yeoman, who, with his colleague the Sergeant Yeoman, supervises all The Queen's travel arrangements, is responsible for seeing that the right number of footmen move with the Court when it goes to Windsor Castle, Balmoral or any of the other royal residences. As his title implies, he travels with The Queen wherever she goes – on board *Britannia*, the Royal Train or The Queen's Flight – looking after all the royal luggage. This can amount to up to five tons for a full foreign tour, so it is easy to see how important his job can be. A trip on board the Royal Yacht is considered the highlight of the year for any footman, so they all try to catch the eye of the Travelling Yeoman when carrying out their normal duties in the hope of being chosen. *Britannia* is the most relaxed of all the royal residences and although the standard never falls, the pleasant atmosphere affects even the most junior servant. Everyone loves to have a spell on board and looks forward to the next time.

Any young man who joins the Royal Household is given an introductory talk by the Palace Steward and is taught what to do when he meets a member of the Royal Family. The first greeting should always be 'Your Majesty' or 'Your Royal Highness' and subsequently they should be addressed as either Ma'am (to rhyme with jam) or Sir. Everybody in the Palace bows or bobs whenever they meet a member of the family – except the Private Secretaries who are in and out of The Queen's office perhaps several times a day – and if a footman passes, say, Prince Philip, in one of the corridors, he will stop until the Prince has moved on but will never speak until he has been acknowledged.

The strange thing about life at Buckingham Palace is that although on the surface life is very formal, underneath there is a complete lack of formality. The team spirit runs from the Lord Chamberlain down to the most junior footman and it is only in front of strangers that an air of sober and serious servility is displayed. Perhaps the least formal relationships of all are those between The Queen and her closest servants. Her Majesty calls them by their Christian names, and even though they are always aware of her position, they are relaxed in her presence – and that is what she prefers. If people are nervous around her it makes her irritable; if they are relaxed she too is able to be more at ease.

The Palace Steward may be the senior of The Queen's domestic servants but he is not the highest paid. That distinction lies with the man who actually prepares Her Majesty's food – the Royal Chef, Lionel Mann. As with many of the world's leading hotels, where the head chef is second only to the general manager in terms of importance and salary, so it is at the Palace. The Royal Chef, who rules the ground-floor area where the vast kitchens are located, takes second place only to the Master of the Household himself. His salary may not match that of his opposite numbers at the Savoy or Claridge's, where the head chefs earn up to £60,000 a year, but he certainly makes more than anyone else 'below stairs' – though his actual earnings are a closely guarded secret in order not to provoke too much jealousy among his colleagues.

The kitchen staff are organised on military lines. The Royal Chef is Commander-in-Chief and everyone else is arranged in 'Brigades' of between eight and twenty, depending on the demands of the day. If a State Banquet is being prepared they work in Brigades of ten – a Head Chef, Sous Chef, Chef de Partie, Vegetable Chef, Fish Chef, Sauce Chef, Apprentice Chefs and Scullery Hands. The chefs at Buckingham Palace are the only servants who have to provide their own working clothes. They all wear full whites on duty while the remainder of the kitchen staff wear overalls which are provided free of charge.

Because of the need to economise, not all the staff who work in the kitchens are full time. For special functions extra help is engaged, mainly as kitchen hands. Occasionally advertisements are placed in the *Evening Standard*, but more often the Head Chef and the Chief Assistant in the Master of the Household's office know who is available from previous functions and offer the opportunity of earning around £3 an hour for an evening's work.

All the washing up after a State Banquet is done by hand, the priceless crystal glasses and delicate china being handled very carefully in the wooden sink units in the Glass and China Rooms. There are no stainless steel sinks in this area to avoid any accidental chipping.

The washing up is done by members of the Royal British Legion from the Fulham Road Branch. No one knows just how they came to corner this particular market but they have done the job as long as anyone can remember.

A chef hoping to be employed in the Royal Household undergoes a rigid examination in a series of interviews. All have been through a training course at one of the recognised catering colleges and each one will be asked to prepare a number of dishes for the Royal Chef to sample. This can be a nerve-racking experience for a youngster, and even experienced chefs have been known to shake a little under the unrelenting gaze of the man who cooks The Queen's meals. His word is law. Even if the Master of the Household is satisfied that an applicant is suitable, he will not be offered the post until the Royal Chef has given his own personal stamp of approval.

Domestic staff at Buckingham Palace tend to stick together in little cliques. Footmen become friendly with other footmen and the kitchen staff rarely fraternise with anyone outside their group. As one of the most senior of The Queen's courtiers has said about the royal kitchens: 'It's a different world.' To anyone coming in from outside it is, indeed, a different world. Even those who have worked in some of the world's greatest hotels sometimes find it strange that, in times when economy is the watchword in almost every establishment, nothing is allowed to mar the standard in this house. Only one criterion is demanded by the Master of the Household and implemented by the Royal Chef – perfection. The Vegetable Chef knows that when he is preparing the sprouts for the royal table, each one must have exactly the same dimensions as its neighbour. And although today the apples and currants for the Dutch apple tart are apportioned by computer, their quality is the responsibility of the Pastry Chef who will not hesitate to throw the lot out if they are not quite up to the standard he expects.

The kitchens are probably the last place in Buckingham Palace where standards have remained at the level of a hundred years ago. But now they have been converted to North Sea gas and there are dish-washing machines for everyday use, while for more than twenty years now there have been only two main kitchens: one for pastry and one for all other food.

In the old days cost was never a consideration. Staff stayed for life and were suitably grateful for the security and prestige that working in the royal kitchens offered. Even today there is something special about being able to say that you are a royal chef, while on those occasions when a full State Banquet is taking place, something of the glamour and magic of a bygone age is captured once more.

Of course the royal kitchens today, and the numbers who work in them, bear no comparison with those of previous reigns. Oliver Everett, The Queen's Librarian, has retained in his records a letter written in 1927 by one of his predecessors, Sir John Fortescue, in which he described the domestic arrangements at Windsor Castle: 'The royal kitchen kept sixty souls busily employed. In the steward's room – a room contemporaneous with the cloisters of Westminster Abbey and roofed with the like vaulting – there were two dinners of one hundred each for the upper servants. In the servants' hall – a fourteenth-century building with columns and vaulting of the period – there were two dinners of two hundred each for the lower servants.'

The majority of domestic servants employed in the Royal Household are male; just over ten per cent are women and they all work under the Chief Housekeeper.

It was in January 1970 that the Master of the Household decided to streamline the work of housekeeping at all the royal residences by creating the position of Chief Housekeeper. Her job is to oversee the work of all the housemaids at Buckingham Palace, Windsor Castle, the Palace of Holyroodhouse, Balmoral Castle and Sandringham. Buckingham Palace had had its own housekeeper before this but there was no one to supervise and coordinate the work at all the other homes. The present Chief Housekeeper is Miss Heather Colebrook, who, although she is still single, within the Palace is given the courtesy title of Mrs.

Twenty-six housemaids are employed at Buckingham Palace as well as a small number of cleaning women who come in daily to help with the dusting, polishing and making of beds. Most of the work is done in the early morning, and the Chief Housekeeper issues a rota so that each one knows exactly what she has to do several weeks in advance.

Any lady staying in the Palace, royal or otherwise, has an early morning tea tray delivered to her bedroom. It is carried upstairs by a footman, but a housemaid always takes it into the bedroom itself. At Buckingham Palace, footmen are not permitted to enter a bedroom occupied by a lady.

The job of keeping house at Buckingham Palace is a massive undertaking which never seems to end. The Chief Housekeeper looks after the linen for bedrooms and dining rooms, the condition of the curtains and carpets and the laundry. Most of the Royal Family's laundry is done by Sycamore Laundry in Clapham, south-west London, as it has been for nearly a hundred years; but the day-to-day sheets and towels are still laundered in the basement washrooms where the Chief Housekeeper has installed a battery of washing machines. Surprising as it may seem, the Chief Housekeeper does not have an open cheque book when it comes to replacing worn equipment. If a carpet sweeper, vacuum cleaner or washing machine breaks down, the maintenance men in the Palace workshops try every means to repair it before a new item can be bought.

At the beginning of every year, the Housekeeper sends a list of her expected requirements for the next twelve months to the Master of the Household, and if he agrees with the list, he then has to obtain the approval of the Keeper of the Privy Purse before the money is spent. Every member of the Royal Family, from The Queen down, has the reputation of being careful with money, and the Royal Household is possibly more cost conscious than any other in the world. The Queen will sometimes suggest that sheets can be darned and used again, and the age and condition of some of the curtains and carpets would shock many people who only see the Palace from the outside. As one of the housemaids has been heard to say, 'It's amazing what you can do with a little make-do and mend.'

Housemaids at Buckingham Palace rarely come into contact with the Royal Family. They are occasionally seen but never heard. Even today most of them will go to extraordinary lengths to avoid being seen by The Queen or Prince Philip, dodging into an alcove or hiding behind a curtain if they notice one of them approaching. There is no reason why they should react in this way, and it is certainly not because of any instructions issued by The Queen or her husband. It's just that tradition dies hard in the Royal Household, and in the old days any female servant seen anywhere near the royal quarters after midday was instantly dismissed without a reference – the equivalent of a death sentence to a member of the Victorian working class.

Another tradition that is faithfully followed is that the living quarters of male and female staff are carefully segregated. Some of the women live on the mezzanine floor while others are housed in the attics near the men but in an entirely separate section. But the housemaids at Buckingham Palace have managed to breach one former golden rule. They no longer have to remain single if they wish to keep their jobs. In the early days of The Queen's reign every housemaid had to be unmarried and remain so if she was to stay in royal service. A number of relationships developed between footmen and housemaids and there have been quite a few marriages. But the rule was never broken or even bent. Thirty years ago a former Palace Steward married a housemaid who had several years' experience but once they were married she was asked to leave. Wives were always welcome as guests at staff social functions and even at The Queen's Christmas party, but not as working members of her Household until a few years ago. Nowadays staff who marry are offered flats or cottages as an inducement for them to stay.

Conditions for domestic staff in the Royal Household have improved immeasurably in recent years, as has the attitude of their employers. One of the longest-serving footmen still recalls the occasion when as a very junior servant he experienced the short temper of the late Duke of Gloucester, the third son of King George V, who was very much one of the 'old school' in that he believed that servants should be neither seen nor heard. In those days His Royal Highness and the Duchess (now Princess Alice) lived in an apartment in St James's Palace and it still had open fireplaces. One winter's afternoon the Duke was sitting in an armchair in front of the fire when a piece of hot coal jumped out onto the carpet. It lay smouldering for a time, the hole in the carpet getting larger and larger, and His Royal Highness apparently watched this happening, without in any way attempting to do anything about it. Eventually this young footman came into the room in the normal course of his duties and in order to stoke the fire. Seeing the burning carpet, he immediately rushed to pick up the offending piece of coal and stamp out the burning rug. The Duke said to him, 'Where the hell have you been? I've been sitting here for hours waiting for someone to turn up.' The footman was obliged to say nothing in his own defence. It simply had not occurred to the Duke to use a pair of tongs to pick up the coal himself or even to ring for the footman to come and do so. As the footman said nearly thirty years later, 'Things had to change.'

Wages in every Royal Household are poor when compared with what could be earned in industry – even in catering, which itself has always been regarded as the 'Cinderella' of the service industries. But the pay has become more realistic of late and the free accommodation and meals make up a great deal of the discrepancy. A junior house-maid on a little over £6,000 a year in the Royal Household would probably only earn about thirty or forty pounds a week more outside. She would never be able to afford a room in central London or pay for three good meals a day out of the extra money, so it all works out reasonably fairly in the end.

When young women or junior footmen leave the Palace it is not always because of the money alone. Many do not like the enforced isolation of long periods spent at Balmoral (eight miles from the nearest village and forty miles from Aberdeen) or Sandringham, where there are few 'off-duty' attractions for modern youngsters. The days when a dance in the local village hall was considered the high-light of the social week have gone for ever. Today, young people from even the humblest homes demand something more sophisticated such as a wine bar or a disco.

But for many men and women service to the Royal Family is a matter of pride and honour that far outweighs any monetary reward. Perhaps they are seduced by the aura of history and glamour that permeates Buckingham Palace and the other royal residences. It's a fever that, once contracted, can last a lifetime.

7

THE
LADIES-IN-WAITING

'WANTED – part-timers for irregular work. Hours – anything from 7 A.M. to midnight. Plenty of travel; no wages but meals provided on duty. Qualifications: impeccable breeding; good dress sense; ability to mix with dustmen and dukes, absolute discretion and above all a sprinkling of good humour. Apply with references.' That might be the way in which some of the most sought after positions in the world would be advertised – if they ever were advertised at all, which they are not! And if you did become one of these part-timers, you would join one of the world's most exclusive 'clubs'. It is so exclusive that there are less than eighty members, all women, and each one has been personally invited. You cannot apply – you have to wait to be asked, either by The Queen herself or by one of the other ladies in the Royal Family.

They are, of course, the Ladies-in-Waiting to the female members of the Royal Family. Those almost invisible but quite indispensable aides without whom, on a public engagement, The Queen, the Princess of Wales, the Princess Royal and all the other senior ladies in the family never venture forth. And because the Royal Family undertakes so many public engagements these days it is necessary for them to have a large number of Ladies-in-Waiting to share the duties.

The Queen has fourteen, in different categories, not nearly as many as might at first appear because they take it in turns to be on duty, while for three of them the appointment is purely honorary. This is the case for Mrs Michael Wall, who was appointed a Lady-in-Waiting after serving at the Palace as Assistant Press Secretary for twenty-seven years. The other two honorary ladies are Mrs John Woodroffe and Lady Rose Baring.

These days the demands of royalty have to fit in with everyday responsibilities to family and home, and The Queen is well aware of, and sympathetic to, such considerations. In fact Her Majesty is the only constant female figure at her Court. All her Ladies are able to take a break from the routine at some time; for The Queen, it never stops.

Queen Elizabeth, the Queen Mother has ten Ladies-in-Waiting, seven regular and three extra, all of them acquaintances of many years' standing but none approaching her own great age. Princess Margaret has ten, and the Princess Royal needs nine, for she heads the league table in royal duties. Princess Alice, Duchess of Gloucester has seven Ladies-in-Waiting and the Princess of Wales six. Next come the Duchess of Gloucester and the Duchess of Kent with four each, while Princess Alexandra and Princess Michael of Kent manage with two each.

The Queen, of course, has the most formal and rigidly structured schedule and her Ladies-in-Waiting work to a different pattern from that of the Ladies serving other members of the Royal Family, where the system is fairly relaxed and flexible. In Her Majesty's Household the Ladies-in-Waiting enjoy job-titles which date back many centuries. At the top is the Mistress of the Robes, who by tradition is a Duchess. At present the Duchess of Grafton holds this position. In bygone days the Mistress of the Robes was a political appointment, and at times of a Queen Regnant the Mistress of the Robes could, and did, exert considerable influence through her daily access to the reigning monarch. But since the early days of Queen Victoria the appointment has been made personally by The Queen and the duties are mainly of an honorary nature. Nominally, however, the Mistress of the Robes is in charge of the roster of the other Ladies-in-Waiting and is always kept informed of any serious changes concerning her colleagues while a lady clerk looks after the day-to-day administrative details.

The Duchess of Grafton has been Mistress of the Robes since 1967 but she has been a member of the Household since 1953, when she was appointed a Lady of the Bedchamber. Born in 1920 as Ann Fortune-Smith, she married the Earl of Euston in 1946, who became by inheritance the 11th Duke of Grafton in 1970. Her badge of office is a miniature of The Queen set in a jewelled oval brooch which is worn below the left shoulder.

It is part of the duties of the Mistress of the Robes to be in attendance at State functions and a number of informal events. She attends The Queen at one of the Garden Parties, but no longer has to personally present to The Queen the wives of foreign Ambassadors, a task now performed by the Marshal of the Diplomatic Corps. Undoubtedly the most important occasion when the Mistress of the Robes is on duty is at the State Opening of Parliament, when she supervises the Robing of The Queen in the Throne Room at the House of Lords and leads the other Ladies-in-Waiting in the royal procession. They then stand alongside the throne while The Queen reads her speech and follow Her Majesty back to the Robing Room.

The atmosphere in the House of Lords can be very hot and humid so the Ladies-in-Waiting need to have plenty of stamina. A former Mistress of the Robes offered the following advice to her colleagues before they left the Palace: 'Always go to the lavatory as late as you can, and keep a bar of chocolate handy in case you feel faint.' So far none of the Ladies has been seen munching in the Mother of Parliaments, and indeed this gastronomic advice is totally ignored by modern Ladies-in-Waiting, one of whom says, 'We never eat chocolate on such occasions – it's too messy and makes you feel sick!'

By modern custom the wife of a new King appoints four Ladies of the Bedchamber and four Women of the Bedchamber. Ladies are always peeresses and Women of the Bedchamber usually the daughters of peers. However, The Queen has only two Ladies of the Bedchamber: the Countess of Airlie (wife of the Lord Chamberlain) and the Lady Farnham, with two Extra Ladies, the Marchioness of Abergavenny (pronounced Abergenny) and the Countess of Cromer. As a reigning monarch The Queen needs fewer Ladies than, for example, did her mother as Queen Consort. The Ladies-in-Waiting to the wife of King George VI did much of the clerical and administrative work which is today performed in the Private Secretary's Office or by one of the other departments in the Royal Household which exist solely to serve the Sovereign, male or female. If the Sovereign is a Queen Regnant, much of her correspondence is official, hence the assistance of government departments and the Household. When the Queen is the wife of a reigning monarch she does not have the help, or the need, of such professional advisers. Her work is more of a social nature and her Ladies-in-Waiting are quite capable of handling anything that comes within that orbit of responsibility.

Most of the duties are in fact carried out by the four Women of the Bedchamber. They are the Hon. Mary Morrison, Lady Susan Hussey, the Lady Elton and Mrs John Dugdale. If things get too hectic they can call on the services of two Extra Women of the Bedchamber: Mrs Robert de Pass and Lady Abel Smith.

The women of the Bedchamber are on duty one at a time and operate a shift system of 'two weeks on, four weeks off'. When on duty they may, if they wish, 'live in' at Buckingham Palace or wherever The Queen is in residence at the time. At present only two of the Women of the Bedchamber do so as the others have homes nearby. Inside the Palace they are accommodated in a delightful suite of rooms on the second floor, quite close to the Princess Royal's office.

Apart from accompanying The Queen whenever she goes out in public, the main duties are to deal with Her Majesty's official entertaining, audiences, lunches and dinners and with a lot of her correspondence. Letters from children and old people are invariably answered by the Ladies-in-Waiting for it is felt that perhaps an answer written by one of the Private Secretaries would be a little too formal. The Woman of the Bedchamber also undertakes some of The Queen's personal shopping.

At Buckingham Palace Ladies-in-Waiting usually see The Queen only when she sends for them – which is quite frequently – at certain meals, audiences and on any outings Her Majesty might make, for they are of course more companions than servants. When not required they spend their time in their private sitting room and usually take their meals in the Household dining-room with other senior members of the Royal Household. But at the other royal residences, life is far more informal.

At Windsor the Lady-in-Waiting acts as a personal guide to female guests of The Queen, showing them to their rooms, and ensuring that the guest is comfortable, and they too are treated more as guests, lunching and dining with the Royal Family every day. The same applies at Sandringham and Balmoral where The Queen likes to maintain a 'country house' atmosphere.

The one quality all the Ladies share is devotion to The Queen. It's not a slavish, blinkered devotion that can see no wrong, but an admiration that has grown through years of close association with someone who 'works much harder than any of us'. As one senior and very experienced Lady-in-Waiting who has spent more than a quarter of a century with The Queen says, 'I cannot remember a single occasion when I have been ordered to do something. It's always in the form of a request – and she usually manages to make you feel that you are doing a favour.'

Over the years Lady Susan Hussey, who is the sister of the politician William Waldegrave, has become an old and trusted friend of all the Royal Family and she is godmother to Prince William. When Princess Anne was starting out in public life she had no household of her own so The Queen 'lent' Lady Susan to show her daughter the ropes. She is married to 'Duke' Hussey, Chairman of the BBC, and as such is often included on the guest list at official functions when not on duty herself. She is also perhaps more in contact with the outside world than most in The Queen's inner circle and consequently has had the task of keeping her mistress informed on all sorts of touchy subjects, including, in the early days, the driving habits of Princess Anne and, more recently, about the choice of brides for both the Prince of Wales and the Duke of York. Hers is one of the most delicate jobs in the Palace. The fact that she has done it outstandingly for more than twenty-five years and is still a good friend to all members of the Royal Family speaks volumes in itself.

The days when Ladies-in-Waiting were political appointments have, happily, long gone. No Prime Minister today, or any party, would dream of trying to influence The Queen in the choice of the female members of her Household, and it is equally certain that The Queen cares very little about their politics. Because they all come from similar backgrounds and are socially of the same class, it would be easy to generalise in assuming that the Ladies are all upper-class Conservatives. But whether they are or not is a matter of supreme indifference to The Queen – and it has probably never occurred to anyone to ask.

For the other members of the Royal Family the system of choosing Ladies-in-Waiting is slightly different – as is the job they do. Most are of similar age to the person for whom they work and generally, but not always, they are friends of long standing with like interests. Caroline Wallace (the former wife of Major Malcolm Wallace and now Mrs William Nunnerly) and Jane Holderness-Roddam were riding colleagues of the Princess Royal long before they were invited to become Ladies-in-Waiting, but Celia Innes and Rowena Feilden had met her only occasionally when they were recruited by someone close to the Princess. And that is usually the way the approach comes. An informal enquiry is made on behalf of the member of the Royal Family so that both sides are spared the embarrassment of a direct refusal if the lady approached does not wish to be considered.

Shân Legge-Bourke, one of the Princess Royal's Ladies-in-Waiting, has a refreshingly open view about being one of the Royal Family's most trusted helpers – and the manner in which she and her colleagues are treated by others. 'It ranges from dripping sycophancy to supreme indifference,' she says. 'Sometimes we are looked upon as the answer to every local dignitary's prayer and at other times they could not care less. We almost get knocked down in the rush. It is really all great fun.'

Most of the Ladies-in-Waiting are not paid a salary, but they do get their travelling and any other expenses. An exception is Anne Beckwith-Smith, who acts as personal secretary to the Princess of Wales as well as Lady-in-Waiting. She is paid a full-time salary plus expenses. Even so, no one does it solely for the money, and for each and every one of these invaluable companions, the main reward is knowing that by doing their jobs efficiently and unobtrusively, they are in the end helping The Queen with her unceasing round of royal duties.

8

THE KEEPER
OF THE PRIVY PURSE

THE MONARCHY is expensive to run – a little over a million pounds a week – and the finances of the Royal Family and their Households are under constant scrutiny. Rarely a week passes without some reference to the costs of maintaining The Queen's Flight, the Royal Yacht *Britannia* or one of the many other expenses associated with royalty, for the Press can always rely on a reaction, favourable or otherwise, whenever they print something about the amount of money spent by, or on, the Royal Family. Parliament debates the royal budget regularly, and there are several backbenchers who know they can attract headlines (when otherwise they would be ignored) if they attack the lesser members of the Royal Family purely on grounds of their alleged extravagance.

When the Duke and Duchess of York moved into their new home in Windsor Great Park, built at an estimated (but not confirmed) cost of £5 million, critics of royal expenditure had a field day. There were plenty of houses available close to Windsor Castle already, so why wasn't one adapted for their use? Why did they have to build something new and in a style completely out of keeping with what most people thought of as a royal home? Where did the money come from? How much came from the taxpayer? Who would pay for the security, said to cost around £300,000 a year? The fact that the house was a gift from Her Majesty's private funds was almost completely overlooked. It was a good story, so why let the facts spoil it? Another detail about the house which was not given much prominence was that while The Queen paid for the construction and gave the building

113

to her son and daughter-in-law, it was not, in fact, owned by them at all. Realising that if she handed over the deeds to the property and it was registered in the Yorks' names, it would be liable to tax when they died, Her Majesty did the obvious thing on the advice of her financial experts. As The Queen is the only person in the country exempt from both capital transfer and income tax (although she does pay tax on certain capital gains and also Value Added Tax on all purchases), she prudently retained ownership of the house in her own name. So there is no question of the Duke of York being able to sell the property.

The same thing happened in 1976 when Princess Anne moved to Gatcombe Park in Gloucestershire. Again it was a private purchase, and no one outside the Royal Household actually knows the real price paid. Speculation ranged from a quarter of a million pounds to over two million, but the price was nearer half a million, and that's as close as any outsider is likely to get. When Captain Mark Phillips said, in an unguarded moment, 'We are just like any other young couple with a mortgage,' he was inviting the shoals of critical articles that immediately appeared. But the loan to which he referred was arranged to finance certain alterations to the house and additions to the stable block; it did not in any way affect the ownership of the property.

In fact The Queen's investment in the Gatcombe estate was a brilliant move on the part of her advisers. It is now worth in excess of £3 million.

The finances of the Royal Family are complex and highly secret. The details of The Queen's assets are known to only a few people and none of them has ever disclosed, by so much as a whisper, how much she is worth or where her fortune is invested. However, it is generally acknowledged that Her Majesty is one of the wealthiest people in the world and probably the richest woman alive. Her fortune is said to be around six and a half billion pounds while a recent newspaper report suggested that, even if she did nothing but leave the money on deposit in the bank, her resources would increase at the rate of £1.8 million a day. But this is pure speculation, of course, and the figures have probably been grossly inflated. When Lord Cobbold, the then Lord Chamberlain, gave evidence to a House of

Commons Committee examining royal finances in 1972, he said that, 'Estimates of Her Majesty's private wealth as being between £50 million and £100 million are highly exaggerated.'

If this was true, and nobody raised any doubts about the veracity of the statement at the time, or has done so since, it is highly unlikely that The Queen's wealth even approaches £6 billion in the early nineteen-nineties. That she is a very wealthy woman is beyond question, but to claim that her income could be £1.8 million a day is plainly ridiculous, even though she does enjoy unique tax advantages that allow her assets to increase in a way denied to any other person in her realm.

Another common myth about The Queen's property holdings is that she owns large chunks of prime real estate in the United States, including skyscrapers on Park Avenue in New York. I have been given categorical assurances by the Royal Household that Her Majesty does not own any property in the United States or anywhere else outside the United Kingdom; nor has she ever done so.

One of those who knows better than most the extent of The Queen's wealth is the man responsible for all Her Majesty's financial affairs, the Keeper of the Privy Purse and Treasurer to The Queen, Major Sir Shane Blewitt KCVO. He holds what is obviously one of the most important positions within the Royal Household and ranks next to Her Majesty's Private Secretary in the order of precedence at Buckingham Palace.

As Keeper of the Privy Purse, Sir Shane looks after The Queen's private financial affairs, controlling, with her agreement of course, her bank account. It's held at Coutts in The Strand, now part of the National Westminster Group, who, although they have provided Her Majesty and all the other members of the Royal Family with their cheque books since 1760, when George III became the first British monarch to open an account with them, still do not hold a Royal Warrant. And they never will. The reason is that bankers, like solicitors and doctors, are not considered to be 'tradesmen' and it is only those 'in trade' who qualify for Royal Warrants. The Keeper is also responsible for the finances of the royal estates, the royal stud and The Queen's racing expenses.

There really is a Privy Purse, made of tapestry, and at the coronation of the Sovereign, the Keeper carries it in the ceremonial procession in Westminster Abbey. After the coronation it traditionally becomes his property. Part of the Keeper's duties in centuries past was to distribute money to the poor *en route* to the coronation, and for this purpose a hundred silver coins were kept in the Purse. These coins were, in theory, given by the Sovereign, but in practice were provided by the Keeper of the Privy Purse himself, who was expected to regard it as a privilege to subsidise the Sovereign in this manner. The custom was allowed to lapse many years ago, certainly before Queen Victoria's coronation in 1837.

As Treasurer to The Queen, the Keeper of the Privy Purse is responsible for all Civil List finances, the amount voted by Parliament to fund the running of the Royal Household and other costs incurred in the course of The Queen's duties as Head of State.

Land was the original source of wealth for British monarchs. Successive Sovereigns acquired vast tracts of ground and huge estates either through right of conquest or, later, by more conventional methods, so that in the mid-fifteenth century, said to be the peak of royal ownership, the monarch owned more than one-fifth of the total land area of the United Kingdom. This happy set of circumstances remained – except during the time of Cromwell's Protectorate – until 1689, when Parliament invited the Dutch King William to occupy the British throne in partnership with his wife Queen Mary, the daughter of Queen Anne. In an attempt to control the excesses that had characterised past regal expenditure a fixed sum was allocated for each year, and this system operated, with some changes, until 1760 and the accession of George III, who surrendered his income from nearly all the lands he owned in return for a fixed allowance from Parliament. This allowance was, and still is, known as the Civil List.

George III's government appointed a Board of Commissioners to administer the land as profitably as possible. The income went to the Exchequer, while the land itself remained the property of the Crown, which is still the case today. The Crown Estate remains part of the hereditary possessions of the Sovereign in right of the Crown; so while the Government does not own it, neither is it the private property of the reigning Sovereign, and The Queen could not sell any part of the Crown Estate for her own benefit. It's a complicated situation but one that appears to work satisfactorily at the present time and is yet another of the many financial problems dealt with by the Keeper of the Privy Purse. One might argue that the country makes a profit out of the monarchy because the revenue from the Crown Estate exceeds the amount paid in Civil List allowances. In 1989, for instance, the net income surrendered to the Treasury's Consolidated Fund amounted to £55 million – just about the same sum as the total cost of the monarchy over the same period.

Contrary to what many people think, both in the United Kingdom and more especially abroad, the Civil List is not a salary for The Queen and no part of it is paid into her private account or those of other members of the Royal Family who receive allowances from it. Every penny has to be accounted for and it is all spent on expenses. From time to time a great deal of fuss is made over the fact that no income tax is paid on Civil List allowances. But as tax is never charged on what the Inland Revenue regards as legitimate expenses, and since nearly 65 per cent of the Civil List goes to pay the salaries and wages of staff and Members of the Royal Households, who are in turn taxed in the normal way, a proportion of the money returns to the Treasury anyway.

It has only been in this century that the Sovereign has been relieved of the burden of paying income tax. Queen Victoria paid income tax, as did her son Edward VII, but in 1910, when King George V came to the throne, Parliament voted to abolish income tax for the Sovereign. As Chancellor of the Exchequer, the fiery Welsh politician Lloyd George persuaded the House of Commons that it was pointless to hand over money to the Sovereign with one hand and then take it back with the other, and succeeding monarchs have had great cause to be grateful for this particular piece of Celtic financial logic. Even so, King George V paid some form of income tax, though no figures have been released as to how much, and it was not until the reign of George VI, from 1936 to 1952, that the Sovereign paid no income tax whatever.

Other members of the Royal Family are exempt from tax on their Civil List allowances but do pay tax on all other sources of income; their tax returns are filed with the Inland Revenue in exactly the same way as those of any other member of the public. The Queen alone

117

pays no tax at all on any part of her private wealth and income, apart from any capital gains made, for example, from the sale of stocks and shares.

The Privy Purse Office also has responsibility for the accounts of all other Households within the Royal Family, with the exception of that of the Prince and Princess of Wales; and the Keeper also liaises with the various Government departments who share the cost of the monarchy, as the Civil List is by no means the only source of finance for official expenditure. In fact some three-quarters of the total cost of maintaining the monarchy is met by public departments – including the £6.7 million it takes every year to operate The Queen's Flight (and the £40 million spent over the past five years on three new BAe 146 aircraft); plus, in 1990–91, an estimated £825,000 for the fares of members of the Royal Family and their Households travelling on civil airlines when an aircraft from The Queen's Flight is either not available or is unsuitable. These and the £9.2 million annual costs of the Royal Yacht are paid for entirely by the Ministry of Defence, who also provide the Royal Equerries at £192,000 a year.

The Queen and the Duke of Edinburgh have four equerries between them while the Queen Mother and the Prince and Princess of Wales have one each, as does the Duke of York. These young officers are almost invariably single, which is just as well as they sometimes work very unsocial hours, and are selected from among the 'high-flyers' in their respective service units. They stay at the Palace for three years during which time they handle, in conjunction with the Royal Mews, all the transport arrangements for the Royal Family and are in attendance at all formal occasions. A spell at Buckingham Palace can be a great help to a service career, but in terms of what they cost one should remember that these officers serve on temporary attachment, and the bulk of this sum goes to pay the salaries which they would receive anyway, wherever they were posted.

The Queen is charged for using the Royal Train, which is owned by British Rail, but she is reimbursed (in 1990 to the tune of £2.3 million) by the Department of Transport. In 1986 £7 million was paid to provide new coaches and a further £18 million in 1990 in order to strengthen the security of the train against possible terrorist attack. This too came from Department of Transport funds.

The Department of the Environment pays for the upkeep of most of the Royal Palaces: Buckingham Palace, Windsor Castle, Kensington Palace, Holyroodhouse, St James's Palace and Hampton Court; an estimated £25.6 million in 1990–91. (There are some strange anomalies. For example, the Master of the Household employs the men who change the light bulbs at Buckingham Palace but the Department of the Environment provides the bulbs.) The Foreign Office picks up the bills every time The Queen or any other member of the Royal Family makes an official visit overseas, while the Central Office of Information pays an estimated £376,000 a year for publicity – providing official hand-outs, information sheets and other associated press items both at home and abroad.

And while it is true that the Prince of Wales's income is provided by the Duchy of Cornwall, it is not entirely accurate to say that he and the Princess of Wales do not receive any money at all from the Civil List. The cost of the clothes they wear when on official visits overseas is met by the Foreign Office, and as the royal couple spend part of every year on foreign tours this presumably adds up to a significant amount. Neither the Foreign Office nor the office of the Prince and Princess will reveal precisely how much is involved but it has been estimated that most years it runs into six figures.

Other items of royal expenditure covered by public departments include all postal services for The Queen, members of her family and official correspondence for the Royal Household. These are all paid by the Post Office, who also pay for staff and other costs of the post office within Buckingham Palace, while the accounts for all telephone calls from all royal residences are settled by the Department of the Environment.

Security is a massive problem and all members of the Royal Family are surrounded by teams of bodyguards who work in shifts. They belong to a division of the Metropolitan Police, and their salaries and expenses, even when travelling abroad on behalf of, or with, a member of the Royal Family, are met by the police authority. It comes to a substantial amount, but whatever it is the Metropolitan Police refuse to disclose the details.

Another task of the Keeper of the Privy Purse is to handle the finances of the Duchy of Lancaster, for two exceptions were made to the surrender of land by George III – the Duchy of Lancaster and the Duchy of Cornwall, both of which remain the personal property of the Sovereign.

The vast wealth of the Duchy of Lancaster and its possession by the monarch goes back to the fourteenth century, when by a series of brilliant marriages with many of the other great land-owning families in Britain and even by marrying into royalty, the earls and dukes of Lancaster had built up a family fortune to rival that of The King himself. Their family holdings stretched right across England from the Irish Sea to the Wash and their ambitions knew no limit. Henry of Bolingbroke, Duke of Lancaster, wanted the throne, and in 1399 he got it, by dispossessing his cousin, Richard II, and having himself crowned as Henry IV. Since then the Duchy has been attached to the Crown.

One of Henry's earliest acts as King was to bestow the Dukedom of Lancaster on his eldest son, Henry of Monmouth, who amassed an even greater fortune. But when he in turn became King Henry V in 1413 he decided the dukedom would remain forever in the possession of the Sovereign. This has been the case ever since the fifteenth century, and the lands of the Duchy of Lancaster are recognised as a private inheritance. Proceeds from the Duchy are kept entirely separate from any other form of allowance for The Queen, are used solely to provide an income for the Sovereign and are not subject to tax. The laws of Britain state that all the land in the country, even that which is held as freehold, is owned technically by the Crown. There is only one exception, the Duchy of Lancaster. For these estates the Land Registry shows the owner as the Duke of Lancaster. The fact that for more than five hundred years Crown and Dukedom have resided in the same person merely underlines the unique position the Duchy holds in the British legal system.

The income from the Duchy of Lancaster is still paid directly to The Queen and provides her with some £1.5 million a year. The estate consists of large areas of land in several counties: Lancashire (where The Queen is still recognised as the Duke of Lancaster), Yorkshire, Lincolnshire, Northamptonshire, Cheshire, Shropshire and Staffordshire, plus the jewel in the crown – the ground on which stands the Savoy Hotel in London – easily one of the most valuable freeholds in the world.

The money the Duchy earns goes into the Privy Purse to meet The Queen's private expenses. For example, all the clothes in Her Majesty's wardrobe are paid for from this source; so too are her many private donations to charity. Balmoral and Sandringham are private homes, owned by The Queen herself, not by the Crown, and she pays for their upkeep out of the income from the Duchy. A large part of the Duchy money goes each year to reimburse the Treasury for allowances paid to certain members of the Royal Family who are not on the official Civil List but who carry out duties on behalf of The Queen from time to time. These include the Duke of Gloucester, Princess Alice, Duchess of Gloucester, the Duke of Kent and Princess Alexandra. The Queen pays all their expenses herself and rigorously checks the figures of all Duchy accounts to make sure the money is well spent.

The estates are managed by a council appointed by The Queen, while the Chancellor of the Duchy of Lancaster is a political appointment of Cabinet rank, the office usually held by the Chairman of whatever party is in power. The Chancellor is nominated by the Prime Minister of the day and it is his responsibility to approve the annual accounts. The Keeper of the Privy Purse is Receiver General of the Duchy of Lancaster, and a member of the Council of the Duchy of Cornwall, the other exemption to the Crown Estate which, although owned by the Sovereign, exists solely to provide an income for the Prince of Wales. This has been the case since King Edward III created his son Edward (the Black Prince) the first Duke of Cornwall in 1337.

Prince Charles is the 25th Duke of Cornwall and has received all the income from the Duchy since his twenty-first birthday in 1969. The Duchy is mainly an agricultural estate, but its most publicised holdings are The Oval, home of Surrey county cricket club in the heart of London, and Dartmoor Prison in Devon. The Prince and Princess of Wales do not receive an allowance from the Civil List but retain the income from the Duchy of Cornwall instead. There is no compulsion to pay income tax as the Duchy is exempt, but since his marriage in 1981 Prince Charles has voluntarily given 25 per cent of his income to the Treasury. Even so, he has made a good deal as under normal taxation regulations as a higher rate tax-payer he would pay up to 40 per cent.

The Keeper of the Privy Purse has what is in some ways a thankless task: that of explaining as tactfully but firmly as possible why certain proposals put forward by other members of the Household – which they, no doubt, consider essential – cannot be proceeded with simply because the money is not available. However, he does not always have his way. On one occasion in the mid-seventies there was a disagreement between the then Master of the Household, Sir Peter Ashmore, and the then Keeper of the Privy Purse, Sir Rennie Maudsley. Sir Peter felt that visitors to Buckingham Palace should not be confined in the tiny, claustrophobic closet used as a waiting room at the time and proposed that a brand new waiting room should be built with money that was available from that year's annual estimates in the Royal Palaces vote. 'The money was there,' said Sir Peter, 'so there was no reason why the work couldn't be done.' But there were strenuous objections from Sir Rennie on the grounds that public money should not be spent on such frivolities at a time when the country was going through a period of financial crisis.

Sir Peter Ashmore felt that his colleague was over-reacting – and for an entirely different reason. 'The new waiting room would have been right outside Rennie Maudsley's door and I'm quite sure he didn't relish the thought of all that building work going on for six months.' It was an impasse and no one seemed able to resolve the issue until one day The Queen herself instructed the Master of the Household to see that the work was carried out. No one knew how Her Majesty had come to be aware of the disagreement between two of her most senior courtiers, but as always, her decision was final. That today, visitors to Buckingham Palace are able to wait in comfort is due entirely to the fact that The Queen considered their convenience to be more important than saving money.

Together with the Prime Minister and the Chancellor of the Exchequer, the Keeper of the Privy Purse is also a Royal Trustee, and when the Royal Trustees published their accounts in October 1990 they estimated that the total cost of the Royal Family and the services it uses would be £56 million in 1991. The figure includes The Queen's Civil List payment, now fixed at £7.9 million a year for the next ten years, £2.52 million in annuities for other members of the Royal Family and £46 million from various Government departments. Since 1975 the Trustees have paid extra amounts to the Royal Family, over and above the Civil List allowances, in order to meet any approved increases in salaries and wages paid to staff working in the Royal Household.

About 70 per cent of the money received by The Queen in the Civil List is spent on staff costs and salaries, which in the last five years have increased by only 4.2 per cent a year, compared with the national trend on salaries of 8 per cent. The Royal Trustees expected these efficiency savings to continue in the coming years.

The Master of the Household has the biggest wage bill: an estimated £1,667,462 for 1990, which means that the men and women under him, mainly kitchen and domestic staff, earn an average of just over £8,000 a year. Next come the departments of the Private Secretary and the Treasurer, which together account for some £922,346 a year, with the Royal Mews in third place with an annual wage bill of £484,777. Bringing up the rear is the smallest department in the Royal Household, the Office of the Lord Chamberlain, whose members were expected to earn £368,748 in 1990.

The Royal Trustees Report contains details of The Queen's Household expenses, listing each department and the amount spent every year. The most recent report reveals that the four Buckingham Palace and Holyroodhouse Garden Parties cost an estimated £213,650, while the royal kitchens ran up a bill of £200,783. The housekeepers in the Royal Palaces expected to spend £180,557 on replacing furniture, including curtains and carpets, while the royal laundry bill totalled £63,700. This might seem an exorbitant amount to the average family, but when one realises that it includes all the linen used at State Banquets to which 170 guests are invited at a time, plus the uniforms of the domestic staff, it does not seem quite so outrageous. The livery worn by the footmen, butlers, chauffeurs and grooms is expensive. As we have seen, a full set of livery as worn by a footman on duty at a State Banquet costs around £1,000, and although some worn today have been handed down for generations – there are even some dating from the reign of King Edward VII at the beginning of the century – during 1990 the cost of providing new livery accounted for some £88,100.

The royal cellars are among the most extensive in the world, containing at least one hundred dozen bottles of Krug champagne alone. The Master of the Household, in conjunction with the Keeper of the Privy Purse, regards the laying down of wine on Her Majesty's behalf a judicious investment for the future and a wise precaution against inflation. During 1990 £71,250 would be spent in this way and also on providing new stock to replace what had been drunk, mainly, it should be added, by The Queen's official guests.

Other items detailed in the Royal Trustees report are: £37,950 for flowers; £34,000 for official presents (given by The Queen when she and Prince Philip make a State Visit overseas); and £13,532 for newspapers – or £260.23 a week.

The Royal Mews cost nearly a quarter of a million pounds to run in 1990: to be precise, an estimated £238,342. It is divided into two sections. Under Horses and Carriages £16,000 was allocated for new horses and equipment, but the repair and maintenance of the existing stock cost a further £149,025. Motor Cars proved much less expensive. One new vehicle was bought and several hired when the Mews could not provide sufficient transport from their own resources, at a cost of £37,042; while a modest £36,275 was spent on garage bills. So the 'Green' lobby should be happy that Her Majesty spends more on her horses than she does on motor vehicles.

The office expenses of the Royal Household include items such as data processing equipment at £123,150; stationery and supplies, estimated at £138,900 for 1990 (down nearly £50,000 on the previous year owing to the computerisation programme) and £29,000 on insurance. The Queen's donations (apart from her private gifts to charity which are not published) and the cups and prizes which are awarded in her name accounted for £9,500, and there is an intriguing item in the household expenses listed as Allowances and Gratuities, amounting to £30,933.

The total expenses for the Royal Household (without counting the salaries and wages) were estimated to be £1,607,167, and every penny had to be justified by the Keeper of the Privy Purse. He and his colleagues constantly look for ways of improving efficiency and thereby cutting costs. For example, the financial consultants Peat Marwick McLintock have been retained to advise on refining management systems in an effort to reduce the £25.6 million annual cost to the Department of the Environment of maintaining the occupied Royal Palaces. One of the company's senior partners, Michael Peat, has been seconded to the Royal Household for two years as Director of Finance and Property Services, a new branch within the office of the Keeper of the Privy Purse which has been set up to take on the management and supervision of these palaces. His brief is to make them run more economically, if not at a profit. This, however, does not include any exploitation of the Royal Family for commercial purposes. There will be no opportunities for social-climbing parents to hire the State Ballroom at Buckingham Palace for their daughter's 'coming-out' ball or for high-flying business tycoons to hold sales conferences in the Waterloo Chamber at Windsor Castle. As the Palace themselves put it: 'The Royal Palaces are not about to be transformed into commercial tourist attractions . . . the reduction in costs will take place only in a manner compatible with the dignity of the Crown.'

Another of Michael Peat's responsibilities will be to assist in the new arrangements for The Queen's Civil List. Under an agreement reached in Parliament which will last until the year 2000, the Civil List is to be standardised at £7.9 million a year. This has been calculated, on figures submitted by the Keeper of the Privy Purse and estimates prepared by the financial consultants, as the amount it is believed it will cost to run the Royal Household for the next ten years, taking into account an annual rate of inflation of 7.5 per cent. For the last seven years increases in the Civil List have been consistently below the annual rate of inflation. Now any savings made during the early years of the decade will be set aside to offset possible deficits in the late 1990s.

The office of the Keeper of the Privy Purse looks after payments made from The Queen's private funds as well as all official expenditure. One example of this private spending is the many donations Her Majesty makes to charities; sometimes to large organisations, but occasionally to individual cases which have been brought to her attention and which she considers worthy. The payments are made by the Keeper of the Privy Purse with only one condition: the recipients must never reveal where the money has come from and publicity is never given as to the amounts involved.

All salaries and wages are paid from the Keeper's office and, as Treasurer to The Queen, her Keeper of the Privy Purse works closely with the royal bankers, Coutts, and with the royal Solicitors Farrer and Company. The Queen's solicitor and chief legal adviser is Sir Matthew Farrer, who is also a trustee for all the royal children, keeping an eye on both the legal and the financial details of their various trust funds. Based at Lincoln's Inn Fields in London, where they have been for nearly two centuries, Farrer and Company was founded in 1701. Sir Matthew has been called upon to act for the Royal Family in matrimonial matters, breach of contract cases, libel (when a former royal servant tried to sell his story to a national newspaper) and a wide variety of legal issues including tax planning and business advice. When The Queen buys a property for one of her children or for a member of her staff (as she did with number 49 Gloucester Street, Pimlico, when Michael Shea was her Press Secretary) Sir Matthew Farrer or one of his many partners handles all the legal documentation.

The Privy Purse office is highly automated. All those working on the Royal Family's finances are thoroughly professional, and the accounts are overseen by expert accountants and book-keepers. Together they handle tens of millions of pounds every year and with the large amount of overseas travel undertaken by the family and Household, a knowledge of the world's currencies is a necessary requirement. Money is moved around the world constantly and by judicious timing the Keeper of the Privy Purse is able to save considerable sums in foreign exchange. The office also handles all the Value Added Tax concerns of the Royal Family and their Households.

Apart from her Private Secretary, the person who is probably in closest and most frequent contact with The Queen is her racing manager, the Earl of Carnarvon. 'Porchy' as he is called by Her Majesty (he was Lord Porchester until he succeeded his father in 1988) has been in charge of the royal bloodstock interests for more than a quarter of a century, and not many days pass without them speaking together. During the season he will telephone The Queen several times a week to discuss form, the next day's racing or a possible buying opportunity. Her Majesty has extensive investments in pedigree bloodstock and is regarded as one of the most knowledgeable owners in the racing world. She has been tremendously successful with her string of thoroughbreds – though she has still to achieve her ultimate ambition and breed a Derby winner – and all the finances relating to her racing interests are ultimately dealt with by the Keeper of the Privy Purse.

Lord Carnarvon, whose grandfather discovered the tomb of Tutankhamen earlier this century, lives at Highclere in Berkshire, from where he is in constant touch by computer with the leading racing agencies in the world. If there is anything The Queen needs to know about virtually any horse anywhere, 'Porchy' Carnarvon can find the necessary information in minutes.

From time to time, members of the Household are permitted to use the Queen's Box at the Royal Albert Hall. On such occasions they have to apply to the Privy Purse office which controls the allocation of seats. The office also supervises the running of the Royal Mausoleum and Private Burial Ground at Windsor, and if anyone wants to name a flower after The Queen or any other member of the Royal Family, the Keeper of the Privy Purse looks after the delicate negotiations.

Within this department, with its ultra-modern approach to twentieth-century financial matters, there is also an ancient-sounding sub-department known as the Royal Almonry. It is headed by a man with an equally historic title, the Lord High Almoner, the Lord Bishop of St Albans. In centuries past the Royal Almonry was responsible for distributing alms to the poor on behalf of the Sovereign. These days the task is basically the same, except that it is more a ceremonial formality and takes place once a year during the annual Maundy Service.

On this day, the Thursday before Easter Sunday, The Queen gives a bag full of coins, one for each year of her life with an extra coin for 'the year of Grace', to the same number of men and women in a particular parish. The coins, which are specially minted for the occasion, are rarely spent and the recipients, who are no longer necessarily 'the worthy poor' but people who have done good works in society, regard them as precious gifts to be treasured for life. The Royal Almonry looks after the administrative details of the Maundy Service, a secretary and an assistant doing the day-to-day work, as the three positions of Lord High Almoner; Hereditary Grand Almoner, who is the Marquess of Exeter; and Sub-Almoner, the Reverend William Booth, one of The Queen's chaplains, are purely ceremonial.

Another little-known duty of the Keeper of the Privy Purse is to supervise the distribution of Balmoral Bursaries – the scholarships endowed by The Queen to enable the children of her estate staff to go to schools and universities in Scotland. And if you have ever wondered how people come to sit in the Queen's Box at the Royal Albert Hall, the man with the answer is the Keeper of the Privy Purse. He is responsible for the allocation of seats and also for choosing and paying for the presentation prizes, medals and cups given by the Royal Family. In addition he looks after one of the most valuable parts of The Queen's private fortune, her stamp collection, said to be the most important private collection in the world.

When The Queen attends the State Opening of Parliament at the beginning of each new session, she is attended by four Pages of Honour, wearing red coats covered with gold lace, white breeches, white stockings and black shoes with silver buckles. They are usually the sons or grandsons of distinguished members of her Household and their appointment carries with it the honour of being physically closest to Her Majesty, while at the same time being the youngest members of the Court. In 1987 a slight problem arose in the selection of suitable boys to perform this role. Prior to this the only formal qualification was to be between the ages of 13½ and 16½, at which age a boy had to retire. The problem arose after The Queen had seen a recording of herself at that year's State Opening of Parliament. Three of the Pages were fine but one, although he was only thirteen and three-quarters, was nearly six feet tall and consequently dwarfed not only his colleagues but The Queen herself, who immediately saw how ridiculous it looked. From that date she issued an order that no Page of Honour was to be taller than she is – 5 feet 4 inches. When Sir Rennie Maudsley was Keeper, his son Piers was invited to be a Page and it fell to Sir Rennie to write to his son to inform him of the appointment. The letter was duly despatched in the most formal of terms, the Keeper making no distinction between his own son and the other boys. These days the Keeper of the Privy Purse makes these appointments in consultation with the Lord Chamberlain, who is also involved with one other category of royal patronage: the thirteen Military Knights of Windsor.

Attached to the Order of the Garter, the Military Knights of Windsor were formed in the same year, 1348. Originally they were called Poor Knights for the very good reason that they had lost everything when large ransoms were paid for their release during the wars in France. As compensation they were given small pensions by the Sovereign and living quarters for life within Windsor Castle. In return they had to attend morning service in St George's Chapel as representatives of the more prosperous Knights of the Garter. It was worship by proxy. In 1833 King William IV changed their designation to the Military Knights and granted them their present uniform of scarlet tail-coat with white cross sword belt, crimson sash and cocked hat with plume.

These days the Military Knights are all retired army officers and they live in attractive houses just inside King Henry VIII's Gate, the main entrance to Windsor Castle. Their point of contact with the Royal Household is via the Keeper of the Privy Purse. He is also Secretary of the Royal Victorian Order, the Sovereign's personal Order of Chivalry, in which he works closely with the Lord Chamberlain who is the Order's Chancellor.

One task the Keeper no longer has to undertake is to issue cheques in Her Majesty's name to the mothers of all triplets or quadruplets born in Britain. Until 1957 it was a royal custom that the parents would receive £1 for each child. The gift was known as The King or Queen's Bounty for Triplets and in the early part of the century made a welcome addition to the family kitty. However, with the coming of the Welfare State in the late nineteen-forties the need for the money in practical terms disappeared, and it was found that the recipients were failing to cash the cheques, preferring to keep them as mementoes. The Keeper of the Privy Purse at the time argued that even such small amounts were disrupting his accounts and The Queen was persuaded to abandon the practice.

A total of forty-six men and women work in the office of the

Keeper of the Privy Purse with a Deputy Treasurer who looks after such items as Household pensions. A further seventy-three staff work in the Finance and Property Services Branch. The Chief Accountant is male while his Deputy, the four accountants and seven clerks are all women. The Palace personnel office is located within the department and there is one clerk whose sole responsibility is to look after the masses of stationery used by the Royal Family and the Household.

Everyone who works for The Queen becomes eligible for a pension and the pension schemes are operated by the Keeper of the Privy Purse. The salaries of those staff above junior clerical grades are paid on a scale analogous to similar ranks within the Civil Service and many of the domestic servants belong to the Civil Service Union. However, recognising their unique position, the Union exempts its members who work for The Queen from taking part in any industrial action. So far there has never been a strike at Buckingham Palace.

Two other important members of the Household who work to the Keeper of the Privy Purse are the Land Agent at Sandringham, responsible for all matters concerning The Queen's private estates in Norfolk, where she owns some 20,000 acres, and the Resident Factor at Balmoral, who does the same job on Her Majesty's 50,000 acres in Scotland.

The Royal Palaces Presentation Fund looks after the various commercial enterprises with which The Queen is involved (for more details see the chapter on The Royal Collection). Visitors to the State Apartments at Windsor Castle and Holyroodhouse and to the Royal Mews and Queen's Gallery at Buckingham Palace pay an entrance fee, and the royal book shops are highly profitable outlets for all manner of memorabilia. One book alone, *The Queen and Her Family*, which has been in print for more than five years, has sold over a million copies so far, and a small royalty payment from each one is paid into the Presentation Fund. The Queen's Gallery at Buckingham Palace is one of the main tourist attractions for visitors to London, its turnover amounting to hundreds of thousands of pounds a year. By contrast the State Apartments at Kensington Palace, Hampton Court and the Tower of London come under the Historic Palaces Agency and all revenues from these buildings go to the public exchequer.

Another little-known business activity is the Royal Gardens enterprise at Windsor. Many of the fruit and vegetables grown are sold at market prices; in 1989 they contributed £30,000 to Royal Household expenses. Another source of income is the game and fowl shot on the royal estates. Sandringham is a large supplier of Christmas trees, another boost to the royal finances, and even the royal kennels do their bit to bring in a little extra money. Puppies bred from The Queen's famous gun-dogs are highly sought after and fetch high prices in a very tight market.

All these businesses have to be supervised. Their administration occupies the attention of a number of people on a full-time basis, and each one works under the aegis of the Keeper of the Privy Purse.

The Queen is landlord to a large number of people, including members of her own family and past and present members of the Royal Household who live in Grace and Favour homes, of which there are 135 altogether. These houses or apartments are occupied at Her Majesty's discretion, and range from tiny pieds-à-terre in St James's Palace used by Household members during the working week to extensive apartments in Kensington Palace, the London homes of several of The Queen's relations. Probably the grandest of all Grace and Favour homes is Clarence House which has been occupied by Queen Elizabeth the Queen Mother since 1952. There are houses owned by The Queen in Pimlico and close to the Tate Gallery in London, large and difficult to heat flats at Hampton Court where many of the tenants are elderly widows of former distinguished public servants, and elegant mansions within Windsor Home Park. Those who live in these Grace and Favour residences pay no rent but are required to contribute something towards the maintenance and, in certain cases, depending on the location, for heating and lighting. The exceptions are the occupants of houses or flats in the Royal Palaces themselves where all services are paid for by the Department of the Environment.

The Keeper of the Privy Purse is responsible for the administration and allocation of these living quarters, with one exception, and that is the Royal Mews. This is the private kingdom of the Crown Equerry who has complete responsibility for all matters, including housing, in the Royal Mews at both Buckingham Palace and Windsor Castle.

As the man who writes The Queen's cheques and obtains cash for her on the few occasions when she handles money, the Keeper of the Privy Purse is one of Her Majesty's most valued and trusted aides. He sees her whenever it is necessary, sometimes in company with her bankers, when they discuss all aspects of her expenditure and income. He knows more details of the royal finances than anyone else alive and, in an organisation where discretion is taken for granted, no one is better at keeping secrets.

9

THE PRIVATE
SECRETARY

THE OFFICE OF Private Secretary to the Sovereign is of far greater importance than is sometimes believed to be the case. The very title of the position can be misleading in that some people might even assume that the Private Secretary answers The Queen's telephone and types her letters. In fact he is the closest aide The Queen employs and is privy to more confidential information regarding the monarchy than anyone in the land. It would be difficult to overestimate the importance of The Queen's Private Secretary, who shares secrets with her that are unknown even to Prince Philip, Her Majesty's husband and consort.

It was not always so. Until his death in 1861 Queen Victoria's closest adviser was her husband, Prince Albert, who assumed the responsibilities and duties of Private Secretary without ever calling himself, or being called by others, by that title. As her Consort (though he was not given the title Prince Consort until 1857), Albert had access to every State Paper delivered to The Queen and it was generally accepted that she took no major decisions without first consulting him. It was a unique position and one that Prince Albert created for himself. His early years in Britain were inactive and, in his own opinion, totally unproductive. This was through no fault of his; it was simply that the Government of the day saw no reason to involve a foreign prince, even one who was married to the Sovereign, in what they regarded as purely British affairs of State. But Queen Victoria felt differently. When she first came to the throne, she sought the advice of her immediate predecessor's Private Secretary,

Sir Herbert Taylor. What should she do about a Private Secretary? His answer was blunt and straight to the point. 'Is Your Majesty afraid of the work?' he asked. On being told that she was not, he replied, 'Then don't have a Private Secretary.'

However, when the young Queen needed advice that was, in her opinion, beyond the capabilities of her ministers, it was natural that she should turn for help to the person she trusted more than any man on earth, her husband, and gradually it seemed equally natural that he should help his wife to shoulder the burdens of constitutional monarchy. This he did so successfully that it soon became apparent that he was influencing every decision she made. Indeed, it was claimed that, although Victoria reigned as Queen and sole Sovereign over the greatest empire the world had ever known, in reality she and her husband ruled side by side; he was King in all but name, in effect her unofficial Private Secretary, closest adviser and consort all rolled into one.

Prince Philip has never enjoyed the same power or influence. He does not see any State Papers and neither does he involve himself in the day-to-day business of the monarchy. He acts as a valuable support to his wife and appears by her side on all ceremonial occasions, but there has never been a need for the sort of help that Queen Victoria obviously required. Prince Charles is the only other member of the Royal Family to have access to State Papers, and those he sees are limited, selected by The Queen for their usefulness to her son's training for his future role as King. However, there is no question of his influencing his mother's decisions or acting in any capacity as an extra Private Secretary.

The first Sovereign to employ a Private Secretary was King George III, who chose Sir Herbert Taylor to be his link between Crown and Government. It was a decision he took alone and was another bone of contention between him and a Parliament which was suspicious of his motives in appointing an adviser who might exert undue influence over him.

A similar row broke out in 1812 when George III's son, the Prince Regent, appointed Colonel McMahon to be his Private Secretary at the then enormous salary of £2,000 a year. One Member of the House of Commons said the office was 'dangerous and unconstitutional, rendering the person holding it the secret adviser of the Sovereign with a degree of influence over his mind totally at variance with the forms of Government in England'. It was also claimed that 'the office would be destructive of a fundamental principle of the constitution, which was, that no one ought to use the name of the Sovereign, give him advice, or be the bearer of his commands, unless he be one of the responsible ministers of the Crown, and answerable for his conduct to Parliament'.

The matter went to a vote and the Prince Regent received the permission of Parliament by a majority of seventy, a total of nearly 300 Members being present. However, when he became George IV, Parliament refused to allow McMahon to become Private Secretary, believing him to be 'not responsible enough to advise the Sovereign', and Sir Herbert Taylor, who by then had proved himself, was recalled. With such an aura of suspicion surrounding the office, successive Private Secretaries have been careful to keep the lowest of profiles, and to maintain cordial relations with both Whitehall and the Palace of Westminster.

The qualities looked for in that first Private Secretary were exactly the same as those required today. He must be above all things non-political in order to gain – and keep – the trust of the government ministers with whom he is in daily contact. Governments change and consequently so does the advice given to the Sovereign by her prime minister, which he or she is constitutionally obliged to accept. The Private Secretary is the only constant in the otherwise ever-changing hues of political affairs and must show no political bias whatever. It would be unrealistic to suppose that each of the paragons of virtue who have held this office have never had leanings towards one party or another (and they certainly have not all come from the Tory stable as is commonly supposed), but one of the necessary regulations imposed when they enter royal service is that they must forget any such inclinations – even that they once possessed them. The Private Secretary's sole responsibility is to the Sovereign; he or she must be able to trust him implicitly, and it is equally important that he inspires the same confidence in the ministers of the Crown.

Queen Victoria's most celebrated prime minister, Benjamin Disraeli, once remarked when speaking about Sir Henry Ponsonby, one of the four Private Secretaries who eventually served her, 'I can only say that I could not wish my case stated to The Queen better than her Private Secretary does it . . . he is scrupulously on his guard to be absolutely fair and lucid.'

Queen Elizabeth II has been served by six Private Secretaries so far in her reign: Sir Alan Lascelles, Sir Michael (later Lord) Adeane, Sir Martin (now Lord) Charteris, Sir Philip (now Lord) Moore, Sir William Heseltine and the present incumbent, Sir Robert Fellowes. Each has been successful in his own way and each has brought to the office his own unique contribution.

Her Majesty's first Private Secretary, Sir Alan ('Tommy') Lascelles, a brilliant man with an independent mind, was, together with his many other attributes, known for his sometimes intransigent attitude and a willingness to air his views no matter whom he was addressing. During the time he was Private Secretary to the Prince of Wales (later Edward VIII) he earned a reputation for tendering unpalatable advice even when he knew that all His Royal Highness really wanted to hear was confirmation of his own opinions; and many years later he had a violent disagreement with Group Captain Peter Townsend over his relationship with Princess Margaret, maintaining that as Equerry to The King, and a much older married man, the Group Captain had betrayed a trust in allowing a romantic love affair to develop with the young princess. In fact, throughout his long and distinguished royal service he had violent disagreements with just about all his colleagues in the Household.

Educated at Marlborough and Trinity College, Oxford, Lascelles was originally destined for the Foreign Office but failed in part of his entrance examination. He opted for the City of London where he became a broker just before the First World War. At the outbreak of hostilities in 1914 he joined the Bedfordshire Yeomanry, winning the Military Cross and being wounded at Cambrai. In 1919 Lascelles went to Bombay as Aide-de-Camp to his brother-in-law, Lord Lloyd, who was Governor. While there he met and married the daughter of the Viceroy, Lord Chelmsford, and returned to England to begin his many years of royal service. His first position was as Assistant Private Secretary to the Prince of Wales (later Edward VIII), with whom he remained for nine years, accompanying him to Canada, the United

States and Kenya. He became an invaluable aide and on at least one occasion, in 1926, enhanced the Prince's reputation and earned the appreciation of King George V, when he wrote a speech which the Prince of Wales delivered as his own before the British Association. Concerned that his son's intellectual limitations would be revealed before such a prestigious audience, The King had advised him not to attend. However, it proved too late to pull out and the success not only enhanced His Royal Highness's credibility, it did no harm to his Assistant Private Secretary either.

It is a great advantage for anyone hoping to become Private Secretary to the Sovereign to have worked overseas for a time. Lascelles followed his term of office with the Prince of Wales with two years as Private Secretary to the Earl of Bessborough when he was Governor-General of Canada, and his experience of living and working in India and Canada stood him in good stead when the time came for him to return to royal service as Private Secretary to King George VI, an office he occupied throughout the Second World War. In fact it was towards the end of the war that he made himself highly unpopular with both The King and the Prime Minister Winston Churchill.

As the date for the invasion of Normandy approached in 1944, both King George and Churchill announced that they intended to be present, watching from a Royal Navy warship. Sir Alan was horrified at the prospect and asked in direct terms whether His Majesty had explained the procedure of succession to Princess Elizabeth. He also wanted an assurance that arrangements had been made to appoint a new prime minister if Churchill should be killed. It was difficult for the Private Secretary to disagree with both the Head of State and the Head of the Government, but he stuck to his guns and eventually they saw the sense of his arguments and agreed to withdraw.

Lascelles continued to serve The King until his death in 1952 and then offered his resignation to the new Queen. It is customary for every member of the Royal Household to resign on the death of a Sovereign in order that a new Household may be appointed, but in the event Sir Alan remained at Buckingham Palace for the first year of The Queen's reign. Then during Coronation year, 1953, he was succeeded by Sir Michael Adeane, whose family had served the Royal

Family for generations. His grandfather was Lord Stamfordham, one of the most famous of all Private Secretaries, and his own son, Edward, would eventually become Private Secretary to the Prince of Wales (though not for long as he left after a fundamental disagreement about his role). Sir Michael's father had been killed in action in the First World War while serving in the Coldstream Guards. Michael Adeane followed him into the regiment after graduating from Cambridge University, where he gained a First Class degree in History, and during the Second World War he rose to the rank of Lieutenant-Colonel. He was wounded fighting in North-Western Europe and mentioned in dispatches.

One of the longest-serving of all The Queen's Private Secretaries, Sir Michael had completed nearly twenty years in the post when he retired in 1972. But his service to the Royal Family had begun many years before that. He was appointed Page of Honour to King George V when he was just thirteen, and in 1937 his full-time career at Buckingham Palace started when he became Equerry and Assistant Private Secretary to George VI. During his time in royal service he became the epitome of the selfless civil servant, a role which was exemplified in his authoritative statement to a Select Committee of the House of Commons on the 'burdens of Sovereignty' when MPs were debating the Civil List allowance in the early 1970s.

When Sir Michael retired, at his own request, at the age of sixty-one, he was succeeded by the man who had been his assistant for the entire twenty years that he had been Private Secretary. Sir Martin Charteris was another Lieutenant-Colonel, but not in the Brigade of Guards. His regiment was the King's Royal Rifle Corps. He had another thing in common with his former superior: his father, Lord Elcho, had also been killed in action in the First World War, but in other ways the two men could hardly have been more different. Charteris had, and has, an exuberant style and flashing wit which he used to great effect when writing The Queen's speeches. He was the first man to put a joke into the royal mouth and he never failed to lead the laughter and applause. And no one enjoyed the joke more than he did himself when he took up his appointment as Private Secretary on 1 April 1972 (All Fools' Day).

Throughout his career he suffered from indifferent health but this did not deter him from enjoying life or from carrying out his duties. On one occasion he was confined to King Edward VII's Hospital for Officers. The Queen was abroad and Charteris conducted the intricate business of the Counsellors of State from his bed, with no embarrassment and apparently no ill-effects – on himself or the monarchy.

Martin Charteris is a natural aristocrat. His grandfather was the 9th Earl of Wemyss and his wife is the great-granddaughter of the 6th Earl of Buckinghamshire. Educated at Eton, from where he has recently retired as Provost, a post to which he was appointed by The Queen in 1978 shortly after he relinquished his position as her Private Secretary, Lord Charteris of Amisfield was perhaps the most outspoken of all the Private Secretaries at a time when discretion was considered second only to loyalty. He also showed considerable gifts of diplomacy and tact. For example, in 1959 he had to break the news to President Nkrumah that The Queen would have to postpone her State Visit to Ghana since she was expecting the birth of Prince Andrew. Charteris, in conjunction with Sir Michael Adeane, arranged that the President, who had been hoping for some much needed favourable publicity and prestige from the visit, should be placated with a personal invitation to Balmoral, and arranged that he should be made a Privy Counsellor.

Among his many talents is one rarely found in Private Secretaries; he is a skilled sculptor of professional standard who has had a work accepted for showing at the Royal Academy. He remains a very social animal who has always greatly enjoyed entertaining. On one memorable evening in 1952 burglars broke into his house while he was giving a dinner party. All the lady guests had their fur coats stolen from a bedroom – happily they were all eventually recovered – and Charteris dined out on the story for many years afterwards.

In his professional life at Buckingham Palace he bridged the gap between the 'old-school' type of traditional courtier and the new, modern and thoroughly professional adviser as epitomised by Sir Philip Moore, the first civil servant to be accepted into the Private Office of The Queen.

Philip Moore, who took over the Private Office in 1977, after being Assistant Private Secretary for five years, came from a very different background. His father was in the Indian Civil Service and

Philip won a Classical Exhibition to Brasenose College, Oxford from Cheltenham where he was a Scholar. His education was interrupted by the outbreak of war, and in 1940, when he was nineteen, he volunteered for the Royal Air Force and became a pilot in Bomber Command. In 1942 he was shot down and taken prisoner, remaining in captivity until 1945. Returning to Britain, he resumed his studies at Oxford where he excelled at sport, being awarded 'Blues' for rugby and hockey and playing cricket for the county of Oxfordshire. In 1951 he capped a brilliant sporting career when he was selected to play rugby for England.

His professional career took off after he joined the Civil Service and within a few years he had been appointed Principal Private Secretary to the First Lord of the Admiralty. He then moved to Singapore to become Deputy High Commissioner, in which post he met the man who was later to become his superior in the Royal Household, Sir Charles (later Lord) Maclean. At that time Maclean was Chief Scout of the Commonwealth and he had been warned by Philip Moore that Lee Kwan Yew, the Prime Minister of Singapore, intended to disband the Scout movement on the island as a relic of British Imperialism. Moore's timely warning gave Maclean the opportunity to prepare his defence before he met Lee Kwan Yew. It turned out that the Prime Minister's main objections were to the traditional short trousers and old Baden-Powell type hats. Maclean immediately changed the uniform to smart long trousers and a military type beret. Honour was satisfied on both sides and today Scouting thrives in Singapore.

Sir Philip's final post before joining the Royal Household was as Chief of Public Relations at the Ministry of Defence. This last must have been an agonising job as Sir Philip was known throughout his time at Buckingham Palace for his distrust of journalists and thorough dislike of anything that smacked of public relations. He was an efficient Private Secretary whose Civil Service background made him appear an extremely cautious man, but on a personal level he was friendly and warm with the most perfect manners.

Bill Heseltine represented another radical change. The son of a schoolmaster, he was educated at Christ Church Grammar School, in Claremont, Western Australia and the University of Western

Australia where he obtained a First Class degree in history. Originally brought over from Australia on temporary attachment to the Buckingham Palace Press Office, he quickly learned the ropes and his way around the royal corridors of power. After a brief return to his native land to work in Sir Robert Menzies' private office, he was asked back to Buckingham Palace where his feet were placed firmly on the ladder of success. His Antipodean forthrightness was like a breath of fresh air and he alone has been credited with opening the doors of the Palace to a wider cross-section of people than ever before. Nevertheless, when he finally reached the pinnacle of success in the Royal Household and became Private Secretary to The Queen, he did not, as expected, revolutionise the office. By that time he had adapted to the ways of the Court as if he had been born to them, all traces of any brashness that might have existed when he first arrived from Australia long since eliminated. He was the first and, so far, only person from a Commonwealth country to be appointed Private Secretary to The Queen.

His successor, Sir Robert Fellowes, comes from a much more traditional background. Since his father was Land Agent to The Queen at Sandringham he was brought up knowing most of the Royal Family from birth, and he is married to the sister of the Princess of Wales. Before entering royal service he was a successful discount broker in the City of London, and his promotion has been rapid. In fourteen years he has progressed from Assistant Private Secretary, or number three in the office, to become the most important figure in The Queen's Household. For make no mistake, although the Lord Chamberlain is titular head of the Royal Household, there is no doubt as to where the real power lies.

Sir Robert is supported by a Deputy, Sir Kenneth Scott, a former diplomat who was British Ambassador to Yugoslavia. There is also an Assistant Private Secretary, Robin Janvrin, a former naval officer who spent three years as Press Secretary before being promoted to the Private Office. These three divide their duties without any 'compartmentalisation', so that when Sir Robert is away, either his Deputy or his Assistant can stand in for him in every respect.

As the closest and most influential of all The Queen's servants, it would be difficult to overestimate the Private Secretary's importance, not only in the Royal Household but far beyond the confines of the palaces. Indeed he is probably one of the most influential people in the country, having the ear of the Sovereign at all times, and being in a position to guide ministers of the Crown, foreign statesmen and even other monarchs and heads of state when it comes to dealings with Her Majesty. Apart from The Queen herself, he is easily the most important person in the working of the monarchy, and he alone is responsible for Her Majesty's programme of events and for arranging audiences. Nobody outside her immediate family sees The Queen without his knowledge and consent, not even the Lord Chamberlain who is in theory his superior. (There is, of course, one notable exception to this rule – 'Bobo' McDonald, The Queen's dresser, who is a law unto herself. She would never dream of asking anybody's permission to see her mistress, and in the days when she was mobile would turn up whenever she wished.) He sees every piece of correspondence that is addressed to Her Majesty, and, together with his two assistants, drafts all the replies to official letters and telegrams.

When a foreign country wishes to invite The Queen to make a State Visit, they first of all contact the Foreign Office, but once the decision is made all the arrangements, which in some cases may take years to complete, are in the hands of the Private Secretary. He accompanies The Queen on all overseas visits, allying his considerable diplomatic skills with his equally important talents as an administrator. Absolute discretion is demanded and no Private Secretary has ever revealed, even by so much as a hint, what Her Majesty's views might be on some of the many contentious issues she has faced during her long reign. Nor has any of them been tempted to publish his memoirs – despite the fact that publishers would surely pay very large sums of money for exclusive rights to any book written with the sort of authority such an author could command.

The Private Secretary to The Queen acts as her link with Government, though he is not present at the weekly meeting between Her Majesty and the Prime Minister. Those Tuesday evenings represent the sole occasions when State secrets are kept exclusively between the two principals: the Head of State and the Head of Government. But the Private Secretary is in regular contact with his opposite numbers: the Secretary to the Cabinet and the Prime Minister's Private Secre-

1 Postillions getting dressed in their State uniforms prior to a rehearsal for the wedding of the Duke and Duchess of York. Note the 'half-wig' which is worn under the hat. The coachmen dislike these wigs, as in the summer they tend to make the head very hot and uncomfortable

2 The stables in the Royal Mews are home to thirty horses these days, including the Windsor Greys, so called because they were originally stabled there. At one time nearly a hundred horses were kept in the Mews both for ceremonial and everyday use, but over the years the number has been reduced to its present level

3 The interior of one of the five Rolls-Royce limousines in the Royal Mews being cleaned before being driven to collect The Queen. The tape collection usually includes many of Her Majesty's favourite recordings of military music

4 Royal Bodyguards are chosen partly for their ability to mix with people from all walks of life and every social level. A group from the Royalty Protection Department in formal morning clothes before leaving for Royal Ascot

5 One of The Queen's longest-serving Ladies-in-Waiting, Lady Susan Hussey, who has been in Royal service for more than a quarter of a century, riding in an open landau with Sir Robert Fellowes, Her Majesty's Private Secretary, the man who, apart from the Royal Family themselves, is easily the most important person at Buckingham Palace

6 The Queen's racing manager, the Earl of Carnarvon, greets the Princess Royal at Royal Ascot. Known as 'Porchy' to all his friends, as he was Lord Porchester before he succeeded to the Earldom, his ambition is to provide Her Majesty with her first Derby winner

7 The Prince and Princess of Wales's office is one of the busiest in the Palace, with hundreds of letters to be read and answered every day. The Lady Clerks are all proficient in using word processors which cut down on the amount of files they have to keep

8 With more than 100,000 items of mail being received at Buckingham Palace every year from all over the world, the various offices become a stamp-collector's paradise. Nothing is thrown away and many of the stamps are sent to charities to be sold on their behalf

9 *Left:* The backbone of the Press Office, Felicity Murdo-Smith, is the longest-serving member of the Palace press team and as an information officer her experience and knowledge have been invaluable to countless journalists and Royal watchers

10 *Above:* One of the Master of the Household's staff makes sure the balcony is in pristine condition before The Queen arrives with other members of the Royal Family following the sovereign's Birthday Parade

11 *Right:* The Queen's Deputy Private Secretary, Sir Kenneth Scott, formerly British Ambassador to Yugoslavia, joins Sir Paul Greening *(right)*, the Master of the Household, on the balcony at Buckingham Palace

12 Two of The Queen's most confidential servants, Sir Robert Fellowes *(left)*, her Private Secretary, and Robin Janvrin, the Assistant Private Secretary who was promoted from the Press Office at Buckingham Palace

13 *Left:* Philip Mackie is employed as a Press Adviser to the Prince of Wales and is paid directly by the Duchy of Cornwall. Based in Scotland, he makes frequent visits to the Prince's office in St James's Palace and often accompanies His Royal Highness on overseas visits

14 *Below:* Inspector Ken Wharf, the Princess of Wales's Police Officer, dresses the part as he accompanies his boss to a sporting event. An umbrella is an indispensable item of the policeman's equipment

15 A Lady-in-Waiting to The Queen has to be flexible and as comfortable in the country as she is on more formal, State occasions. Happily, the Hon. Mary Dugdale shares a love of country pursuits with Her Majesty

tary. In fact, there is a long-standing joke in the Palace about their relative positions. One or two previous Private Secretaries to The Queen have pretended a friendly rivalry with their counterparts in Government, who are usually paid a great deal more and enjoy several 'perks' such as chauffeur-driven limousines.

As Keeper of The Queen's Archives the Private Secretary is responsible for the filing and cataloguing of all The Queen's correspondence for eventual retention in The Queen's Archives, which are housed in the Round Tower at Windsor Castle. Most of the day-to-day work is the responsibility of his Assistant Keeper, who is also The Queen's Librarian and is based at Windsor. At present this post, regarded as one of the most interesting in the Royal Household, is occupied by Oliver Everett, a former Foreign Office 'high-flyer' who was previously Assistant Private Secretary to the Prince of Wales.

Since 1964 a senior serving officer of one of the armed forces has always been attached to the Royal Household as Defence Services Secretary. General Sir Rodney Moore was the first officer to be appointed, following the rearrangement of Ministerial responsibility for Defence matters set out in the Defence (Transfer of Functions) Act of 1963. Since that time the post has rotated between the Army, Navy and Royal Air Force and each Defence Services Secretary serves at the Palace for three years. During this period he is a member of Her Majesty's Household with an office on the north-west corner of the first floor which is approached via the Chinese Luncheon Room. It is one of the most fascinating rooms in the Palace as it also houses a vast collection of knives, bayonets and spears.

The Defence Services Secretary provides a link between The Queen, other members of the Royal Family and their Households, and the Ministry of Defence on all military, naval and air force matters. All the senior royals have strong connections with all three services and many of their official engagements involve service units. So in order to avoid any possible confusion, all contact with the Palace from the services is channelled through the Defence Services Secretary, and he also accompanies The Queen on important visits to service establishments. He keeps Her Majesty informed of any senior service appointments and advises the Household on matters relating to military and naval protocol.

The Buckingham Palace Press Office also falls into the Private Secretary's area of responsibility, and although there is a full-time Press Secretary, with direct access to The Queen, no major decisions concerning the media coverage of the Royal Family are taken without the Private Secretary being consulted first. A fairly recent addition to the Private Office is the Court Circular. For many years this account of the daily events and programme of the Royal Family was issued by the Master of the Household, but it was decided a short while ago that it would make more sense if the person responsible reported to the Private Secretary, and so these days it is prepared by the Information and Correspondence Section, who then submit it to The Queen for her approval before releasing it to the newspapers.

Within the Private Office there is another tiny but vital section called the Information and Correspondence section. It's run by a lady who has been made a Member of the Royal Victorian Order for her services to The Queen, and when you realise the extent of her duties, it's easy to see that the award was fully justified. Apart from the official correspondence, The Queen receives around 250 letters every day from members of the public. The writers range from young children asking Her Majesty if she wears her crown to bed and American matrons wanting to know how they can become Ladies-in-Waiting, to inmates of one of Her Majesty's prisons begging for royal intervention in their case: sackfuls follow a visit to a particular part of the country or an overseas tour. There are letters from people informing Her Majesty of a significant anniversary and hoping for a letter of congratulation, others demanding information about The Queen's corgis, horses, homes, dresses, eating habits and wealth. The flow never stops, close on a hundred thousand pieces of mail every year to be sorted, checked and answered by the seven women who operate the section. Everyone receives an answer. It may only be a polite acknowledgement but nothing that arrives addressed to The Queen is discarded without being read and sent to the appropriate department for action.

Of course the offices in the Palace are now highly automated and all letters are written on word processors, something which would have been a godsend in the days of King George V and Queen Mary. One of Her Majesty's Ladies-in-Waiting wrote an account of her day in 1932: 'There were piles of letters which never seemed to dwindle and it was rare for me to lay down my pen before 1 A.M. Often it was much later. I can even remember finishing letters at 8 A.M., having a bath and coming down to breakfast at 9 A.M. to start a new day.'

Even in the latter days of Queen Victoria's reign and throughout the reign of Edward VII, all correspondence from Members of the Royal Household to the Sovereign had to be handwritten, the Private Secretary even laboriously making his own copies. A file in the Royal Archives reveals that the first typewritten letter to be dispatched from the Private Secretary's office was dated as late as 30 June 1897, though the typewriter had been in commercial use in Britain for more than fifteen years at the time.

One thing common to every Private Secretary is the fact that, while history may be made, to a lesser or greater extent, during his period in office, it is never made by the Private Secretary himself. True, many have been present when historic decisions have been taken, sometimes affecting entire countries or, in one or two exceptional cases, the world. But history is made by prime ministers, kings and queens, and however great might be the contribution of the Private Secretary on such occasions, no matter how long he may toil or how significant his share in the discussion, the final word is never his. Anonymity is the watchword among private secretaries to the Sovereign. Fame has never been sought – nor has it ever been bestowed.

The appreciation of the Sovereign, in some, not all, instances, is the only recognition the Private Secretary can expect, and occasionally the grateful thanks of an appreciative government. For while the Sovereign and her ministers are busy making history, the Private Secretary is merely acting as a conduit between them. He is always ready to assist when called upon; anxious to offer the best, impartial advice of which he is capable. But if that advice is not acted upon, even if he knows without a shadow of a doubt that he is right and the Sovereign wrong, he is obliged to remain silent – the keeper of secrets, a source of wisdom that might be ignored, but never the source of rumour or gossip. Unlike the advice given by a government minister, which the Sovereign must accept, the Private Secretary's counsel is not binding, though few monarchs would ignore advice offered by their most trusted and confidential aide.

Under the present system of constitutional monarchy, the Private Secretary is also the line of communication between The Queen and the governments of all her seventeen realms within the Commonwealth. Their representatives do not have to go through the Foreign Office or any other British ministry to obtain access to The Queen. A direct route via the Private Secretary's Office leads straight into the office of her Majesty. It is a privilege jealously guarded by all The Queen's overseas prime ministers and cherished equally by Her Majesty herself.

With fifty countries in the Commonwealth, The Queen regards her position as Head of the Commonwealth as almost equally important to her role as the British Sovereign. And while The Queen is the present head of this great family of nations, she is not there by right of succession. She was appointed to the role by common consent; in a way this is one position to which Her Majesty has been elected. And since there is no divine right of succession as with the British Throne, when Prince Charles succeeds his mother he will not necessarily follow her as Head of the Commonwealth. In all probability this will happen, but it is not automatic.

The Queen takes her role within the Commonwealth very seriously. Her relationship with the prime ministers of those Commonwealth countries of which she is Head of State is exactly the same as with her chief minister within the United Kingdom. She is required to accept their advice in precisely the same way, and her Private Secretary liaises with her Commonwealth prime ministers just as he does with the Prime Minister of Britain.

There is one further link between the Private Secretary and the Commonwealth and that is through the Secretary-General. The Secretariat of the Commonwealth is located in London, in Marlborough House, the former home of Queen Mary, which has been placed at the permanent disposal of the Commonwealth by The Queen. The Secretary-General is in frequent contact with Buckingham Palace, briefing The Queen's Private Secretary on a wide variety of delicate matters which call for clear thinking, good judgement and a deep knowledge of the problems facing people of vastly different cultures.

No Sovereign could manage without a Private Secretary and nowadays no Sovereign with any sense would ever try. They are indispensable to the working of the monarchy and the influence exerted by the Private Secretary is no less important for being known only to a select few.

The Queen's great-grandfather King Edward VII openly admitted that he preferred to conduct affairs of State on a personal level and liked to talk to people face to face whenever possible. He used his private secretaries as extra eyes and ears, collecting information for him from various sources and from the many contacts they made outside the Palace.

Queen Elizabeth II, who was prepared for the throne in a much more thorough manner, still relies on her private secretaries today for the same kind of advice and information. A 'yes-man' who told her only what he thought she wanted to hear would be of no use whatever and would soon find himself unemployed. As the monarchy moves towards the twenty-first century the needs of the Sovereign become more widespread than ever before. It is no longer possible or practicable for the Head of State of any one country to isolate himself from his or her opposite numbers in other parts of the world. The Queen's Private Secretary will remain a man of great influence in this country and perhaps, with the lowering of national boundaries, particularly in Eastern Europe, of even greater global importance. In 1991 President Gorbachev of the USSR was received at Buckingham Palace, the first such visit by a Russian leader since the Revolution in 1917. Sir Robert Fellowes was responsible for the arrangements between the two Heads of State.

Since it is his responsibility to keep the Sovereign informed on all possible aspects of the political situation, he will, for example, take informal soundings among politicians to help The Queen determine her own course of action. His role is crucial here, for while The Queen cannot be involved in the wear and tear of party politics, it is imperative that she should know the mood of Parliament and that both Government and Opposition parties are canvassed for their opinions. The Private Secretary is the only person who can bridge this gap and to give himself the fullest possible picture he talks not only to current Members of Parliament but also to former politicians and Members of the House of Lords whose experience he values.

If the Private Secretary to The Queen is the inconspicuous power behind the throne, seldom noticed and even more rarely recognised, he remains an indispensable part of the constitution without whom the orderly and efficient operation of the monarchy could not continue, and privately they have all been appreciated greatly by their royal masters and mistresses.

Sir Arthur Bigge, Private Secretary to the Prince of Wales (later George V), received a unique tribute from the Prince in a letter written from Sandringham on Christmas Day 1907.

> What would have happened to me if you had not been there to prepare and help me with my speeches, I can hardly write a letter of any importance without your assistance . . . I offer you my thanks from the bottom of my heart. I am a bad hand at saying what I feel, but I thank God I have a friend like you, in whom I have the fullest confidence and from whom I know on all occasions I shall get the best and soundest advice whenever I seek it.

The political scientist Harold Laski once described the role of the Sovereign's Private Secretary as 'dignified slavery'. But perhaps Sir Alan Lascelles defined the job better than anyone else when he said, during the latter part of King George VI's reign, 'It is not by any means beer and skittles. The Private Secretary's work, both in volume and responsibility, is continually increasing . . . the office compares unfavourably with the relative opposite numbers in the Civil Service, as regards man-hours per day, as regards pay and as regards leave. We serve, may I remind you, one of the very few men [The King] in this world who never gets a holiday at all and who, unlike the rest of us, can look forward to no period of retirement at the end of his service, for his service never ends.'

Words which were spoken more than half a century ago but which are still as relevant today.

10

THE PRESS OFFICE

THE PRESS SECRETARY is one of The Queen's closest aides. He is in daily contact with her and other members of the Royal Family, and as we have seen he has direct access to Her Majesty. On his desk is a telephone console connecting him with the room on the floor above where The Queen works at her desk, and when she wants a word with him, she has only to press a button and she is through at once. Similarly, if he needs to speak to her, either on the telephone or in person, he does not have to obtain the permission of the Private Secretary or go through any other third party. It is a unique and privileged position, but one which carries with it the responsibility for all news emanating from Buckingham Palace – and there's a great deal of that!

There is actually no such thing as *the* Press Office. It is a collection of small, and not-so-small, rooms located on the ground floor of the Palace. Much to the astonishment of journalists, especially those from overseas visiting for the first time, who expect to see armies of press officers, all in a state of highly charged tension, rushing all over the place, there is no large office with telephones ringing, facsimile machines buzzing and computers whirring away.

In fact the atmosphere, in keeping with that throughout the Palace, is calm and dignified. The only indication that one is in the presence of people who need to be in contact with one another at all times is the fact that the press secretaries carry personal 'bleepers' and mobile telephones, the only members of the Royal Household to do so.

The Press Secretary himself occupies a large, pleasant room next door to the waiting room and immediately opposite the Privy Purse door, which means he is separated from the rest of his staff by the entrance hall and a corridor. For thirty years the Press Offices were located along the principal corridor adjacent to the rooms of the Private Secretaries, but when the Prince of Wales moved his offices out of Buckingham Palace and into St James's Palace, this all changed. The Lord Chamberlain's department, which had lost its prime location in St James's, moved to Buckingham Palace and took over most of the space previously devoted to the Press Office.

There are certain advantages to the move, however. Visitors to the Press Secretary no longer have to be escorted past the offices of the Private Secretary's department, where, with its policy of never closing its doors, it was possible for inquisitive ears to pick up isolated snippets of information. But there is one distinct disadvantage. Previously the Press Secretary's office opened directly onto the garden and its ever changing views. Today all he has to look out on is the Palace forecourt, which has been taken over as a Household carpark. On the other hand, the Deputy Press Secretary, John Haslam, did quite well out of the change. Instead of the poky, claustrophobic little room he once used, he now enjoys a spacious, airy office at the front of Buckingham Palace where he works to the accompaniment of a military band as it parades for the Changing of the Guard outside his window at 11.30 every morning.

Charles Anson is in fact only the tenth person to hold the office of Press Secretary since F. J. Prior was appointed in 1918. In 1931, King George V decided he had no use for a Press Secretary and the post was abolished, what few press matters there were being attended to by the Assistant Private Secretary of the day. But in 1944 King George VI realised the importance of good public relations (he had seen the way in which Winston Churchill used the media to such magnificent effect) and re-established the position. Nowadays the Press Secretary has a Deputy and two Assistant Press Secretaries to help him deal with the queries which arrive at the Palace from all over the world, twenty-four hours a day, 365 days a year.

Although the office of Press Secretary is a comparatively new one in the Royal Household, there had been an official called the Court Newsman since the days of King George III. His Majesty became so annoyed with what he called the 'inaccurate reporting of the move-

150

ments of the Royal Family' that he appointed someone whose sole duty was to distribute the Court Circular, which newspapers were required to publish without changing or omitting a single word. The records show that in 1899 the Court Newsman was expected to attend Buckingham Palace personally every day, both afternoon and evening when Queen Victoria was in London, and once a day (Sundays included) when Her Majesty was away. He was also required to attend any Court functions at St James's Palace and Buckingham Palace, and during the Court season he reported to the Lord Chamberlain's Office a number of days before State balls or concerts, where he would sit down and personally copy out the invitation lists. Similarly, after levees and drawing rooms, he was given the invitation cards so that he could make lists to deliver to the offices of the various newspapers. In 1886, his salary for these duties amounted to £45 a year, but even this sum was considered excessive and in 1909 it was reduced to £20. However, the position was not so badly rewarded as at first appears because the newspapers, even then, were prepared to pay the Newsman for information about royalty, and an enterprising official could make a steady living out of the titbits he gave to his favourite editors. Strangely enough this practice was not frowned upon by the Sovereign but recognised as a legitimate way for the Court Newsman to enlarge his meagre earnings. Also a number of ambitious ladies and gentlemen who wanted their names to appear in the same column as The Queen would quietly slip the Newsman the odd guinea so that he wouldn't forget them. George III's order that no word should be omitted or altered had been conveniently forgotten by then.

The position of Court Newsman cannot have been so humble as one might suppose for there was certainly a lot of competition for the job and nepotism was an accepted route to appointment. The first Court Newsman was a Mr Doane and the next name the records show as occupying the post was a Mr Beard who was a grandson of Mr Doane. He served from 1864 to 1886 and was succeeded by A. Phillips, 1886–9, who handed over to his son, W. Phillips. This Mr Phillips looked after Court Press matters until 1909 (when the salary was reduced). The last Court Newsman was H. C. North, who served until 1918 when the office of Press Secretary was established.

The Court Newsman worked under the jurisdiction of the Master of the Household, and as we have seen, until very recently, the Court Circular, which contains the engagements of the Royal Family for the previous day, and which *The Times*, the *Daily Telegraph* and the *Independent* publish every morning, came not from the Press Office but from the office of the Master of the Household. It was a chore that successive Press Secretaries were delighted to be spared, especially when there was a long list of foreign visitors to Buckingham Palace, and the spelling of every name had to be checked. However, when Sir William Heseltine became Private Secretary to The Queen in the late nineteen-eighties, he felt it would be more suitable for what is essentially a press matter to become part of his department. So today the Court Circular is prepared by the Information and Correspondence Section, where the lady responsible for it answers to the Private Secretary to The Queen and not to the Master of the Household.

Of course, the business of reporting royal events has changed beyond recognition since those days of King George III and the first Court Newsman, and even since the early days of our present Queen's reign. The comings and goings, the romances, marriages and divorces of the Royal Family have become required daily reading for millions of people, not only in Britain but throughout the world. Writing on the Royal Family has become big business and many of the journalists and authors who have joined the 'royal watchers' squad have become rich, famous and personalities in their own right.

The way in which the duties within the Press Office are distributed are as follows:

The Press Secretary looks after the affairs of The Queen himself, accompanying her on all State Visits abroad and overseeing the media requirements for every major State occasion, as well as annual events such as The Queen's Christmas Day broadcast. He spends a good deal of his time abroad as he makes an advance or 'recce' trip before every official visit to an overseas country The Queen undertakes. This can mean up to three months of every year is spent away from home. In addition he heads the Buckingham Palace Press Office and, as such, helps to coordinate all press matters on behalf of all the immediate Royal Family, acting as the point of contact between the Palace and the media throughout the world. No interview is granted, no official photographs are taken and no radio or television programmes involving the Royal Family are broadcast without his knowledge and consent. It is a position of awesome responsibility when one considers the amount of coverage that is devoted to The Queen and her family, and journalists throughout the world who want the cooperation of the Palace are all anxious to obtain and keep his goodwill.

For a major overseas royal tour, as many as a thousand applications for accreditation can be received, from reporters, photographers, cameramen, television presenters, radio commentators and their back-up teams. Each one needs that coveted little plastic square on which the Royal Cypher is embossed and which enables them to be as close as possible to the royal party; and the Press Secretary has the final word on which organisations and individuals are favoured.

During a royal 'walkabout' he will need to keep the press party in check to make sure they do not stray from the agreed route, and he also needs to keep an eye and ear open for hidden microphones. With modern sophisticated technology long-range microphones can easily pick up conversations between The Queen and her hosts which are strictly 'off-the-record', and certainly not intended for other ears. There is also a fair measure of 'camera-bashing' – the physical restraining of press photographers who will always try for that extra shot by getting too close to the royal person. However, both sides know the game rules and actual incidents are rare.

The Deputy and Assistant Press Secretaries report directly to the Press Secretary but in practice have their own responsibilities, allocated by him, and divided in the following way: The number two in the office, John Haslam, a former BBC radio executive, looks after the press affairs of the Princess Royal and the Duke of Edinburgh, while Geoffrey Crawford, an Australian who was initially on temporary attachment to Buckingham Palace but is now a full Member of the Household, concentrates on the Duke of York, Princess Margaret and Prince Edward. There is always someone from one of the Commonwealth countries working in the Press Office, usually an Australian, New Zealander or Canadian. It gives the man a useful insight into the workings of the Royal Household and at the same time enables The Queen to add an extra dimension to her domestic arrangements. It is also useful in another, more practical fashion. The temporary attachee remains on the payroll of his own government while he is at Buckingham Palace and so the Press Office gets an extra pair of hands at no additional cost. The other Assistant Press Secretary, Dickie Arbiter, works practically full time for the Prince and Princess of Wales. Nevertheless, he and the others are all employed directly by The Queen, and it is to Her Majesty that their ultimate responsibility lies.

The Prince of Wales also has a Press Adviser who works only for him. He is Philip Mackie, a former Scottish newspaperman who had written many articles about Prince Charles when he was plucked from obscurity and invited to become Assistant Press Secretary to The Queen – to work for the Prince of Wales. Mackie moved from his home in Edinburgh to London but within a few months realised he had made a mistake – not in accepting a position within the Royal Household, but in trying to set up a new home in a strange environment. He is older than the other people working in the Press Office and found the transition hard to make. He told the Prince of Wales of his unhappiness and His Royal Highness agreed that Mackie could leave the Household. However, the Prince did not want to lose the services of someone he had come to value in a comparatively short time and a compromise was reached. Mackie became a part-time adviser to the Prince of Wales, travelling to London or wherever he is needed as required. When Prince Charles was involved in a tragic skiing accident in Switzerland in 1988, Mackie was with him and took charge of the extensive press coverage. His assistance is greatly valued by the Press Office as it helps to relieve the pressure when their resources are stretched. He is paid directly by the Prince of Wales's office and belongs to His Royal Highness's personal Household – not to that of The Queen.

The Queen Mother has her own Press Office at Clarence House, while Princess Alexandra, the Duke and Duchess of Kent, the Duke and Duchess of Gloucester and Prince and Princess Michael of Kent all have Private Secretaries who handle Press enquiries on their behalf.

Visitors to the Press Office at Buckingham Palace are surprised to find that its entire complement is so small. There are the four Assistant

Press Secretaries and four lady clerks (who are now designated Information Officers with a starting salary of £14,000 a year), one or two of whom have been there for more than twenty years and would themselves be more than competent to act as Press Secretary should the need arise. But women in the Royal Household have not been very successful in climbing to the top. In fact only one has ever risen to the rank of Assistant Press Secretary. This was Mrs Michael Wall who worked in the Press Office for twenty-seven years. She was passed over for promotion several times during her stay at the Palace, each time for a man, and knew that she would never become Press Secretary to the Sovereign. It's a man's world around The Queen, and Mrs Wall accepted that fact, though in fairness, it should be added that when she retired from royal service she was rewarded. She was made an Extra Lady-in-Waiting to The Queen and admitted to the Royal Victorian Order, the Sovereign's personal order of chivalry.

As with so many of the men and women who serve The Queen today, in the Press Office professionalism is the key-word. They may be small in number but in terms of productivity the staff's output is prodigious. But this has not always been the case. In the early days of The Queen's reign, the Press were treated like tradesmen; never on friendly terms with the members of the Household and expected to be grateful for whatever titbits they were fed.

In those days the Press Secretary was one of the last of the old-style courtiers, the legendary Commander Richard Colville. He was ex-Royal Navy, punctilious, prickly but with beautiful manners – and almost no knowledge whatever of newspapers and journalism. He was well-meaning but didn't know what news was all about – nor did he want to know! Any enquiry about what The Queen felt about a particular subject, or even what she might be doing, apart from a public engagement, was met with the comment, 'That is a private matter. I'm sorry, I can't help at all.' His main job, as he saw it, was to protect the Sovereign from these suspicious characters, these dubious figures, the pressmen. Indeed, most of Fleet Street gave up telephoning the Press Office at Buckingham Palace and Commander Colville became known as 'the Abominable No-Man'.

On the surface, the Press Office today appears completely different. The telephones seem never to stop ringing and each enquiry is greeted with a polite answer, even if the person at the Palace cannot always supply the information required. There is a genuine interest in providing as much help as possible and I have never failed to have a call returned or a letter answered. When I was writing a biography of Princess Anne, I would sometimes ring the Press Office eight or nine times a day, and yet always received the same courteous cooperation – even though the staff might be groaning inwardly because I was taking up so much of their time with my idiotic questions and seemingly irrelevant queries.

Probably the only journalist who regularly receives a welcome at Buckingham Palace is the Press Association Court Correspondent. This is a unique position and is greatly valued and jealously guarded, for the Press Association is the accredited news agency which handles all press releases from the Palace and is the organisation which is called in first whenever there is a major royal story. All announcements of births, marriages, deaths, engagements and appointments are made via the Press Association, and the men and one woman who have been their Court Correspondents have all enjoyed very privileged positions in the world of journalism.

The PA Court Correspondent also deals with the official announcements from Clarence House regarding the Queen Mother, those from York House for the Duke and Duchess of Kent and from Kensington Palace for Princess Margaret and the Gloucesters. He makes a daily call to the Press Office at Buckingham Palace and accompanies The Queen on all overseas visits. To be successful in the job he needs to build up a close working relationship with the members of the Press Office and also with several other senior members of the Royal Household. This can take years to achieve and the relationship can quickly turn sour if a story appears which the Palace would have preferred to be kept out of the newspapers. It may not have come from the Press Association; in fact it almost certainly will not have. However, when things go wrong, the entire press is blamed, with no exceptions. Nobody is ever left in any doubt that where the Palace and the press are concerned it is entirely a 'seller's market'.

The first official Press Association correspondent was listed simply and formally as Mr F. Smith, who served from 1894 until 1927. He became one of the best-known reporters of his day and, like one or two others who have had the good fortune to become close to the Royal Family, some of the 'regality' rubbed off. He soon earned the sobriquet 'Royal Smith' – a nickname which stayed with him for the rest of his life. The job must have been popular because each of the first three Court Correspondents remained for more than twenty years, and two of them, Louis Wulff, who occupied the post from 1927 to 1950 and Ronnie Gomer Jones, 1950–71, were honoured by the Sovereign as MVO and CVO respectively. 'Dougie' Dumbrell was Court Correspondent for only five years, 1972–77, but he became one of the great characters among royal reporters and when he left he too was awarded the MVO. Grania Forbes, the only woman to become Court Correspondent, had a sympathetic but straightforward approach to the job that earned her tremendous respect not only from the Press Office at the Palace but among her colleagues in Fleet Street, who haven't always regarded those who write about royal events as on the same journalistic level as themselves.

The current Court Correspondent for the Press Association is Tom Corby. He sees himself as not simply the man the Palace calls in when they want something published, but as a genuine newsman whose job is to seek out the stories the public wants to read. He says, 'I am not some sort of substratum courtier. This is strictly a news appointment and my job is to report the news as it affects the Royal Family. It's a great running story. No other country has a royal family quite like ours – two superstars [The Queen and the Princess of Wales] – it's all there. Everybody wants to know about them; they all love to read about them, whether they are pro, anti or luke-warm.' Corby acknowledges that the relationship between himself and The Queen's Press Secretary is good and friendly, but even he would like to see what he calls 'a little loosening up on the dividing line on what is private for the Royal Family and what is public'. He feels that if there were this relaxation more sympathetic stories would be written. He gives an example: 'The joint twenty-first birthday party for Prince Edward and Lady Helen Windsor at Windsor Castle was classified as a private function so there was no facility for *any* Court Correspondent to go in for even half an hour to set the scene. Now that was a nice, warm, sympathetic story of young people enjoying themselves. Half an hour in the room getting the feel of it wouldn't have hurt,

157

but the dividing line is there – and I expect it will always be there.'

The Queen has been served by a number of outstanding press secretaries. Some have been closer to her than others, but with one exception they have all established warm working, if not personal, relationships. And they have come from a variety of backgrounds.

As has already been mentioned, Commander Colville was a former career officer in the Royal Navy with that service's particular attitude to both royalty and the 'lower decks' – where, so far as he was concerned, all members of the Press belonged.

By contrast his successor, the Australian Bill Heseltine, was considered a brilliant press secretary. It was he who persuaded The Queen (with the help of Prince Philip) to allow BBC television cameras to follow her around for a whole year and make the film *Royal Family* produced by Richard Cawston. The programme was seen in almost every country in the world and opened up the monarchy to the general public in a way that was considered astounding in its day.

It is since that film was made, in 1969, that much other media coverage of the Royal Family has developed into the intimate 'fly-on-the-wall' programmes we take for granted today. The Prince and Princess of Wales have become television 'superstars' largely through their agreement to take part in very detailed accounts of their work and lifestyle, and by cooperating with the media to an extent far greater than any member of the Royal Family has ever agreed to in the past. But there are still many people in royal circles who feel that the Press has too much access to the Royal Family, and that if this continues part of the magic of the monarchy may disappear. The Duke and Duchess of York came in for more than their fair share of criticism when they invited press photographers to their home and allowed enormous freedom in showing how they lived.

Today the press takes for granted the fact that when members of the Royal Family appear in public they will make themselves available for pictures and interviews. When they do not they are attacked; when they do, another section of society says they are too open. Whatever the rights and wrongs of the situation, one thing is clear. It all began with Bill Heseltine. So he has to take the credit (or blame) for allowing a greater insight into the extraordinary lifestyle of what was previously a reclusive family.

The man who occupied the Press Secretary's office for the shortest time was Robin Ludlow, who was there for just over a year in the early nineteen-seventies. He is also the only senior member of The Queen's Household to leave without an honour. Ludlow was working at the Palace during the time when Princess Anne became involved with Mark Phillips. Now the Palace Press Office has a policy of never deliberately telling lies. They often issue denials about stories which are subsequently proved true, but in every case the reason for the denial is that the Press Office has not been told all the facts – for the very reason that they can then claim no knowledge with absolute honesty. The exception came about early in 1973. For months there had been tremendous speculation in the press about a possible romance between Princess Anne and Captain Phillips. It seemed the more the Press wanted them to announce their engagement, the more determined they became not to do so. The 'will they – won't they?' stories went on for months, so much so that the Palace issued a denial – the only official denial of the engagement. It came at the end of January 1973 when Robin Ludlow, The Queen's Press Secretary, told John Knight of the *Sunday Mirror* that 'an engagement is not expected at this time' – which was perfectly true as far as he knew. The trouble was he didn't know enough. This was barely ten weeks before the official announcement of the engagement was made by Ronald Allison, who had replaced Ludlow as Press Secretary meantime. Allison was emphatic that he had never issued a denial. But the *Sunday Mirror* had published the story as told to John Knight by Robin Ludlow, and they were quite justifiably furious when the eventual truth was revealed. Robin Ludlow admitted after he left the Palace that there had been difficulties with some of his colleagues in the Royal Household, mainly because he saw himself as a pressman with an equal duty to serve both the Royal Family and the Fourth Estate, a state of affairs the Palace could not and would not contemplate. But he did not resign over the issue of the denial. This was pure coincidence and Allison had been canvassed as a replacement some months before.

When Ronald Allison became Press Secretary, the appointment was greeted by Fleet Street with sighs of relief. Here at last was one of their own, a reporter who knew their problems and who would ease their path through the royal labyrinth.

Allison had been Court Correspondent for BBC television for five years when the offer came from Sir Philip Moore, The Queen's Private Secretary. His coverage of royal events had earned him a reputation as a good, objective reporter with an eye for a news story that would not be clouded by proximity to royals. In other words, he was in no danger of suffering from 'Red Carpet Fever' – the ailment that strikes at so many of those who come in close contact with Buckingham Palace and its inhabitants.

One thing that Ronald Allison was adamant about when he accepted the post was that he would not remain longer than five years. He felt it was important to return to the 'real world' and resume his career in journalism. Anything longer than five years would mean staying at the Palace for good – which would not have been in the best interests of either himself or The Queen.

He became one of the most popular courtiers of modern times. Sir Philip Moore described him as 'pure gold'. The Queen quickly recognised his unique talent for putting people at ease and with his large frame and soft Hampshire burr he managed, with no apparent effort, to quell the unruly elements in the ranks of royal watchers with firm but good-humoured tact. Besides, his period at Buckingham Palace happened to coincide with a time of 'truce' in the constant battle between the Palace and the Press. The Royal Wedding of Princess Anne was a happy media event, and this was before the intrusion by the tabloids that subsequently marred the relationship. Allison managed to maintain his role as press adviser to the Royal Family while at the same time appearing to be on the side of those reporters and cameramen whose very presence could be the cause of great irritation and annoyance to the people he was supposed to be protecting. It was a delicate balancing act and one he perfected during his five years in the Press Office top job.

He also kept his own identity and sense of proportion by declining The Queen's offer of a Grace and Favour house, preferring to live in his own semi-detached home near Hampton Court Palace because, as he put it, 'I did not want to live over the shop.' He also never tried to be anything other than he was. He had come from a modest background and he knew it would be difficult to compete socially with some of his colleagues from families with great fortunes and even grander titles. It was the right decision. Because he never tried to put on airs and graces and because he was always perfectly natural, everybody knew where they were with him and respected him for what he was – a thorough professional. But he could be tough. I once heard him give an absolute roasting on the telephone to the Private Secretary of a member of the Royal Family because the man had authorised a press interview without first consulting him.

Having been the BBC's Court Correspondent for five years Ronald Allison was in a unique position to judge the Royal Family's attitude to the media. 'The Queen was very aware of what was being said about her in the Press,' he remembers. 'She always took a great interest in what was happening and she would frequently ask why a certain event had been reported in a particular way – or sometimes, why something had not been covered.'

When the time came for Allison to leave royal service the search for his successor ranged through many countries. It might be helpful at this point to explain the process by which senior members of the Royal Household are recruited. For example, when a post such as Press Secretary to The Queen falls vacant it is usual for a preliminary 'trawl' to take place among candidates known to existing Members. These are usually people who have come into contact with the Royal Family in the course of their duties. They may have assisted in the arrangements for a foreign tour or an event in the United Kingdom. If they have carried out their tasks in an exemplary manner The Queen's Private Secretary will make a note for future reference; it might be years hence, but it will not be forgotten. Prime Ministers of Commonwealth countries may be asked if they have someone who might be suitable for royal service and distinguished journalists are also canvassed.

Once the first 'trawl' has been completed a long 'short list' is drawn up. This consists of around half a dozen or so from which the serious contenders emerge. The final two or three are invited to Buckingham Palace for a talk with the Private Secretary and Assistant Private Secretary. It could not be classed as an interview because very little about the job itself is discussed. Rather it is just an informal chat to enable the two members of the Household to discover whether the man they are meeting is the sort to fit in with life at Court. It's an important point because, no matter how professional he might be at arranging press coverage and public relations, if the candidate does not know the form, or is unable to adapt to a particular lifestyle, he will simply prove to be a disruptive element in a very smooth-running organisation. There is nothing snobbish or elitist about this form of selection. The Royal Family and, perhaps to a lesser extent, their Household, care little about the social background of their servants or colleagues. They are satisfied so long as the best available person is chosen. It just so happens that the same families have provided generations of courtiers for many years, and until fairly recently even the jobs of the domestic staff were handed down father to son. Each one knew his place and so long as he or she did not try to be anything other than they were there were no problems. The Royal Family, The Queen in particular, have a knack of detecting 'phonies' at a glance.

One of the first questions all prospective members of the Royal Household were asked until a few years ago was: 'Are you divorced or likely to be?' This was because until the late nineteen-seventies no divorced people were employed. By then the rule had become impracticable and today a number of royal servants, including several at very senior level, are men who have been involved in divorce proceedings – and remarried. When Anne Hawkins, The Queen's Assistant Press Secretary and a niece of Princess Alice, married a man who had been divorced, there was strong pressure to remove her, even though her husband had been the innocent party. It was only when her then boss, Ronald Allison, interceded on her behalf, that The Queen relented and Miss Hawkins (now Mrs Michael Wall) was permitted to remain in her post.

The question of the candidate's commitment to the monarchy is examined fairly carefully and a reassurance is sought that no major changes are planned in the way in which the Press Office will be run. When Michael Shea arrived at Buckingham Palace in 1978 he wanted to alter the work-pattern and office accommodation so that the entire Press Office would be located in one large room with himself in a glassed-off section. In this way, he felt, everyone would be more aware of what the others were doing, making for a more efficient operation. But he hadn't reckoned on the reaction of the Private Secretary, the Master of the Household and the Keeper of the Privy Purse, each of whom had to be consulted before such a radical change could be introduced. For various reasons they were all completely opposed to the plan and it died. Such is the way of things in the Royal Household. Change takes a long time and anyone with revolutionary ideas, even those meant to improve the organisation, is better advised to keep them to himself – or to be very patient.

Returning to the selection process for a new Press Secretary, once those on the short list have been seen, two final candidates are chosen. One is the first choice and the second a reserve; and each is seen again: this time by the Private Secretary alone who explains the finer points of the job and the conditions. The salary is on a scale analogous with the equivalent rank in the Civil Service (the Press Secretary is on the same grade as an Assistant Secretary), the holidays are about the same, but as we have seen there is no company car. There will, however, be one major advantage. Once a trial period has been successfully completed, the Press Secretary will be allocated a Grace and Favour home. It might be an elegant house or apartment within Kensington Palace, such as that occupied by John Haslam, the Deputy Press Secretary, at the present time. Or, if the man concerned lives in a different part of the country and needs just a *pied-à-terre* in London during the working week, a one-bedroomed flat in nearby St James's Palace – with all fuel bills paid. Since 1980 the Press Secretary has occupied a handsome terraced house in Pimlico. It is built on four floors and The Queen first bought it, for an undisclosed sum believed to be slightly less than £200,000, for Michael Shea. He had lived in another Grace and Favour house, near the Tate Gallery, but this was thought to be too far from the Palace and Her Majesty sold a house she owned in Hampstead for around the same amount as she paid for the property in Pimlico.

At the final interview one serious disadvantage is emphasised – the extraordinary amount of time the Press Officer will be expected to spend away from home and family. As we have seen, for every overseas visit undertaken by a member of the Royal Family, a member of the Press Office goes with the advance team that carries out the 'recce' trip in order to prepare the programme. This means they actually travel twice as often as their principals because they always accompany them on the visit itself. In practice each of the press secretaries can expect to spend up to three months of the year away from home. If this is likely to cause family problems, now is the time to speak up.

Once the domestic details have been agreed and the Private Secretary is satisfied that he has chosen the best candidate, the person is invited to meet The Queen. It is virtually a 'rubber-stamping' formality as Her Majesty relies on the advice of her senior staff for all such appointments. However, to safeguard herself, and spare the successful candidate any possible embarrassment, she always says that they should give each other a trial period, 'so that if at the end of a few months we find we hate each other, we can say "goodbye" without any hard feelings'. And that is how one of The Queen's most trusted and confidential aides is appointed to his job.

This was the process by which a successor to Ronald Allison was found. After a prolonged search which took several months, Michael Shea, the Deputy Director of the British Government Information Service in New York, was recruited. Shea could not have been more different from Ronald Allison. A Foreign Office 'high-flyer', he supplemented his Civil Service pay by writing novels under the name of Michael Sinclair. From the start, in 1978, he let everyone know he was different from the usual run of Palace courtier by insisting that he should be allowed to continue writing fiction in his spare time. The Queen agreed, even telling Shea that she enjoyed his books.

A Scotsman married to a Norwegian, Shea had lived in many countries and, on his own admission, enjoyed 'the good life'. The successful handling of a royal visit to the United States in 1976 had singled him out for future favour (as did a similar service, but in India, for his successor Robin Janvrin eight years later). Shea was in his element at Buckingham Palace. He thoroughly enjoyed the high profile he attracted and, unlike his predecessors, never seemed to shrink from the publicity that followed him. He was widely quoted in the Press; his picture appeared frequently in newspapers and magazines and he featured in the gossip columns. He even warranted a profile in the *Sunday Times* which he must have approved himself because friends such as Sir David Steel, at that time Leader of the

Liberal Party, contributed, and he and others would not have done so without the subject's knowledge and permission.

One or two of Shea's more senior colleagues were not entirely happy about his apparent fascination with headlines. They felt it would be more appropriate for The Queen's representative to assume a slightly more anonymous role. Others, however, realised that Shea was performing an important task in deflecting attention away from the Royal Family and taking most of the criticism himself. Whether this was his intention is unclear. It clearly worked. Whenever an unfavourable story about the Royal Family appeared in the Press, Michael Shea would reply in words that immediately transferred the attention of the media to himself. It was a brilliant strategy and one that had never been used before – or has been since. On numerous occasions he himself became the story. On a State Visit to Canada a reporter claimed that Michael Shea told her that The Queen sometimes put on a 'Miss Piggy' look when she was displeased and the story was printed in newspapers throughout the world. Shea denied this, saying he would never use such a phrase, and apparently The Queen believed him, as he still occupied a favoured position at Court.

He again made headlines in October 1980 during The Queen's State Visit to Morocco. On one occasion Her Majesty had been kept waiting by her host King Hassan for more than two hours in suffocating heat. She was, understandably, furious, and the accompanying Press corps began berating Shea for the delay. Finally, unable to stand it any longer, he shouted to the BBC's Keith Graves, 'You've been buggered about, The Queen's been buggered about and I've been buggered about.' The quote made the day for the reporters – and their editors.

From 1978 to 1983 Michael Shea remained on the staff of the Foreign Office. They paid his salary, which was reimbursed by the Privy Purse. When this term was ended The Queen offered him a permanent position within the Royal Household and he relinquished his Foreign Office status. In 1988 he was asked to join the Hanson Group as its spokesman (at a salary said to be at least four times greater than his Buckingham Palace pay), and he resigned. But he has remained on excellent terms with the Palace; his company even paid for the Duchess of York to learn to fly a helicopter.

Shea's departure was rather swift and placed the Private Secretary's office in something of a dilemma. They had already appointed Robin Janvrin to be a replacement for Victor Chapman as Assistant Press Secretary. Chapman was a Canadian who spent most of his time at the Palace looking after the Press affairs of the Prince and Princess of Wales, and as such was number three in the office. He retired to Canada because of ill-health and died shortly afterwards.

So between his appointment and the date when he actually started Janvrin, who had expected to join the Household as the Press Office's new number three, was promoted to be Press Secretary to The Queen. It was a meteoric rise; easily the fastest promotion in royal history. John Haslam, the Deputy Press Secretary, was apparently not considered for the top job even though he was, and remains, the most experienced media man in the Press Office. He has now served under three Press Secretaries: Shea, Janvrin and Anson.

Robin Janvrin was the archetypal civil servant. He had obtained a First Class degree at Oxford and served as an officer in the Royal Navy and in a number of overseas postings as a Foreign Office diplomat. He brought to the Press Office a meticulous attention to detail and a natural courtesy which made him many friends among the world's media. His was a difficult task, following such a high-profile figure as Michael Shea. He is reserved, cautious but with a determined streak in his make-up, and the tough reporters of Fleet Street and the television news teams soon found he was not the easy target they at first thought. One of the things that distinguished him from some of his colleagues and predecessors was the fact that he genuinely wanted to help the Press – so long as by doing so he did not in any way compromise his position as guardian of the royal image.

He also pleased the more traditional members of the Household by reverting to the practice of being merely 'a Palace spokesman' instead of using his own name. When Michael Shea answered the telephone he always gave his name. Robin Janvrin invariably said, 'Press Office'. He quickly earned the respect of his colleagues and of The Queen, and his quiet but firm manner ensured that under him the Press Office operated as efficiently and effectively as ever. The secret of his success lay in his ability to get things done without any apparent effort. He always had time to talk to visitors and even if he never felt completely at home with the Press, it did not show.

Janvrin's time in the Press Office was comparatively short – just over three years. Then in 1990 Sir William Heseltine, The Queen's Private Secretary, announced that he was retiring to return to his native Australia. Sir Robert Fellowes, his Deputy, became Private Secretary, and the Assistant, Sir Kenneth Scott, also moved up a rung. The vacancy as Assistant Private Secretary to The Queen has been filled by Robin Janvrin, who moved to a position for which he is eminently suited when still only in his mid forties. Clearly Robin Janvrin is destined eventually for the top job.

The present Press Secretary, Charles Anson, has impeccable credentials for someone entering royal service in a highly confidential yet 'high-profile' role. With twenty-one years in the Diplomatic Corps and four years in the City, he combines the twin talents of traditional Civil Service reticence with a 'street-wise' credibility that enables him to deal with equal facility with those representing other world leaders and also with fast-talking news reporters. During his period in the Civil Service, he worked in the Press Office at No. 10 Downing Street from 1979 to 1981 under prime ministers James Callaghan and Margaret Thatcher. He was then Spokesman at the British Embassy in Washington from 1981 to 1985, handling two of The Queen's visits to the USA – to the West Coast in 1983 as a guest of President Reagan and a private visit to Kentucky the following year – and must then have come to the attention of Her Majesty's Private Office.

After leaving the Diplomatic Service Anson joined the banking firm of Kleinwort Benson, becoming Director of Corporate Affairs from 1987 to 1990 before he was invited to join the Royal Household. He brought to the Press Office a reputation for straight talking and a respect among City journalists that is rare among people whose job it is to distil the gold from the sometimes undiluted nonsense emanating from many eminent financial institutions. He comes from a family background where proximity to royalty is not uncommon, so he was comfortable and at ease in Buckingham Palace from the start. But he made headlines himself, in a very unfortunate manner, in March 1992, when he was handling the media coverage of the separation of the Duke and Duchess of York. Remarks he made were apparently authorised by The Queen, but this proved not to be the case, and Anson had to make a public apology to The Queen and the Duchess.

The world's media has a voracious appetite, and the Palace Press Office has to deal with a continuous stream of enquiries from national and local newspapers, weekly and monthly magazines and literally thousands of freelance writers and reporters. However, nothing has brought the monarchy to the attention of the world so much as television. The BBC and ITV both have Court Correspondents who are accredited to Buckingham Palace and accompany The Queen on every State Visit overseas, reporting back the trivial as well as the important aspects of the tour. If they can find something offbeat to report, so much the better. The two main broadcasting organisations take their royal coverage very seriously and monitor each other's programmes to see if one has received more cooperation and better facilities from the Palace than the other. Today nearly every major State occasion is seen through the lenses of cameras placed at strategic points inside the palaces and along the processional routes. The public has become as familiar with the sight of The Queen and her family at banquets, opening Parliament and attending weddings and other services at Westminster Abbey and St Paul's Cathedral, as they have with the daily happenings on television programmes such as *Coronation Street* or *EastEnders*.

Television has played a vital part in portraying the splendour and ceremonial of the monarchy and its value is fully realised by The Queen and her advisers. When the idea of televising the Coronation was first mooted forty years ago, Her Majesty was concerned that the magic and mystique of the Crown might in some way be diminished. She is also a very shy person who did not relish, and still does not, appearing before the cameras. Her advisers in those early days were of the same mind, distrustful of this new technology and convinced that it would be wrong to allow such intrusion into the solemn moments of such a ceremony. But when she was eventually persuaded by Sir Winston Churchill, who was never slow to seize the opportunity to exploit any public relations event, to allow the cameras to record every moment, even the act of crowning itself, Her Majesty involved herself enthusiastically in every aspect of the project. It has been the same ever since. Each time a royal wedding or other State occasion has been seen on television, it is only with the express permission of The Queen, who is advised on each stage of the proceedings by her Press Secretary.

Whenever a television programme is planned by the BBC or ITV in Britain, a set routine has to be followed. No producer or writer is allowed direct access to the Palace without first going through the official Palace liaison officers both organisations employ. The system suits both the Palace and the broadcasting companies, as with regional autonomy there are now so many different branches, departments and individual programme makers that there has to be a central control point. Otherwise scores of people could be writing to or ringing up the Palace, all perhaps suggesting similar ideas.

As Head of Outside Broadcasts at the BBC, Jim Moir is responsible for all royal broadcasting on radio and television. He supervises with just one assistant, Miss Jane Astell, The Queen's Christmas message, the State Opening of Parliament, all royal weddings, funerals, Royal Ascot, the Royal Maundy Service and anything else that might occur, and his office looks after all requests for interviews with members of the Royal Family and programmes involving royalty.

If a producer wants to make a programme about the Royal Family, he will first of all write to Jim Moir giving as many details as possible about the proposal. This is then forwarded to Charles Anson at Buckingham Palace for further consideration. If the project is considered in the best interests of the Royal Family – and this is the only criterion – the producer will be invited to the Palace for a talk. Then follow many more detailed discussions about what is and is not allowed until eventually the programme is made. The Palace sometimes imposes certain conditions on the programme makers: they will want to see the finished production before it is transmitted so that any changes they want can be made; they will decide which part of the subject's lifestyle can be shown on television and which parts remain strictly 'off limits'. Occasionally there is a financial agreement by which some of the proceeds are given to a charity nominated by the particular member of the Royal Family who is taking part.

Such was the case when Sir Alastair Burnet of Independent Television News was chosen to interview the Prince and Princess of Wales at their home in Kensington Palace. The film was sold to a large number of countries and was shown in the USA at peak time, coast to coast, achieving audience figures even greater than the leading soap operas *Dallas* and *Dynasty*. Burnet wrote a book based on the interview, which was published in record time to coincide with the television programme in September 1986, and one of the Prince of Wales's charities benefited to the tune of several hundred thousand pounds. The Palace was so pleased with the results that Burnet was again selected to present an intimate portrait of the royal couple a year later. By now he had become one of the world's experts on the Royal Family, with a newly established reputation eclipsing anything he had previously achieved in a distinguished career in journalism.

The BBC film *Elizabeth R*, shown in 1992 to celebrate the fortieth anniversary of The Queen's Accession, also generated a great deal of money. It was sold throughout the world, and profits are expected to eventually reach well over £1 million, which will be divided equally between the BBC and a number of charities nominated by Her Majesty, who has prudently retained all copyright.

So far as Independent Television is concerned, most royal programmes are made by ITN, the news organisation jointly owned by all the independent companies. Their Court Correspondent keeps them up to date with possible programme ideas. If one of the other companies in the group wishes to make a programme about or involving the Royal Family, the suggestion is discussed at the monthly meeting of the network committee and then forwarded to the Palace.

Foreign television companies constantly bombard the Palace Press Office with requests for interviews with the Royal Family; some are lucky. Prince Philip and the Princess Royal have both taken part in programmes in which they have been interviewed in either French or German – Prince Philip is fluent in both languages; the Princess speaks reasonable French.

The American networks are among the most persistent. Their reporters and producers, who are used to total access in their own country, find it hard to understand why they cannot interview The Queen or film behind the scenes in Buckingham Palace. But the Palace Press Office is quick to point out that members of the Royal Family do not compete in the 'ratings war', nor do they consider themselves players in a soap opera – even the most successful one in the world. As a former press secretary said: 'There is an extremely arrogant statement which keeps being made by one or two so called royal watchers, who say that if it wasn't for them the Royal Family would be terribly worried and if they didn't do their job, the popularity of the monarchy would fade away overnight. I think everybody would agree that's total rubbish. The monarchy to survive does not need the sort of prurient and/or sometimes quite adulatory coverage it gets.' But the very presence of a Press Secretary who is one of the Queen's closest advisers indicates that the Royal Family takes more than a passing interest in what is being said and written about them.

When the Prince and Princess of Wales visited America in 1985, more than a thousand reporters and cameramen applied for accreditation to cover the tour. And The Queen's visit to the West Coast of the USA the previous year received more coverage than the last Presidential election. Why should this be? What is this *worldwide* fascination with the British Royal Family? Is it just gossip and the fact that so many of us like to hear tittle-tattle about the most famous family in the world? Are we genuinely interested in the serious aspects of the monarchy, or just in what goes on behind the scenes? And why should this curiosity extend overseas as well as being prevalent in Britain? Nowadays nothing sells newspapers or magazines like royalty. A survey of national periodicals in Britain in 1985 showed that a photograph of The Queen or the Princess of Wales on the cover could mean an increase in sales by as much as 10 per cent. A similar survey in 1980 showed that pictures of Princess Margaret or Princess Anne could have exactly the opposite effect.

There has only been one occasion when The Queen has taken legal action to prevent a story involving a member of her family being published. It happened on 21 February 1983 when the *Sun*, one of the most popular of Britain's tabloid newspapers, printed an exclusive article about the antics of Prince Andrew and his then girl-friend Koo Stark. The story revealed how they lived it up in Buckingham Palace when The Queen was abroad and how Miss Stark, who, incidentally, has never said one word to the Press about her relationship with the Prince, romped through the corridors and ran barefoot in and out of the State Rooms. The articles also promised further revelations about the Princess of Wales. The source of this material was a former employee in the Royal Household, who had worked for a little over two years as a junior storeman. Within three weeks of leaving Buckingham Palace he had sold his story for what was said to be several thousand pounds, in spite of the fact that all employees in royal service sign an undertaking not to disclose any information they might come by during their period of employment.

When the story broke, The Queen was *en route* for the West Coast of America on board the Royal Yacht, and as soon as she was informed, she decided, on the advice of her then Private Secretary, Sir Philip Moore, to apply for an injunction to prevent any further disclosures. The application was actually made in the name of Mr (now Sir) Russell Wood, Deputy Treasurer of The Queen's Household, the man who paid the storeman's wages. The injunction was granted and the newspaper stopped the offending articles.

The case was given a tremendous amount of coverage by all the other national newspapers, every one of which was secretly delighted that one of their competitors had received this public 'slap on the wrist'. But the *Sun* didn't come out of it too badly either. Even though they had to stop printing the story, the amount of free publicity they received as a result of an action instigated by The Queen was worth far more than they would have made if the story had been published.

On this occasion the Palace decided that the rules on what they regard as decent and responsible reporting had been breached, and moved swiftly to abort what might have proved to be the birth of a monster. If they had failed to prevent this particular former servant from telling his story, who knows who else might be tempted into revealing behind-the-scenes gossip at other royal homes? Already a former valet to the Prince of Wales had published in America a book giving intimate details of his time with the heir to the throne. Stephen Barry became probably the most famous and certainly the richest defector since 'Crawfie', The Queen's governess, the first royal servant to sell her story to the Press. Barry made more than a quarter of a million pounds from his book *Royal Service*, which so far has not appeared in Britain. The author did not live long to enjoy his new-found wealth; he died a few years later.

Probably more books have been written about members of the Royal Family than anyone else in the world. In 1981, when Lady

Diana Spencer became engaged to the Prince of Wales, no fewer than eighty books were produced about her alone. They ranged from tiny children's booklets which had been put together in a matter of weeks to serious, well-researched biographies. And each year since then at least one title has been published on the same subject. There are authors who specialise in writing about royalty and a select few are welcome at Buckingham Palace and given remarkable facilities in their research. Elizabeth Longford has written what many people regard as the definitive biography of The Queen, *Elizabeth R*. It contains nearly 500 pages and catalogues in chronological order the life of The Queen, her work and the various aspects of the constitutional monarchy. Lady Longford could not have written the book without the utmost cooperation and she acknowledges this in her foreword. The Queen has never given interviews but both Queen Elizabeth the Queen Mother and Princess Margaret were interviewed by Lady Longford, and there is no doubt that they agreed to this only after discussions with The Queen herself; they would not have dreamed of talking to an author without the permission of Her Majesty.

The whole question of cooperation from the Press Office at Buckingham Palace is one that has puzzled journalists for many years. Where factual information is required the necessary answers are always forthcoming. But you have to ask the right questions. The Press Office does not normally volunteer information beyond the questions asked. The Press Secretary might suggest a radio or television programme to a producer, as in the case of the celebrations to mark the Queen's Silver Jubilee in 1977 or the arrangements for a State Visit, but for every suggestion he makes, he receives a hundred or so from outside. He would not, however, offer unsolicited advice to someone who wanted to write an article or book about a member of the Royal Family. That is not how the press officers see their function. They believe their role is to supply relevant facts to journalists in the interests of accuracy. Within the Press Office there is an extensive filing system listing almost every known detail about present members of the Royal Family, and they are delighted to give this information when requested. The difficulty arises when they are asked questions about what they regard as purely private matters. They will never, for example, tell anyone what The Queen and Prince Philip give each other for Christmas or on birthdays – even if they know, which is in any case highly unlikely. They will never reveal whether Her Majesty offers the Prime Minister a glass of sherry during the weekly audience on Tuesday evenings. Nor will they discuss the private finances of the Royal Family. On that subject they stick rigidly to the official line about the Civil List.

As we have seen, it is a common myth among editors in Fleet Street that the Royal Family needs them more than they need the Royal Family. Perhaps a more realistic assessment would be that both need each other. We live in a world where not only the Royal Family but holders of high office throughout the world have to be seen to be doing their jobs. There needs to be a line of communication to the ordinary reader and viewer of television. One of the most difficult tasks of the image makers – and the Press Office at Buckingham Palace is as much in the business of image making as any commercial public relations company, though its members would be horrified at the suggestion – is to keep control, so that a balanced view is presented. It is acceptable to let in a little daylight from time to time, but the mystery must be maintained. The Queen is of course the most human of human beings, but she is not like the rest of us. She is the Sovereign and as such must always remain apart, in spite of the so called democratisation of the monarchy. It is patently ridiculous for newspaper editors and reporters to say that were it not for them the monarchy would disappear, but at the same time the Royal Family has a real need for the media. They would find it very odd if, on a foreign tour, there was no cloud of cameras and reporters trailing behind them, and equally odd if a week passed by without one of them appearing on our television screens.

The voracious appetite of the public for scraps of news from the royal table is in no danger of being satisfied; and if the Royal Family felt no need to drop titbits about themselves from time to time, they would have no use for a Press Office. The monarchy has never been as popular as it is today, partly because of the person who occupies the throne, and partly because of the skilful exploitation of the media by one of the most successful public relations machines in the world. It may not be the largest and it certainly is not the highest paid, but it is undoubtedly among the most effective.

11

THE CROWN EQUERRY

WHENEVER THE QUEEN TRAVELS BY ROAD, whether by royal limousine, State carriage or on horseback, the responsibility for making all the necessary arrangements rests with the Crown Equerry, the man in charge of the Royal Mews.

The titular head of the Royal Mews is the Master of the Horse, one of the Great Officers of the Royal Household who ranks third in the order of precedence at Court, behind the Lord Great Chamberlain and the Lord Steward, and in olden days the Master of the Horse actually had day-to-day charge of all the work that was carried on out of doors, including the Royal Mews. But today his duties are purely ceremonial although in State processions he can still be seen riding immediately behind the Sovereign.

The Royal Mews also seem something of a throwback to ancient times. The air of an old country estate still hangs about this south-east corner of Buckingham Palace where the Crown Equerry lives and works. His house is situated immediately inside the large ornate gates to the Mews, on the left as you look at it from the front. It is a splendid three-storey house which would not look out of place nestling amid the rolling countryside of Oxfordshire or Gloucestershire, and it goes with the job, which means it comes virtually rent-free. The only trouble is that these days it is difficult to clean and almost impossible to heat so large a house.

In Queen Victoria's time, the Crown Equerry was given ten servants to wait on him, all of them living in, and paid for by the Crown. Today, his successor manages with a daily cleaning lady whose wages he has to pay himself. One of the most intriguing parts of the house is the kitchen in the basement. It contains cooking ranges which are so large they could not be removed without serious structural alterations to the building. These kitchens have long been disused; a modern kitchen on the ground floor is much more convenient – and economical.

The Crown Equerry is assisted by a permanent Superintendent, who acts as his deputy, and two or three temporary Equerries who each serve for three years. They may be recruited from the armed services and among their other duties, such as attending The Queen at Court and on official visits at home and overseas, they make all The Queen's transport arrangements.

There is also a Comptroller of Stores, a Chief Clerk and a deputy Chief Clerk. To drive and maintain the fleet of royal cars there are mechanics, cleaners and twelve highly trained chauffeurs. Seamstresses and upholsterers work on the livery worn by coachmen and postillions and the interiors of the State Coaches, but the ten gardeners, supervised by the Head Gardener, a man of enormous experience and considerable ability, who used to be responsible to the Crown Equerry, now work for the Master of the Household. In addition a large number of other workers, who are employed by the Department of the Environment but who work within the boundaries of the Buckingham Palace grounds, also answer to either the Master of the Household or the Crown Equerry when they are on the premises.

A hundred years ago, in the days of Queen Victoria, there were more than two hundred horses in the Royal Mews, and the Crown Equerry was responsible for every one. By the time King George VI was crowned in 1937 the number had been reduced to seventy-five and today there are just thirty: twenty Bays and ten Windsor Greys, so called because they were once stabled in the Mews at Windsor Castle. These days all the horses live permanently at Buckingham Palace and are taken by road to Windsor in June for the annual Royal Procession at Ascot.

The thirty horses are sufficient for all ceremonial occasions in the royal diary with the exception of a coronation. Then more than a hundred are required, and at The Queen's Coronation in 1953, several local riding schools and clubs lent their horses to the Crown Equerry for the occasion.

The day's routine in the Royal Mews starts early. The single stable-lads or grooms who live in a dormitory are roused at 5.30 A.M. in order to be on duty promptly at 6.15, their first task to make sure the horses (each man looks after two) have eaten their overnight feed. If they haven't, the Head Coachman, who is the Mews foreman, is informed. Then the grooming begins. Each morning this takes around an hour and a half and it has to be done before the lads can have their breakfast. In the past special categories of worker were employed to muck out the stables, polish the brass and clean the exercise harness. Nowadays everyone, including the coachmen, lends a hand. These are tasks that have to be done throughout the year, and before dawn on cold winter mornings some of the staff find it difficult to maintain enthusiasm for the exacting and unrelenting routine.

After breakfast the grooms are inspected by the deputy Head Coachman, for they must be as immaculately turned out as their charges. Overalls are worn for mucking out, and then they change into working riding gear: black coats, dark breeches, boots and helmets. These helmets are comparatively new and are very unpopular with the riders, for they are bulky and unattractive. But experience has proved that they can prevent serious injury in an accident, so the Crown Equerry insists that they are worn. At nine o'clock the string of horses is ridden to Hyde Park for a canter in Rotten Row. With the increasing flow of vehicles through London's West End, the route has become more and more hazardous over the years, so a mounted police escort 'pathfinds' a way across the island of Hyde Park Corner, cutting out the worst of the traffic across their way.

The exercise period in Hyde Park lasts about an hour and a half and then comes the return journey to the Mews. Once the horses have been examined to ensure none has sustained any injury, they are rubbed down and given a feed. The men then take their mid-morning break.

Every morning during the working year, more than half a dozen carriages are used on a variety of duties. The Messenger Brougham operates twice a day carrying mail and messages between the various

Royal Households. The word brougham came into usage in equestrian circles in the mid-nineteenth century, when Lord Brougham commissioned the coachbuilding firm of Robinson & Cook to build him a light, single-horse carriage capable of carrying two passengers. One has been in constant use in the Royal Mews since 1843, and the Messenger Brougham used today is painted blue and pulled by either a bay or a grey; the coachman wears plain livery of black coat and light fawn breeches on his round.

One of the most popular duties is to collect and later take home an incoming Ambassador or High Commissioner who wishes to present his Letters of Credence to Her Majesty. This takes place some three or four times a week, for with more than seventy diplomatic missions accredited to the Court of St James's there is a lot of coming and going throughout the year. Three carriages are dispatched, the first for the use of the diplomat, who is accompanied by the Marshal of the Diplomatic Corps. The others are occupied by members of the diplomat's family and staff. The duty starts at around 9.45 in the morning and finishes at 12.30 P.M. when the staff in attendance receive the rest of the day off. On the journey back to the residence, the formalities over, there is a very relaxed feeling in the air; and there is always a small celebration in the residence to which the coachmen and grooms are invariably invited. Beer, champagne and spirits are brought out, and more than one coachman has been known to say, 'Thank God the horses know the way back.'

Attendance at Royal Ascot is far less popular because for this the coachmen and postillions have to wear heavy wigs under their hats and elaborate State Livery costing £1,400 a set. In June the weather can be hot and the drive along the course is tedious and tiring. Always polite, the men say that they find this duty 'less interesting' than some others.

The early afternoon is a peaceful period in the Royal Mews and the staff are allowed a break for an hour or two. Then come early evening stables, making sure the horses are fed, watered and bedded down for the night before the day's work ends at about five-thirty in the evening.

Throughout the year there is a constant round of rehearsals for major State occasions and frequent weekend duty when one of the

Royal Family or Household is taking part in horse trials or a carriage-driving event. This extra work is allocated by the deputy Head Coachman, and is not voluntary. It is one of the conditions of employment and overtime is not paid.

During 1991, between 13 March and 22 December, and apart from the normal daily duties, 106 official events were listed in the Royal Mews calendar for which horses, coaches and drivers were required, thirty-nine of which involved weekend working.

The attention to detail which characterises the entire Household is reflected in the instructions issued whenever the Royal Mews goes into action. For example:

The Meet of the British Driving Society – Sunday, 12 May 1991

The Meet was held at Windsor, and the Head Coachman sent out the following instructions to his staff:

1. Sir John Miller
   J. Day (Carriage Groom)
   Goshawk, River Star – Ambassador Harness – Beaufort Phaeton

2. Prince Michael
   Cmn [Coachman] Nelson (Carriage Groom)
   St Patrick, Twilight – Best Harness – Balmoral Dog Cart

3. Prince Ludwig
   M. Chard (Carriage Groom)
   Mulgrave Dante, Ramblers Leah – Ambassador Harness – Maroon Dog Cart

4. Count Andrassy
   H. Nelson (Carriage Groom)
   Alderney, Seville – Best Harness – Demi-Mail Phaeton

5. Crown Equerry
   A. Myers (Carriage Groom)
   Monarch, Barcelona – Ambassador Harness – Iron/Tyred Waggonette

179

The list gives, first, the person who is going to drive, next the name of the Royal Mews attendant, then the two horses, the type of harness required and the type of carriage to be driven.

Then follow the logistic instructions:

DRESS	Black Livery – Kersey Breeches.
STABLING	Box Yard.
TRANSPORT	QB [Queen's Box]. Harness and Equipment. 0930 Friday, 10 May 1991 *Miss Wood* [the Horse Box driver] *Sunday, 12 May 1991* J. Day – St Patrick, Twilight, Mulgrave Dante, Ramblers Leah, Goshawk, River Star, M. Chard. J. Butler – Land-Rover and Trailer with Balmoral Dog Cart
TIMINGS	0900 Depart Royal Mews
	1000 Arrival Windsor – Grooming. Touch up harness. Stow spares.
	1115 All to depart for lunch.
	1230 Harness up.
	1315 Change into livery.
	1330 Bridles on.
	1345 Put to.
	1400 Move off.

J. Butler will see that the above mentioned Carriages are well turned out, and will see they are washed off after the driving event. Deputy Head Coachman Matthews [now Head Coachman] will be in charge of the party.

It all goes like clockwork, but only because everyone knows his or her job backwards and also because the success of the drivers reflects back onto the team. It's very much a matter of pride and one of the more rewarding aspects of Mews work.

Recruitment takes many forms. The Army has always provided a large proportion of the liveried staff (the term applied to all the men who work on the royal carriages), The King's Troop Royal Horse

Artillery being a particularly fruitful source of talent. Some of the senior staff today arrived at the Mews after several years in racing. They may have suffered accidents which terminated a career on the Turf, and have proved highly successful in handling The Queen's more ceremonial horses. More recently, youngsters on Youth Opportunity Schemes have been found places in the stables. Even enterprising young men who turn up on the doorstep and ask for a job are interviewed and, if found suitable, offered work once their references have been checked.

Single men live in dormitories with all meals found and livery provided. They are paid around £140 a week at the start, and that is free of all accommodation charges. Married men are given flats in the Mews, some of which are splendid homes of three or four bedrooms overlooking the Palace gardens.

Whenever someone is taken on in the Mews he is put on probation for six months. This works both ways. If, at the end of this period, he does not want to continue, he is able to leave without any recriminations; and if on the other hand he is found to be unsuitable, he can be dismissed without any comeback. It is unusual for anyone to leave at the end of the probation period; but sometimes a man who has not worked with horses before finds he just cannot adapt to a way of life in which the animal always comes first.

The Royal Mews is a community and its members tend to stick together. Some of the staff come from families boasting generations of service with The Queen. Their fathers and grandfathers have worked at the Palace before them and they stay for life. The compulsory retirement age is sixty, but employment is always found in the stables or yard for any man who becomes too feeble to handle the horses in public. The money at the top is still not very large: a senior coachman earns just over £10,000 a year, but one could easily add a further £5,000 a year by taking the rent-free accommodation and meals into consideration.

The five coachmen who are responsible for looking after the State coaches and carriages are among the most experienced horsemen in the country. Theirs is a skill that takes years to acquire and they belong to a dwindling group of dedicated carriage drivers who jealously guard the privileged positions they hold. The fifteen grooms also act as postillions on ceremonial occasions. As we have seen, each groom looks after two horses and there is tremendous competition and friendly rivalry between them to see who can turn out the best-looking animals in the Mews.

Each employee has his favourite among the Royal Family, but two stand out with them all. All agree that the Queen Mother and Prince Charles are the most appreciative, and always come around to the front of the coach after a procession to say a few words to the driver. The Queen carries lumps of sugar for the horses while Prince Philip can be a little difficult at times, especially if something has gone wrong when he has been driving. Apparently it is never his own fault!

The men and women who work in the Royal Mews enjoy a special relationship with the Royal Family because of their mutual love of horses. Anyone who works with animals will understand this; it's a common bond that links servant and master in a way that sets aside the usual relationship between employer and employee. This feeling of mutual respect is also evident between the Mews staff and the senior Members of the Household, and manifests itself in a variety of ways. The Lord Chamberlain, for example, has racing interests in a number of outside organisations, and knows that most of the ex-jockeys and others in the Mews enjoy a good day at the races. He often arranges for some of them to be his guests at Newmarket or one of the other courses around the country, and they are given the full treatment – champagne, smoked salmon, afternoon tea and the best seats in the stand. On the day they seem to forget their relative positions; they are just good friends with a love of horses, out to enjoy the best that the country can provide.

In addition to the Mews at Buckingham Palace there are also Royal Mews at Windsor Castle, Hampton Court Palace and the Palace of Holyroodhouse. The name mews derives from an ancient French word used to describe a change of feathers, and in medieval times the mews was the place where the Sovereign's falcons were housed during their 'mewing' or moult. The ones in London date from 1825 and are largely unchanged from Nash's original design for King George IV. They are constructed around a quadrangle. The east side is reserved for the State coaches and carriages and the horses are stabled on the north and west. A riding school adjoins the Mews and here the horses are exercised for at least an hour every day. Here also young men who may not have ridden before joining the Royal Household are taught to ride. Somewhat surprisingly, not all those employed in the Royal Mews have grown up with horses. So long as the young man is willing, and shows an aptitude, the Crown Equerry is quite prepared to take him on and provide expert instruction, in both riding and the more difficult skill of carriage driving, free of charge.

The riding school is seventy-five yards long with a firm surface laid on a six-foot deep foundation of faggots and peat. In order to get the horses used to conditions they may encounter during a large procession, lines of brightly coloured flags and bunting are strung across the school from time to time. Stable boys act the part of onlookers, throwing streamers, bursting paper-bags and shouting and cheering while recordings of military bands are played at full volume to accustom the horses to the extraordinary noise that accompanies every major royal ceremonial occasion.

The Royal Mews is also the scene of one of the most popular – and informal – of all Household events. It is the annual Christmas drinks party given by members of the Royalty Protection Department – the Royal Family's bodyguards – to which invitations are keenly sought. And it is not unknown for at least one of the younger members of the family to turn up unannounced, and stay to the very end.

The garages in the Royal Mews contain The Queen's five Rolls-Royce limousines, the most famous of which is the Phantom VI presented to Her Majesty in March 1978 by the Society of Motor Manufacturers and Traders to mark her Silver Jubilee the year before. As all five Rolls-Royces are State limousines, they carry no registration number plates – the only vehicles in Britain with this distinction. They are all painted in royal maroon livery and are fitted with special brackets to hold the shields bearing the royal coat of arms and the personal pennants of their royal passengers. Whenever The Queen is travelling in one of her official cars a solid silver mascot depicting St George and the Dragon is fixed to the front.

The private cars of the Royal Family are also looked after in the Royal Mews, including an unusual vehicle used by the Duke of Edinburgh. It is an electrically powered van which is on lease from the Lucas battery company and its pollution-free motor appeals to the ecologically-minded Duke who used to be seen occasionally driving the vehicle around central London – but not in the last few years, as he rarely drives himself in the capital these days.

The pride of the Royal Mews is undoubtedly the magnificent collection of historic State coaches. The most famous of them all is the Gold State Coach, built in 1762 and seen at every coronation since that of King George IV. The most frequently seen is the Irish State Coach – so named because the man who built it in 1852 was also Lord Mayor of Dublin at the time – which used to convey The Queen to the State Opening of Parliament every year. She used this particular coach because her father, the late King George VI, discovered that the Gold State Coach, which is much heavier and more cumbersome, could travel no faster than three miles an hour, which meant that the journey from Buckingham Palace to Westminster took twenty-five minutes. This is because the Gold State Coach weighs so much that it cannot be pulled at the trot for fear it might run out of control. The Irish State Coach is much lighter and more manoeuvrable, and can travel at the trot, pulled by four horses and covering the same distance in twelve minutes. A former Crown Equerry, Sir John Miller, realised this fact after a number of experimental journeys in all kinds of weather.

The most comfortable of the three major State coaches is the Scottish State Coach favoured by Queen Elizabeth the Queen Mother, with its large windows and glass panels in the roof. Visitors to the Royal Mews are also able to see the beautiful Glass Coach used by every royal bride this century for the drive to the wedding church.

The most recent addition to the Royal Mews is the Australian State Coach, a gift from the people of Australia during the country's Bicentennial year of 1988. It was first used by The Queen and the Duke of Edinburgh on Tuesday, 22 November 1988 for the State Opening of Parliament. Similar in design to the Irish State Coach, the Australian State Coach is constructed of the finest Australian materials – red cedar and matched elm burr veneer. The interior is upholstered in blue silk brocade of which twenty-nine metres were supplied by the Royal Household for the purpose.

The best-known of all Crown Equerries, certainly in this century, was Lieutenant-Colonel Sir John Miller, who was not himself a cavalry man at all. His regiment was one of the Foot Guards, the Welsh Guards. He was in royal service for more than a quarter of a century and became a law unto himself within the Household. As the man who taught most of the younger members of the Royal Family to ride, and who introduced Prince Philip to the sport of carriage-driving when arthritis forced His Royal Highness to give up polo, he created a special niche for himself which, as we have seen, he nurtured with care.

Sir John prided himself that no royal engagement in which he was involved was ever late, even by so much as a minute. So he was horrified when, on the eve of the wedding of the Prince of Wales and Lady Diana Spencer, he received a message that the future Princess of Wales wished to exercise a bride's prerogative and arrive at St Paul's Cathedral a few minutes behind time. He had already been over the route many times, stopwatch in hand, timing to the exact second every step of the way, and he knew that he had everything perfectly prepared. The timetable had been printed and the world's media had been given copies; if he obeyed this soon-to-be royal command, his reputation for punctuality would be in tatters. He consulted the Lord Chamberlain, Lord Maclean, and asked his advice. But this was one occasion when the Head of The Queen's Household decided to leave the decision to his junior colleague.

When the moment for the bride's arrival at St Paul's came she was less than thirty seconds late; it was enough to satisfy her stated wishes but not enough to damage the reputation of the man to whom punctuality was not just the politeness of princes but of their servants also. Lady Diana was feeling a little nervous on the day and her father jokingly suggested as they came out of Clarence House that the carriage should turn right – towards Buckingham Palace – rather than left towards the crowds waiting at St Paul's. Luckily the coach-man took his instructions from the Crown Equerry and all was well.

The collection of State coaches, landaus and carriages is comple-mented by a fascinating exhibition of State harness, together with many photographs and other items of historical interest, all of which may be seen by the public throughout the year. Even so the Royal

Mews remains very much a working showplace, a source of constant pride to those who work there and in particular to the man with overall responsibility for its smooth efficiency – The Crown Equerry.

12

THE ROYAL
COLLECTION

WITH AN ESTIMATED TOTAL of one million items, the paintings, drawings, engravings, furniture, Fabergé eggs and other priceless *objets d'art* that constitute the Royal Collection make up the most important private art collection in the world. Its significance is reflected in the fact that it is now all under the control of a single department, and those who administer the Royal Collection on behalf of Her Majesty are among the world's leading experts in their various fields.

Until 1987 responsibility for the care of the Collection was in the hands of three people, the Surveyor of The Queen's Pictures, the Surveyor of The Queen's Works of Art and the Librarian at Windsor Castle, who worked under the overall jurisdiction of the Lord Chamberlain's Office. Then, when the management consultants Peat Marwick McLintock, who were also auditors to the Privy Purse Office, recommended that a single new department should look after the entire Collection the present system was set up.

The first Director of The Royal Collection was Sir Oliver Millar, a man of considerable experience and with a distinguished reputation in the world of art. He had originally joined the Royal Household as Deputy Surveyor of The Queen's Pictures in 1947, the Surveyor at that time being Sir Anthony Blunt.

When Sir Oliver retired in 1988 he was appointed Surveyor of The Queen's Pictures Emeritus and his place as Director of the Royal Collection was taken by Sir Geoffrey de Bellaigue, who also retains his position as Surveyor of The Queen's Works of Art. There is a

strong family tradition in this branch of royal service, for Sir Geoffrey's wife Sheila holds the post of Registrar in the Royal Archives.
She has worked at Windsor Castle for many years and her knowledge
of historical facts and figures relating to royalty past and present has
proved invaluable to countless authors and scholars who have been
given permission to consult the Archives.

The Deputy Surveyor of The Queen's Works of Art is Hugh
Roberts, whose wife Jane is Curator of the Print Room at Windsor.
The current Surveyor of The Queen's Pictures is Christopher Lloyd.
He came into the Royal Household with an impeccable pedigree,
having been an Assistant Head of Department at the Ashmolean
Library in Oxford.

One of the key positions in the Royal Collection is that of Registrar, who together with his assistant reports immediately to the
Director, although he also helps the Surveyor of Pictures and, to a
lesser extent, the Librarian at Windsor from time to time. The Registrar is in constant contact with outside interests as he is responsible
for granting reproduction rights in pictures and works of art to a wide
range of commercial users, mainly book and magazine publishers and
television companies, from all over the world. For this purpose he
maintains a large and extensive library of colour transparencies (some
2,500) which are lent to customers of the Royal Collection Department on payment of a fee. Every time a photograph of one of The
Queen's pictures or works of art appears anywhere in the world, it
will have come from the Registrar's library – and Her Majesty will
have been paid for giving Her Gracious Permission.

Other duties of the Registrar involve arranging for police escorts
to accompany particularly valuable works when they are in transit,
and the vast amount of paperwork relating to insurance and the other
complex formalities required whenever items are loaned for outside
exhibition. He also acts as Secretary of the Royal Palaces Exhibition
Committee. This is the body that organises the annual displays of
royal treasures in The Queen's Gallery at Buckingham Palace, exhibitions that involve the Registrar in much detailed preparation.

For many years the two Surveyors (of Pictures and Works of Art)
and the Librarian were each allocated a budget for the care and
maintenance of their respective part of the Royal Collection by the

Lord Chamberlain. The money came from profits derived from admissions to and bookshop sales in certain royal residences, namely Windsor Castle State Apartments, the exhibition of Old Master Drawings, Queen Mary's Dolls' House and The Queen's Gallery at Buckingham Palace. But as part of the recommendations suggested by the Peat Marwick McLintock reorganisation the responsibility for these admissions and sales was transferred to a new office under the direction of the Deputy Treasurer to The Queen called the Royal Palaces Presentation Fund. This office, based at St James's Palace and under the day-to-day control of the Superintendent of Public Enterprises, is additionally responsible for all admissions to, and bookshops in, the Palace of Holyroodhouse in Edinburgh and Frogmore House at Windsor, which has recently been opened to the public for the two months every year when the Court is at Balmoral. Towards the end of 1990, the Royal Palaces Presentation Fund also assumed control over public admission to the Royal Mews at Buckingham Palace.

The net profits from the Royal Palaces Presentation Fund are allocated to the three sections of the Royal Collection Department in annual budgets based on forecasts of revenue during the coming financial year. This income is not augmented from any other source, not even the Civil List, so it follows that the cost of maintaining the Royal Collection does not fall directly on the taxpayer.

Progress on the many accounts through the year is strictly monitored by the Royal Palaces Presentation Fund Management Committee, whose monthly meetings are chaired by the Keeper of the Privy Purse and whose members include the Director of the Royal Collection, the Superintendent of Public Enterprises, the Deputy Treasurer to The Queen and the Financial Controller of the Royal Palaces Presentation Fund.

One immediate result of the Gulf War in 1990–91 was a disastrous fall in the number of visitors to London, which in turn meant a substantial drop in admission fees and bookshop sales at all royal venues. The consequent reduction in income for the Royal Collection had far-reaching implications on the amount of restoration work that could be carried out and on buying new items.

As Director of the Royal Collection and Head of one of the six departments in the Royal Household, Sir Geoffrey de Bellaigue sits on the Lord Chamberlain's Committee, the policy-making body for all Household affairs. The department itself is divided into three sub-divisions: Works of Art (i.e. three-dimensional objects), Pictures, and the Royal Library, whose head is Oliver Everett, the former Foreign Office executive who later became Assistant Private Secretary to the Prince of Wales. Like the Director, the Surveyor of Pictures and the Deputy Surveyor of Works of Art, the Librarian is a Member of the Royal Household, all the remaining personnel being Officials or Staff.

THE FURNITURE RESTORATION WORKSHOP AT MARLBOROUGH HOUSE

Two senior conservators of furniture and two conservators work here, together with a single conservator/armourer who has a separate workshop in Marlborough House Mews. This man was formerly employed at the armouries at the Tower of London where he was responsible for the care and maintenance of all the armour and arms held there. All these employees are specialists in their own fields and as such are paid salaries that are graded according to the scale used at the Victoria and Albert Museum. This means that they are relatively better off than others of similar standing within the Royal Household, but it is the only way that craftsmen with their unique talents can be persuaded to work for The Queen's Collection.

The Marlborough House staff are usually engaged on the restoration of the more important items of furniture, many of which may be required for exhibition in The Queen's Gallery or loaned to outside organisations. There is a wide variation in the quality of items in the Collection and consequently a certain overlap between the work carried out by these specialist conservators and that executed by the furniture craftsmen within 'G' Branch of the Master of the Household's staff, who generally look after items of a 'domestic' nature. Inevitably a natural degree of rivalry and jealousy occurs between the

190

two groups as each tries to show the other 'how it should be done'. The Director also makes every effort to allow the expertise of his craftsmen to be shared and from time to time employs students from overseas museums on a sandwich course basis, to give them practical experience.

Most items in the Royal Collection are not kept in ideal or museum conditions but in a normal, domestic environment with its accompanying variations in temperature, humidity and light. Therefore, in a typical year, much of the work in the Marlborough House workshop consists of repairing damage inflicted on furniture as a result of drying out through central heating. The armourer is likewise employed, mainly on maintenance and preparing items for exhibition – in his case the main problem, understandably, is rust!

Occasionally the skills of the restorers are required to repair damage caused by accidental breakage, and this can be something of a problem. A few years ago a young maid was dusting in one of the State Rooms at Buckingham Palace when she knocked over a magnificent Sèvres vase. It broke into several pieces and the poor girl was too terrified to tell anyone what she had done. She hid the pieces, bought a tube of super-glue, and tried to stick it back together. Some time later an official from the Royal Collection happened to be in the room and saw the vase with 'bits sticking out at all sorts of angles'. He realised what had happened and took the vase back to St James's Palace for the experts to examine. But as soon as they tried to take it to pieces they found that the glue was stronger than the porcelain, and without knowing which brand had been used it was impossible to use a solvent.

Since the Master of the Household did not know which of the maids had caused the accident he called a general amnesty – no recrimination so long as the culprit owned up. The unfortunate girl eventually came forward and confessed, and she remembered what type of glue she had used. With this information the experts were able to start the painstaking process of gradually breaking down the adhesive, removing the broken pieces and reassembling them. The work took two years to complete but today the vase is back in its place of honour, in practically its original condition – and the maid is still employed in the Royal Household.

191

FRIARY COURT STUDIO

Friary Court is the small area bounded on three sides by St James's Palace, with the fourth side open to Marlborough Road. Princess Alexandra has her office on the south side while the Headquarters of the Yeomen of the Guard is situated on the north. In between are apartments for members of the Household, and it is from the Brick Balcony above Friary Court that the Proclamation of a new Sovereign is first read.

The paintings restoration studio here employs a senior restorer and two restorers, although, as with works of art, where highly skilled restoration work on a single piece of delicate porcelain can take years to complete, and is therefore too expensive to contemplate 'in-house', some work is undertaken by outside contractors. In the case of paintings this consists chiefly of re-backing and lining, the actual restoration of the picture being carried out in Friary Court. Recently a museum technician has also been employed to work on the picture frames, works of art in their own right, many of which have been neglected for years due to lack of funds.

Some years ago the Surveyor of Pictures had cause to be rather upset by one of his colleagues, the Crown Equerry. A number of valuable paintings had been loaned to the Crown Equerry to decorate the walls of his Grace and Favour house. Shortly afterwards a fire broke out in one of the paint stores in the Royal Mews and it was discovered that several of the pictures, which should have been in the Crown Equerry's house, were in fact in the storeroom, and had been badly damaged.

An exchange of letters on the subject then took place. The Surveyor wanted to know why the paintings were not where they were supposed to be. The Crown Equerry replied that some of the gilt on the frames had been tarnished and he was having them touched up – just about the worst possible thing he could have said. It was bad enough to remove the paintings from their scheduled hanging places without informing the department responsible, whose staff would normally perform such tasks. But to use Mews staff to work on very valuable picture frames was unforgivable, and the tone of the letters became more icy. Eventually the paintings were returned to the Royal Collection department for restoration and the damage was able to be repaired, but it took some time for cordial relations between two of The Queen's very senior courtiers to be restored.

The studio is kept busy checking the condition of paintings to be sent out on loan and performing any cleaning or restoration work required. Many important international exhibitions owe much of their success to contributions from the Royal Collection, and Her Majesty encourages a positive attitude to requests from all over the world. The difficulty is that great care has to be taken of the paintings, particularly when long-distance travel is involved.

These days lack of finance prevents large-scale purchases of famous works of art, but the Royal Collection is still in the market when suitable items become available. Sellers try to inflate the price when they learn who the buyer is, so some of the less well-known members of the department are usually detailed to attend auctions and bid for anything on which the Director has his eye.

The Department also advises members of the Royal Family who are buying paintings for their private collections. They have been particularly successful on behalf of Queen Elizabeth the Queen Mother who is an avid collector in her own right and an enthusiastic supporter of British artists. Her Majesty was an early supporter of the renowned war artist John Piper and during the Second World War invited him to paint, among other subjects, a squadron of aircraft which was based at Smith's Lawn, Windsor Castle, where today the Prince of Wales enjoys his Sunday afternoon polo matches. That painting and several other views of Windsor by John Piper are hanging in Clarence House. Queen Elizabeth obviously had a keen eye for a good investment too as these paintings which she bought for a few hundred pounds each are now valued in excess of £20,000 each.

THE ROYAL LIBRARY AT WINDSOR

The Queen's Librarian is also Deputy Keeper of the Royal Archives which are stored at Windsor. They are not, however, part of the Royal Collection and come under the overall supervision of The

Queen's Private Secretary who is their Keeper. Also at Windsor is the Print Room, in the charge of a curator and a deputy curator, who are responsible for all prints and drawings, while an assistant curator deals with the loan of prints and drawings to outside exhibitions. Unlike Pictures and Works of Art, who tend to lend individual items, the Library will often loan a complete collection of drawings by an important artist such as Leonardo da Vinci, Holbein or Canaletto. Another assistant curator in charge of photographic services deals with the many requests for reproduction rights.

The chief restorer of drawings and his assistant are as well qualified in their field as their colleagues at Friary Court and Marlborough House, and they have specialists to help them – a maintenance and exhibitions conservator, three bookbinders, a paper conservator and, most essential to such an historic collection of books, a bibliographer.

For many years the Royal Library has prepared and published catalogues of various parts of the Royal Collection and for more than twenty years Phaidon Press had an agreement with the Palace to publish books written by or with the cooperation of members of the Royal Household. Sir Oliver Millar wrote a number of works on Tudor, Stuart and Georgian pictures. In the 1980s the agreement lapsed and a new contract was entered into with Cambridge University Press, who in 1986 published Sir Geoffrey de Bellaigue's masterly catalogue of the Louis XVI service of Sèvres porcelain. They also worked with Sir Oliver Millar on his long-awaited catalogue of Victorian pictures, together with a companion volume of Victorian watercolours and drawings by Lady Millar, which at the time of writing were due to be published early in 1992. Perhaps the most successful, and certainly the most popular, book written on a part of the Royal Collection was Sir Oliver Millar's *The Queen's Pictures*, published by Weidenfeld and Nicolson in 1970. It became a bestseller and was reprinted several times in a number of different versions.

As has already been mentioned, it is estimated that there are some one million items in the Royal Collection, and for the past two years the department has been engaged in setting up a comprehensive computer system to catalogue and record every single one. It has been a mammoth task, and for the purpose a computer inventory manager has been seconded from the Home Office to supervise the installation of the hardware and to make sure the programmes are running correctly. The manager has spent much of his time drawing up standard procedures for recording the normal location and movement of items between Palaces, together with a standard form of description. This last has not been easy as many of the works of art have either not been inventoried before, or not for many years.

The inventory photographer has a darkroom in Stable Yard House in St James's Palace and works closely with two inventory assistants who are based in Buckingham Palace. However, there is far too much work for just one photographer, and outside agencies, mainly A. C. Cooper Ltd and Rodney Todd-White Ltd, both in the West End of London, are contracted to do additional photographing, printing and developing.

A military assistant to the Surveyors is also employed, dividing his time between the Royal Library at Windsor and St James's Palace. As his title suggests, his job is to advise the Surveyors of Pictures and Works of Art on the hundreds of military prints, drawings and other items in the Collection. He is steeped in military history and his knowledge of uniforms and badges of rank has proved to be immensely helpful, especially when it comes to identifying portraits of unknown individuals. Sometimes the only way a painting can be placed is through painstaking research among regimental records that produces a clue to some long-forgotten decoration.

Until fairly recently the clocks in Buckingham Palace and the other royal residences were regarded as timepieces and nothing more. As such they were left in the hands of the Master of the Household, who provided the men to wind and maintain them purely as a domestic chore. Nowadays they are considered to be valuable works of art and are in the charge of the Royal Collection. Two clockmakers at Buckingham Palace and another at Windsor Castle look after the extensive collection, said to number some three hundred or so, many of them one-off movements commissioned by past Sovereigns. The busiest times for the horologists are in March and October when they spend an entire weekend altering the timepieces as British Summer Time begins or ends.

The Royal Collection is widely dispersed throughout Britain, for many items are on indefinite or exhibition loan to various institutions. The bulk of the Collection, however, is to be found in what is termed the Occupied Royal Palaces, those which The Queen and her Court use regularly: Buckingham Palace, Windsor Castle and the Palace of Holyroodhouse in Edinburgh; Sandringham House and Balmoral Castle are private residences.

The administration and presentation to the public of the other palaces fall to two agencies which are independent but which ultimately answer to the Secretary of State for the Environment. The first is English Heritage, formed from the Ancient Monuments and Historic Buildings Inspectorate of the Department of the Environment and now the custodian of Osborne House in the Isle of Wight.

Osborne never had the status of a Royal Palace, but was a private house built by Queen Victoria and Prince Albert with money obtained from the Privy Purse. Shortly after Queen Victoria's death, her son King Edward VII handed the house and its grounds to the nation and in 1902 it became a convalescent home. The original household wing has remained a convalescent hospital ever since, but in the twenties the State Apartments were opened to the public. Queen Victoria's private rooms remained closed for a further thirty years and it wasn't until the 1950s that they too were put on view.

The entire contents of the house remain part of the Royal Collection, and the English Heritage custodians work closely with the Department on their presentation and preservation. A recent example of this cooperation was the reinstatement of the nursery floor in the family wing, formerly used as a residence by the House Governor. Considerable research was undertaken by English Heritage, partly in the Royal Archives, to discover as much as possible of the original decorations, and the Department lent some original furniture and pictures to complete the scheme, including the swing cot used by Queen Victoria's children that had been on display in Kensington Palace.

The second body to care for so-called unoccupied palaces was formed in April 1990 from the Royal Palaces Division of the Department of the Environment and is known as the Historic Palaces Agency. This Agency, whose headquarters are at Hampton Court

Palace, is responsible for Hampton Court, the Tower of London, the Banqueting House, Whitehall (the last remaining portion of the old Whitehall Palace), Kensington Palace, Kew Palace and The Queen's Cottage at Kew. Its brief is to narrow the considerable gap between maintenance expenditure and income, thus reducing the cost to the taxpayer of the upkeep of these Grade 1 listed buildings, all of which are of national importance.

Recent enterprises introduced by one or other of the agencies include new and enlarged bookshops at Kensington Palace and Windsor Castle (where the main shop adjacent to the Henry VIII Gate is said to sell more royal books than any other in Britain) and the conversion of the old Mews Block at Holyroodhouse in Edinburgh into a retail complex selling royal memorabilia. Hampton Court is now used extensively for corporate entertaining and both the Tower of London and the Banqueting House in Whitehall can be hired for private functions at competitive rates.

The contents of these buildings remain part of the Royal Collection, although the situation at the Tower of London is slightly more complicated. Most of this ancient fortress and royal palace (for it retains its original status in spite of the fact that no Sovereign has lived there for centuries) has been directly administered by the Department of the Environment for many years. But complications arise over the Royal Regalia – the Crown Jewels – for the Lord Chamberlain is responsible to The Queen for the care and use of the Regalia, while through the Historic Palaces Agency the Secretary of State for the Environment retains responsibility for the presentation to the public of the Regalia in the Jewel House.

When items from the Regalia are required by The Queen and other members of the Royal Family, for example, the Imperial State Crown worn at the State Opening of Parliament or the Maundy Dishes used in the annual Maundy Service, the Lord Chamberlain's Office withdraws them and replaces them after use. The method is distractingly simple; the Comptroller calls a taxi to take him from Buckingham Palace to the Tower. There he signs a chitty and departs with the priceless and uninsured Regalia, then reverses the routine once the ceremony has been performed.

The majority of Royal Collection pictures not in Occupied Palaces are kept at Hampton Court, and the Historic Palaces Agency has appointed its own Curator there to work closely with the Royal Collection department and in particular with its representative on the spot, the Superintendent of the Royal Collection. One product of this close collaboration was the exhibition held at Hampton Court in 1991 that marked the 500th anniversary of the birth of Henry VIII, which had as its centrepiece the magnificent portrait of the King by Hans Holbein the Younger (1497–1543). It was painted in 1536 at the time of Henry's third marriage to Jane Seymour. Strangely enough the painting was never listed as belonging to the Royal Collection and is not included in the official catalogues of 1542 or 1547. It is believed it was given by the King to one of his courtiers and it surfaced in 1641 as the property of Robert Spencer, the 2nd Earl of Sunderland. In 1934, the Earl Spencer (grandfather of the present Princess of Wales) sold the painting for an undisclosed sum to Baron Heinrich von Thyssen, the present Baron Thyssen's father and founder of the Thyssen collection. Today the picture is valued at over £5 million.

The Department lent a series of companion portraits to complement the central painting and a number of artifacts that are usually housed at Windsor, including a small clock commissioned by Henry VIII for Ann Boleyn, complete with original drawings by the designer and the clockmaker's account for a little over three pounds. It also provided Henry's hunting knife used by the Sovereign to slit the throats of deer. A further exhibition on the same theme was held at Greenwich, and for this the Royal Collection provided the centrepiece: the magnificent painting *The Field of the Cloth of Gold*. Its artist is unknown but it was painted in 1545 to record the meeting twenty-five years before of Henry VIII with his rival Francis I of France.

The future of the Royal Collection Department depends greatly on how much money becomes available. Clearly many of its staff believe tough times lie ahead, particularly with regard to the new Civil List funding, for they feel that if economies have to be made within the Royal Household, the Royal Collection will be vulnerable. Already they have been made aware of the need for cuts and the new restoration studio being built in Marlborough House has had its scheduled budget reduced. However, the band of dedicated men and women who spend their working lives caring for the finest private art collection in the world still see opportunities to enhance its preservation. They are looking forward to the implementation of the new computer system and to increasing the number and scope of their programme of exciting exhibitions at The Queen's Gallery, the Palace of Holyroodhouse and many other venues throughout the world. Theirs is truly a global vision and it is shared by The Queen, who believes, as they do, that art is to be appreciated by everyone – not just those who can afford to own it.

13

THE ROYALTY PROTECTION DEPARTMENT

ALTHOUGH NOT STRICTLY within the Royal Household, the Royalty Protection Department (*not* the Royalty Squad, this is simply a tabloid press invention) plays a vital role in its everyday existence. The police officers who provide security for every member of the Royal Family are on duty night and day, working more closely with their royal employers than any other members of the Household.

The department is provided by the Metropolitan Police at New Scotland Yard and is under the personal supervision of a Deputy Assistant Commissioner, the fourth highest ranking police officer in the 'Met'. He also happens to be paid more than anyone else in the Royal Household as he, and all those working for him, remain on the payroll of the Metropolitan Police during their tour of duty with the Royal Family. His current salary is around £50,000, which puts him only slightly behind The Queen's Private Secretary.

The total cost of providing security for the Royal Family and all the Diplomatic Missions in London runs to £30 million a year. All of this comes out of the Metropolitan Police budget, which in turn is financed by the Home Office. It is difficult to separate the actual cost apportioned to the protection of royalty, as the budget is allocated in a single sum. But obviously a major part of the £30 million awarded to the Royalty and Diplomatic Protection Department, to give it its full and correct title, must be attributed to the protection of London's many foreign embassies and High Commissions.

Not only salaries but also all expenses for police officers serving in the Royalty Protection Department are paid by the police themselves.

Nothing is charged to the Civil List or any other source of funding for the Royal Family. Even when bodyguards accompany members of the Royal Family abroad their air fares are paid by the police force. The security at other royal homes is the responsibility of the police authority in whose area the house is located. Gloucestershire Constabulary looks after Gatcombe and Highgrove while the Thames Valley Police fund security at the home of the Duke and Duchess of York.

At Buckingham Palace itself the senior protection officer is a Chief Superintendent who is also The Queen's personal police officer and bodyguard, a job for which he is paid just under £40,000 a year. He accompanies Her Majesty on all visits overseas and he (or one of his colleagues) sits alongside the chauffeur in the royal limousine, makes sure a rug covers the royal knees and carries an umbrella in case of rain.

It may sound as if the personal bodyguard to a member of the Royal Family performs a role that falls between valet and outside butler, and it is true that a certain amount of fetching and carrying is done. But there are also the ever present threats to the Royal Family from terrorists, lunatics or simple seekers of publicity.

Chief Superintendent James Beaton, who recently retired after nine years with The Queen, has first-hand experience of the danger facing a royal bodyguard. He first went to Buckingham Palace as Princess Anne's personal policeman, starting his job on the day she was married in November 1973. In those days there was not the same attitude to security as today and in the main the job consisted of keeping over-curious members of the public at bay and making sure that photographers and reporters were not too intrusive when the Princess was competing at a horse show, for she was a rider of international class at the time. But all this changed on an evening in March 1974 when an armed man made a dramatic attempt to kidnap the Princess in The Mall, just yards from Buckingham Palace. The attempt was foiled, mainly by Beaton, who was shot three times in the incident. He was subsequently awarded the George Cross, the highest honour for bravery it is possible for anyone outside the armed forces to receive.

Today every member of the Royal Family has his or her own team of bodyguards who take it in turn to work around the clock. The

Princess Royal has four police officers, headed by a Chief Inspector who, with a salary of £27,000 a year, earns only slightly less than the Princess's Private Secretary. As the police are not members of the Household they do not qualify for Grace and Favour apartments or houses but when on duty their meals are provided in the staff dining room.

The Royalty Protection Department is divided into two segments: those who wear uniform – around sixty in number, the most junior earning some £14,000 a year, the longest-serving £19,000 – and who look after security inside the Palace: manning the gates, patrolling the grounds with guard dogs and, in the case of a single sergeant, sitting outside The Queen's bedroom all night; and the plain-clothes branch which provides the royal bodyguards. There are just under a hundred of these, most of them inspectors on just over £24,000 a year, but with some sergeants who manage on £19,000.

They are based in a special police station which was built and equipped at a cost of £1.6 million shortly after the break-in to The Queen's bedroom by Michael Fagan in 1982. It is located along the southern boundary of Buckingham Palace between The Queen's Gallery and The Royal Mews. It is shielded from the rest of the Palace gardens by a screen of trees and manned twenty-four hours a day, 365 days a year. Inside is a sophisticated network of electronic equipment providing direct communication with every royal residence. If an incident should occur at Gatcombe Park, the Princess Royal's home, or at Highgrove House, where the Prince and Princess of Wales spend their weekends and holidays, the police office in Buckingham Palace is instantly aware. And even if the main lines of communication should fail, through a bomb attack or an explosion, several back-up systems ensure that the royal homes are never cut off from outside help. Another task is to keep track of all journeys made by vehicles carrying royal passengers. This the Protection Department does by means of electronic homing devices fitted to all the cars in the royal fleet. The proposed route to be taken on every journey is known in advance and any deviation from it will register immediately on the monitor screens back at Buckingham Palace.

The personal protection officers in the Royalty Protection Department are all volunteers and are chosen from the cream of the Metropolitan Police. They go through a rigorous selection procedure before being sent on training courses to equip them to work in this highly specialised division. Each one is an expert in unarmed combat and proficient in using a variety of weapons. They all carry revolvers, even when travelling by air on commercial aircraft – the only people permitted to do so.

When on duty they live in one of the royal homes for eight days at a time. At Gatcombe and Highgrove each has his or her own bedroom-cum-office, complete with private bathroom and colour television set. They eat with the Household and never allow their particular royal charge to leave the house without them. To do so would mean instant dismissal from the police force. So the stories one has read in certain sections of the Press about the Princess of Wales giving her police officers the slip and going off on her own are pure fabrication. Even if the royal personage concerned ordered his or her officer to leave he would not do so – and the royals know this and stick to the rules, although privately they would sometimes love to be left alone for a while.

Members of the Royal Family have grown accustomed to having an armed policeman permanently at their side and generally the attitude is one of resigned tolerance, though there have been occasions when Prince Philip, for example, has flared up in public at what he considered arrogance in a 'minder'. To the outsider, the relationship between, say, the Princess of Wales and her bodyguards might seem casual and easy going. That is the way both parties want it to look; but in reality, nothing could be farther from the truth. The relationship is totally professional: master, or mistress, and servant; and the police officers, all of whom are very experienced men (or occasionally women), would not want it any other way. If there is the slightest sign that a royal bodyguard is becoming over-friendly, or that some of the 'regality' is beginning to rub off, the officer is moved on. It doesn't happen very often but there have been occasions, particularly with younger members of the family, when the relationship has been in danger of developing beyond the professional, and senior officers have moved quickly to nip it in the bud. They know too that because many of these men spend more time with their royal boss than with their own family there is always a danger that the wife

203

and children may feel left out – and are on their guard against such a possibility.

The Royal Family are all too aware of the disruptive effects on normal family life that working for them can mean, and try hard to help. Wives are invited to Christmas staff parties and invitations to a Garden Party are always available. But as the wife of one of the most experienced of the royal bodyguards has admitted, 'There are only so many royal parties in any one year and you soon become disenchanted at having to bring up a family on your own when your husband is away in some of the most glamorous spots in the world.'

There have been exceptions to the rule about 'no fraternising'. When Prince Charles was single his bodyguard and constant companion was Inspector John Maclean. Wherever Charles went in public Maclean was at his side: wind-surfing, swimming, skiing. He became something of a celebrity in his own right, and a close friendship developed over the years between the policeman and his royal boss. Eventually the time came for Maclean to retire and Prince Charles gave a special farewell dinner party in his honour. Queen Elizabeth the Queen Mother gently but firmly reprimanded her grandson on the grounds that it would have been fine to pay for such an occasion, but in arranging the function himself and by being present, the Prince had strayed across the line that divides servants from their royal masters. Obviously this varies with the category of servant, because some years later she herself gave a farewell lunch to the retiring Lord Chamberlain, the late Lord 'Chips' Maclean (and no relation to Inspector Maclean apart from membership of the same clan).

More recently, in the summer of 1991, the Princess of Wales invited one of her police officers, Inspector Paul Smith, whom she affectionately called 'Smudger', to be a guest on a Mediterranean cruise. Inspector Smith was recovering from a serious illness at the time and the invitation was a generous and thoughtful gesture to which nobody took exception.

On paper the work schedule of the royal police officers does not look too gruelling. Eight days on and then, in theory, three weeks off. But what it usually means is that after the eight-day shift, one of the team will find himself either abroad or somewhere in another part of the United Kingdom carrying out a 'recce' trip for a future royal engagement. Another will be attending a refresher course at one of the police colleges to keep him abreast of current developments in security work. A third might be on leave and a fourth at the head-quarters of the Special Air Service in Hereford being briefed on the latest counter-terrorist tactics. If individual members of the team manage to get five free days in a month they feel they have done well. (The SAS keeps detailed photographs of every room in every royal home so that, if a surprise entry has to be made, they will know the exact location of every piece of furniture. It follows that no one may move furniture without informing the SAS.)

Being a bodyguard to The Queen or the Princess of Wales is a high-profile job, and the men who hold these positions receive no special privileges or extra pay apart from a dress allowance to enable them to look the part. Contrary to the public's general perception of them as 'gung-ho' latter-day James Bonds, all the men in the Royalty Protection Department come from the uniformed branch of the police service. They are not detectives at all. It's just that they carry out their duties in plain clothes.

For men and women who stay too long at Buckingham Palace there is a risk of being passed over for promotion. On the other hand, a successful stint in royal service, so long as it is not too long, may help their career. In addition the officer can look forward to some-thing new every day, to first-class travel, exciting foreign tours and, as most admit, a lot of reflected glamour. Some may complain about the unsocial hours and lack of extra pay, but they have to remember that each of them is a volunteer who can return to normal police work at any time. And there is no shortage of candidates to replace them. For every man who is chosen to work with the Royal Family, at least twenty are turned down.

14

GUARDS OF HONOUR

THE YEOMEN OF THE GUARD

THREE ROYAL BODYGUARDS have special responsibility for protecting the Sovereign. The most ancient of these is the Yeomen of the Guard, the oldest military corps still in existence in the world. It was founded by the first of the Tudor monarchs, Henry VII, less than a month after the battle of Bosworth in 1485 in which Richard III was killed – the last English monarch to die in battle – and it has been in continuous service ever since, serving no fewer than twenty-four kings and queens.

In the turbulent days of the fifteenth century King Henry VII needed all the personal protection he could get, but he was determined that the people would not see the new body as an offensive threat, stressing in his Royal Warrant that the Yeoman of the Guard were intended purely for defensive purposes and 'for the upholding of the dignity and grandeur of the English Crown in perpetuity, his successors, the Kings and Queens of England, for all time'. Until the battle of Dettingen in 1743, when George II was the last British monarch to lead his troops in war, the Yeomen always accompanied the Sovereign into battle.

The service demanded of the Yeomen in their formative years was fundamental in that they provided the Sovereign with protection at all times. One of the duties of the Yeomen Bed Hanger was to search the hangings of the royal bed to make sure no intruders were hidden there. At the same time the Yeoman Bed Goer was searching the bed itself for signs of treachery. This was no haphazard business, but one that occupied several men every time the Sovereign was about to retire for the night, and was carried out with all due ceremony, as an account written in the reign of Henry VIII describes:

> 'After bringing in the stuff for the bed then the Esquire or the Gentleman Usher shall command them what they shall do. So, first one of them to test the straw with a dagger or otherwise (that there be no untruth therein), and then the Yeoman to take the straw and lay it plain and draw down the canvas over it straight. Then shall they lay on the bed of down and one of the Yeomen to tumble up and down upon the same for the search thereof . . .' [They go on to attend in great detail to the placing of the sheets, pillow, covers and curtains] 'as shall best please The King . . .' [The order of the day ended with the instruction:] 'Item. A groom or page ought to take a torch while the bed is making, and fetch a loaf of bread, a pot of ale, and another of wine, and bring it without the traverse, where all they which were at the making of the bed shall go and drink together.'

The custom of making the King's bed continued in this way until the middle of the eighteenth century, while the titles Yeoman Bed Hanger and Yeoman Bed Goer are still in use today by senior members of the Body Guard, though of course the duties are now purely ceremonial and the titles honorary.

Discretion has always been a prerequisite of those who would be Yeomen of the Guard, and for the first three hundred years of their history they had ample opportunity to display this characteristic, for until 1775 they were given the fascinating and at times delicate task which became known as 'back-stairs duty'. Every royal residence (and most of those belonging to the aristocracy) was equipped with a secret or private rear entrance which connected directly with the King's apartments. The primary reason was to enable the royal mistresses to come and go without being seen, but this entrance was also used when the Sovereign wished to discuss affairs of State without the knowledge of his courtiers, when confidants were smuggled discreetly in and out. As the Sovereign's most trusted servants, the task of guarding these 'back-stairs' entrances and conducting the clandestine visitors was given to specially selected Yeomen of the Guard, and the custom gave rise to the phrase 'back-stairs influence'.

Nowadays Yeomen of the Guard are chosen from distinguished retired officers, warrant officers and senior non-commissioned officers from the Army, Royal Air Force and Royal Marines. The Navy is not allowed to supply Yeomen because, in the old days, when most sailors were 'pressed' into service, tradition had it that their loyalty to the Crown could not be guaranteed. Former serving non-commissioned officers of the Royal Air Force have only been admitted since the end of the Second World War, the first of these being appointed as recently as 1955.

The Yeomen of the Guard (who are distinct from the 'Beefeaters', the Yeomen Warders at the Tower of London) can be seen on all royal ceremonial occasions standing closest to the Sovereign. The full official title is Yeomen of the Guard (of the Body) of our Lord the King, but for centuries they have been called The King's (or The Queen's) Body Guard of the Yeomen of the Guard. There was, however, one period when this was changed. In the nineteenth century Queen Victoria ordered that the title should be altered to: The Royal Body Guard of the Yeomen of the Guard, and this remained until 1901 when one of King Edward VII's first commands restored the original title.

In 1908 King Edward issued another decree, that the minimum height for officers in the Guard (there are six) should be 5 feet 10 inches, because, he argued, 'the appearance of undersized officers would be marked and unsightly'. Some years ago the Senior Messenger Sergeant-Major, a certain 'Snowy' Baker, former Regimental Sergeant-Major of the Welsh Guards, was introduced to a new officer in the Guard. The recruit was a most impressive figure, and Baker took only one look at him before inviting him to stand at the official measuring device which is kept in the Orderly Room at St James's Palace. When he found that the officer was only 6 feet 5 inches, Baker was delighted. As he put it, 'That's all right, sir. I'm 6 feet 6 inches and we can't have anyone in the Body Guard who's taller than me, can we, sir?'

The officers are led by the Captain, who is a political appointment, usually a Deputy Chief Whip in the House of Lords, the Chief Whip himself holding the post of Captain of the Gentlemen-at-Arms. The remaining five officers have all been commissioned in the Army and are chosen from a list of volunteers kept by the Ministry of Defence. One other qualification, apart from the height requirement, is that on joining officers should be under fifty-five years of age.

To be appointed Captain of the Yeomen of the Guard is a signal honour and the present holder of this ancient post follows in the footsteps of a number of illustrious predecessors. Perhaps the most famous of all Captains was Sir Walter Ralegh, who held the rank no fewer than three times – twice under Elizabeth I and again under James I. He suffered the ignominy of being escorted to the Tower of London by his own Yeomen, first in 1592, for having the temerity to start a love affair with one of the Queen's Ladies-in-Waiting – without asking Her Majesty's permission first – and finally in 1618, when his imprisonment ended with his execution on Tower Hill. The tenure of present-day Captains ends equally abruptly, if not quite so dramatically and finally, for they lose their job if the Government falls.

At one time the strength of the Body Guard was 600 men. It was King Henry VIII who reduced their number to 200 as an economy measure; today they are down to sixty-six: two Messenger Sergeant-Majors, four Sergeant-Majors and sixty Yeomen. All are part-timers apart from the senior Messenger Sergeant-Major, who acts as Company Clerk, looking after all administration, records and correspondence. He also allocates duties and makes out the rosters while finding time to make sure all the uniforms are in perfect condition. As the only full-time member of the Guard, he lives rent free in an apartment on the ground floor of St James's Palace, where his neighbours include Princess Alexandra, the Duke and Duchess of Kent and several senior members of the Royal Household.

To become accepted into the Yeomen of the Guard all candidates must have earned a Long Service or Good Conduct Medal and, like their officers, be at least 5 feet 10 inches tall. The waiting list is long as there are only about three or four vacancies a year. Yeomen usually join shortly after their fiftieth birthday and remain until the compulsory retirement age of seventy.

Once a vacancy occurs the Ministry of Defence summons the candidate to undergo a medical examination, and only after he has passed this hurdle is he invited for an interview with the Body Guard's Clerk of the Cheque who acts as Adjutant. The next step is for the Clerk to submit the man's details to the Lord Chamberlain, where further enquiries may be made before finally the name of the candidate is laid before The Queen. Her Majesty has the last word and her approval is required before any appointment can be made. Thus every Yeoman is personally approved by the monarch today, in exactly the same way as has been the practice for five hundred years. The title and meaning of being the oldest personal bodyguard to the Sovereign in the world is not taken lightly by any of those involved.

Every Yeoman takes an oath of loyalty to The Queen which has varied little in style and content since the fifteenth century:

> I, [name follows] sincerely promise and swear to serve Her Most Sacred Majesty ELIZABETH II, by the Grace of God of the United Kingdom and Northern Ireland, Queen, Defender of the Faith, Her Heirs and Successors lawful Kings and Queens of these Realms both faithfully and truly in the Place and Office I am now called unto, and to be placed in, namely, as one of the Yeomen of the Guard of Her Majesty's Guard of Her Body in Ordinary, and in all things touching Her Honour and Safety, I shall neither myself do, or procure, or give consent to be done by any other, and manner of thing that shall, or may be prejudicial, or hurtful of Her Majesty's Person, Crown or Dignity, or to any of the Royal Family. But if I shall hear of, or by any way understand any such, or that any manner of Bodily hurt, dishonour, or prejudice may be in agitation, contriving, or likely to happen, I shall do as much as in me lyeth to prevent, stop and hinder the same, and besides to disclose and discover it with all speed to Her Majesty, or to such of Her Majesty's Council as I can or may come next unto, or to some or one of my Officers on duty, and by all ways and means I can possibly, to cause the same to be made known.

I swear to be obedient to my Captain and all other of my Officers, of the said Guard in all things concerning my office in her Majesty's Service.

I shall keep The Queen's peace in my own person both in the Court, and all other places, as much as in me lyeth, and shall cause all others to do the same to the utmost of my power.

All these things I shall truly, faithfully and obediently keep and perform: So Help Me God.

Once the new Yeoman has been enrolled he is given a certificate as proof of his membership as '. . . one of the Yeomen in Ordinary of Her Majesty's Body Guard of the Yeomen of the Guard . . .' The certificate also states that he is '. . . to have, hold, exercise and enjoy the said Place, together with all Rights, Profits, Privileges and Advantages thereto belonging.'

One of the 'Rights' today is exemption from all jury service, but any 'Profit', which in olden days meant a Yeoman was allowed to sell his position, has long since disappeared.

The scarlet uniform worn by Yeomen today dates from the reign of Henry VIII. Before that they wore russet cloth for everyday duties and Tudor white and green on ceremonial occasions. The dress has been modified in succeeding centuries and today the familiar uniform is almost identical to the ones worn during the reign of King George IV (1820–30).

The business of donning the full ceremonial garb is a ritual in itself and one that requires outside assistance. First to go on are the breeches and red stockings, with red, white and blue rosettes fastened just below the knee. Next come the shoes; black and buckled and known as Monk Shoes after one of the most famous of all officers in the Yeomen, Exon Roger Monk, a wealthy nineteenth-century businessman who left a bequest to the Yeomen so that a dinner could be held every year to celebrate the Sovereign's birthday. The custom continues to this day. It is called the Roger Monk Dinner and a toast to his memory is drunk after the Loyal Toast.

Next comes the ruff. First introduced by Elizabeth I, then banished by the Stuarts but reintroduced by Queen Anne, it is tied from behind. Then the heavy doublet of scarlet and gold is put on, its royal badge of the symbols of England, Scotland and Ireland, the rose, thistle and shamrock, emblazoned on front and back. The badge is surmounted by a crown and flanked with the royal cypher EIIR. On his chest the Yeoman wears all the decorations to which he is entitled and over his left shoulder the red, black and gold cross-belt. Another belt is fastened around his waist and from it hangs his sword, which is never drawn. The black velvet hat, devised and introduced by Charles II, complete with its ribbons of red, white and blue around the crown, is almost the last item of clothing to be donned before the white gloves complete this ceremonial attire.

Finally the Yeoman is ready to collect his partisan, or long-handled halberd which, unlike the rest of his uniform, is not reserved for his use alone. Weapons are drawn from a pool in the armoury when they are needed. The entire process of getting dressed to attend The Queen takes over half an hour, each man helping his comrades to prepare.

The privilege of being allowed to stand closest to the Sovereign is jealously guarded by all ranks within the Body Guard, and the reasons why they are in attendance on the Sovereign at certain ceremonial occasions sometimes go far back in history. For example, on 15 May 1800, King George III, who survived at least three attempts on his life which were foiled by his Yeomen of the Guard, was attending a performance at the Drury Lane Theatre when a man in the audience fired a pistol at him. The attempt, like all the others, failed, the bullet narrowly missing two Yeomen who were, as always, standing closest to The King. They overpowered the would-be assassin and, as a direct result of this incident, nowadays a detachment of the Body Guard escorts the Sovereign to all Royal Gala performances, which are now held at the Royal Opera House, Covent Garden.

The most recent occasion when a member of the Yeomen of the Guard was personally involved in protecting his Sovereign was on 29 January 1908. King Edward VII was returning to Buckingham Palace from the State Opening of Parliament when a suffragette, campaigning for women to be given the right to vote, ran into the road. She evaded the police and approached the royal carriage shouting, 'Petition . . . Petition.'

The official report of the incident stated: 'She would have reached the coach had not Yeoman Allan Wood, who was marching alongside the near front wheel, seized and held her until the police came up and removed her.'

Of course, there is no evidence that the woman was trying to harm His Majesty. In all probability, she was merely attempting to attract publicity for her cause by presenting her petition. But the Yeoman didn't know that. His job was to protect The King and the very fact that she had managed to get close to His Majesty was enough for Yeoman Wood. She might have been carrying a concealed weapon – and he took no chances.

If such a thing were to happen today, however, the Yeomen would not have the chance to protect The Queen in the same way. 'Wheelmen' are no longer required to march alongside the State Coach in the Royal Procession at the State Opening of Parliament since, as we have seen, a walking pace has now been replaced by the procession 'breaking into the trot', and the Sovereign's Escort of The Household Cavalry are now the 'closest Guard' during this parade. However, at the Coronation of the Sovereign, the Yeomen still perform 'wheelman' duties as the Gold Coach travels at walking pace to and from Westminster Abbey.

The many ceremonial occasions when the Yeomen of the Guard are on duty include the Garter Service, held every June at Windsor Castle, the Royal Garden Parties, State Banquets, State Visits by foreign Heads of State, the Royal Maundy Service, the Epiphany Service and all Investitures held by The Queen and other members of the Royal Family.

The Epiphany Service

The first ceremonial occasion of the year is held on the twelfth day of Christmas in the Chapel Royal at St James's Palace. Until the eighteenth century, the Sovereign took part personally, presenting gold, frankincense and myrrh to the Church as a royal offering. However, this practice ended during the reign of George III. Nowadays two Gentlemen Ushers represent the Sovereign, attended by an escort of a Sergeant-Major and two Yeomen of the Guard. These days the gold coins – sovereigns specially obtained from the Bank of England

– are afterwards changed into bank notes and given in The Queen's name to charity.

The service is short but is carried out with as much solemnity and attention to detail as if Her Majesty were present, and it is surely as impressive today as at any time since it was first held during the reign of William the Conqueror, more than nine hundred years ago. It is also an occasion when members of the public are permitted to take part but, as space is severely limited, applications for tickets must be made well in advance.

The Maundy Service

The Royal Archives which are housed in the Round Tower at Windsor Castle contain a fascinating collection of royal information ranging from the menus used at State Banquets for the past two hundred years to recipes for all royal wedding cakes since the time of Queen Victoria. Details of many royal ceremonies are also recorded in this unique library, among them the Royal Maundy, dating back to the thirteenth century. The first Sovereign to distribute alms to the poor on this day was Edward I (1272–1307), beginning a custom which has been repeated almost ever since. It happens on the Thursday before Good Friday, when the Sovereign gives to the 'well deserving poor' as many coins as she has years, plus one extra representing the hope that God will grant the monarch this additional 'year of Grace'. The coins, which are, of course, worth far more than their face value, are silver pennies to the value of one, two, three and four sterlings – the name of the original penny weight in Norman times. It is from this ancient weight of currency that the description 'pound sterling' is derived today.

The Yeomen of the Guard have taken part in the Royal Maundy Service since they escorted Henry VII to his first Royal Maundy in Lincoln Cathedral in 1486, the year after they were formed. In the early days an essential part of the Sovereign's duties at the ceremony was to wash and kiss the feet of the poor as Christ washed the feet of his disciples on the night of the Last Supper. It was not always a pleasant task, and Queen Elizabeth I, realist that she was, ordered her Yeoman of the Laundry to make sure that any feet presented for her attention were first thoroughly scrubbed with warm, scented water. James II was the last British king to do this at a service in 1685 held in the Chapel Royal of the Palace at Whitehall, and until 1750 the Lord High Almoner was sent in the monarch's place. But early in the present century King George V revived the ceremony in a modified form, and his son and grand-daughter have continued it ever since.

One symbolic link recalls the old washing of the feet in the modern service, when The Queen is presented with sweet-smelling nosegays by children of the parish – a reminder of those far off days when the odours of the poor and diseased were a little too strong for delicate sensibilities. And the Lord High Almoner and his assistants are still girded with linen towels as further reminders of the ancient custom.

The Maundy Service takes place at Westminster Abbey one year and at a cathedral outside the capital the next, an innovation initiated by The Queen herself. It is comparatively short and simple, lasting just over three-quarters of an hour. The Queen's Body Guard of the Yeoman of the Guard are on duty in full ceremonial uniforms, the Senior Yeoman having the honour of carrying the dish containing the alms to be distributed. It is a singular honour but one which becomes slightly more onerous as the years go by, for as the number of coins increases with The Queen's age, the heavier the dish becomes. So the Yeoman undertakes weight training some weeks before Maundy Thursday to strengthen his muscles for the ordeal.

The Garter Service

Since Tudor times the Yeomen of the Guard have taken part in the annual Garter Service on the Monday of Ascot Week in June. Thousands of visitors gather in the precincts of Windsor Castle to witness the spectacular procession as The Queen and other members of the Royal Family walk from the Castle to St George's Chapel down a route lined by dismounted troopers of the Household Cavalry and soldiers of one of the six regiments of Foot Guards. The Military Knights of Windsor in their scarlet uniforms, the Heralds in their colourful tunics, precede the royal party with the Yeomen of the Guard in their customary place immediately behind the Sovereign.

215

As the procession enters the chapel the Yeomen form up inside to guard the main door, and at the end of the service they move to the bottom of the steps at the front of St George's Chapel to salute Her Majesty as she enters her carriage for the journey back to the Castle.

Like all members of the Royal Household, the Yeomen of the Guard are certainly not motivated by financial reward. The pay they receive is nominal and it is only since the nineteen-seventies that they have been reimbursed for any travelling expenses incurred. This could be something of a hardship, particularly when a Yeoman came from the north of Scotland or the far west of Wales and was required for royal duty at St James's Palace six or eight times a year. These days a travel warrant is issued with the summons to parade and Yeomen are also given a small but adequate allowance to cover all meals and overnight accommodation if required.

THE YEOMEN WARDERS

If one thing is guaranteed to send any member of the Yeomen of the Guard into an instant rage it is to be called a 'Beefeater'. This is the term popularly associated with the Yeomen Warders who are based at the Tower of London, and while they are rightly proud of their own ancient and honourable traditions, they are not Yeomen of the Guard.

Yeomen of the Guard were fighting men who accompanied their Sovereign into battle, while the Yeomen Warders were jailers whose first duty was to guard State prisoners in the Tower of London. In modern times the main cause of the confusion in the minds of the public is that the two bodies wear almost identical uniforms – but not quite. There is one vital difference: Yeomen of the Guard wear a gold embroidered cross-belt over their left shoulder; Yeomen Warders do not.

There is some confusion about the exact date of the formation of the Yeomen Warders as a separate body from the Yeomen of the Guard, but there have no doubt been guardians of the Tower since William the Conqueror started to build it in 1078, and records show that in 1509, when Henry VIII came to the throne, he ordered twelve of his personal bodyguard to be stationed permanently at the Tower. They were known as Yeomen of the Tower, but they did not wear the royal livery at the time, although further documents of the period indicate that these Warders were former members of the Sovereign's bodyguard considered too old and feeble to fight.

Once a Yeoman Warder was appointed he remained in the post for life. It wasn't until this century that he was ordered to retire at sixty-five, and there used to be a profitable trade in the sale of appointments. Warders were permitted to sell their posts so long as they themselves remained fit to carry out the duties. In the seventeenth and eighteenth centuries the going rate was around 250 guineas (about £25,000 at today's prices) and many elderly Warders enjoyed a comfortable old age on the proceeds. If a Warder died in office, the job was still sold, but the proceeds went to the Constable of the Tower rather than to the dependants of the deceased. This led to the traditional toast still drunk today whenever a new Yeoman Warder is installed: 'Yeoman Warder, may you never die a Yeoman Warder!'

The Duke of Wellington abolished the practice of buying and selling Warderships when he was Constable of the Tower during the nineteenth century and at the same time ordered that in future all vacancies should be filled by deserving ex-soldiers who had held the rank of sergeant and above. Today, as with The Queen's Body Guards, Warders are recruited from the Army, the Royal Marines and the RAF but not from the Royal Navy.

Nowadays Yeomen Warders are full-time employees, earning around £9,000 a year. They also receive accommodation in the Tower of London which has to be given up once they retire. There are forty of them in the garrison and each one is sworn in as a special constable with police powers within the precincts of the Tower, for the Metropolitan Police do not enter the Tower officially except with the permission of the Governor. As members of the Civil Service Union Warders are subject to the same rules and regulations governing industrial action as any other member, but even though they have been called out on strike on more than one occasion, the union has turned a blind eye when they carried out their principal ceremonial and security duties while officially on strike.

If the Yeomen of the Guard object to being called 'Beefeaters', the term is equally irritating to the Yeomen Warders even though it is the name by which they are most widely known. No one can explain the precise origins of the term although there have been many theories, several of which involve King Henry VIII, who was known for his gargantuan appetite. One story says that the Yeomen Warders were allowed to eat the remains from the King's table, another that they could eat as much beef as they could carry on the blade of a dagger, while even as late as 1813 the records show that rations for the thirty Yeomen then on duty included twenty-four pounds of beef a day. Whatever the reason, the Yeomen have always been regarded as 'great eaters of beef', and despite the unpopularity of the term among the Warders the nickname is likely to remain.

Warders have been on duty continuously at the Tower since its inception and throughout that time have been responsible for all security at the fortress. The routine locking of the main gate at night in the Ceremony of the Keys is performed today as it has been for the past six centuries. But the only State ceremonial occasion in which the Yeomen Warders play a part is the Coronation, when they form a Guard of Honour at Westminster Abbey. With no prisoners to guard in the Tower of London, these days their duties consist mainly of looking after two million or so visitors who flock to London's biggest tourist attraction every year.

THE HONOURABLE CORPS OF GENTLEMEN AT ARMS

Formed by Henry VIII in 1509 as a personal guard who would appear mounted on horseback, carrying spears, the first title of the Honourable Corps of Gentlemen at Arms was The Band of Gentlemen Spears. At its institution, 'The Kynge ordeined fiftie gentlemenne to bee Speres, every one of them to have an Archer, a Demilaunce [who would be armed with a short-handled spear] and

218

a Castrel [or groom], and every Spere to have three greate horses [probably draught horses] to bee attendaunte on his persone.' In 1834 the style 'Gentlemen Pensioners' was further changed by William IV to that of 'Gentlemen at Arms'.

The recruits to Henry VIII's newest royal bodyguard were socially superior to the Yeomen, coming from the 'landed gentry', and in recognition of this The King ordered that they should be given precedence over the Yeomen of the Guard. But as the older bodyguard, the Yeomen fought a rearguard action to preserve their position as Nearest Guard, the arguments continuing, on and off, for more than three centuries until, in 1851, Queen Victoria settled the matter, ruling, 'that the Corps of Gentlemen at Arms whenever we shall command their attendance shall do the duty of the Guards nearest to our royal person and shall attend for the purpose of performing such duty when so commanded upon all State occasions whether in our Royal Palaces or elsewhere and that the Yeomen of the Guard shall be the Corps upon all such occasions doing duty next to the Corps of Gentlemen at Arms.'

Also during Queen Victoria's reign, in 1856, the highest decoration for gallantry on the battlefield, the Victoria Cross, was instituted, and since that date the medal has been awarded to no fewer than twelve Gentlemen at Arms.

As early as 1526 the Household Statutes, made at the Palace of Eltham, described the Band as then complete and fully officered, the officers being (as they are today) the Captain, the Lieutenant, the Standard Bearer, the Clerk of the Cheque and the Harbinger. In addition to the five officers there are twenty-seven Gentlemen, all of them retired officers of the Army or the Royal Marines and on appointment under the age of fifty-two. Retirement from the Corps is automatic on reaching seventy.

With one exception, the Captain has always been a Peer of the Realm, and for the past two centuries this has been a political appointment, changing with the Government, for as his Royal Household duties are not too onerous these days, the Captain combines his role with that of Government Chief Whip in the House of Lords. On appointment the Captain of the Corps is handed a gold stick of office by the Queen, to whom he has the right of direct access on all matters concerning the Corps.

So far only one woman has been appointed Captain. She was the Life Peer, Baroness Llewelyn-Davies, who served in this unique role from 1974 to 1979. She too was given the gold stick of office by The Queen but Her Majesty decided that the ornate uniform worn by all Lady Llewelyn-Davies's predecessors was unsuitable for a woman and a special brooch as her own badge of office was designed.

Second in command is the Lieutenant, who must have reached the rank of Lieutenant-Colonel in the regular Army. He is the senior executive officer of the Corps and handles all matters of organisation and internal discipline. His stick of office is surmounted by a silver head. Next in rank is the Standard Bearer who receives a stick of office identical to that of his immediate superior, as does the Clerk of the Cheque and Adjutant who, as his title implies, issues all the orders for the various duties to the members of the Corps.

The uniform worn by the Gentlemen of the Corps is basically that of a Dragoon Guards Officer of the 1840s. It has a skirted red coat with Garter, blue velvet cuffs and facings, embroidered with the Royal (Tudor) Badge of the Portcullis, and worn with a gold oak-leaf design pouch belt and heavy gold epaulets. The officers wear gold aiguillettes. The overalls are blue with gold stripes, the helmet gilt with long white feather plumes and the gauntlets white. Swords are worn and every Gentleman carries a long ceremonial battle axe, most of which are at least three hundred years old. The duties of the Axe-Keeper and Butler include looking after the battle axes, but these days he is also in charge of the mess at Engine Court, St James's Palace, where members of the Corps hold three dinners every year.

As all the Gentlemen of the Corps are members of the Royal Household, when they dine in the mess, particularly in the presence of The Queen, who joins them once a year, or another member of the Royal Family, they wear the Household Evening Coat. This is unique to Members of the Household and consists of a black tail-coat with velvet collar and brass buttons bearing the Royal Cypher. It is worn with white tie and full formal evening dress.

In 1538 the Gentlemen were reorganised to include foot soldiers who were issued with poleaxes, and the Gentlemen seem to have performed both mounted duties and duties on foot in palaces and as escorts until the reign of King George II, who on 5 December 1745 ordered them to be 'ready with their servants, horses and arms' to march to Finchley to protect the capital against a possible Jacobite attack led by Bonnie Prince Charlie. By the nineteenth century, however, it seems that all duties were performed on foot, and have been so ever since.

It was considered a great privilege to be a member of the Corps, and for many centuries it was possible to buy your way in, until Queen Victoria did away with what she called 'this abuse of a royal system'. Since then the Corps has been made up of distinguished retired officers. They enjoy the unique honour of guarding the body of the Sovereign as it lies in State, and also attend the monarch at the Coronation and other royal occasions. During a Garden Party, as we have seen, Members of the Corps single out guests who are to be presented to The Queen.

THE ROYAL COMPANY OF ARCHERS

This Bodyguard, which escorts the Sovereign on all royal occasions in Scotland, is the youngest of the three Royal Bodyguards and was created in the seventeenth century. The precise date is not actually known, but 1676 is generally accepted because this was the year in which 'an influential body of noblemen and gentlemen' gathered together and drew up the Constitution which still governs the Company today. The Archers are also regarded as the 'baby' of the Royal Bodyguards because they were not officially recognised as 'The Sovereign's Bodyguard in Scotland for all Ceremonial and State Occasions' until 1822.

The first Captain-General was the Duke of Atholl. He and a Drummer and a Bowmaker, one Robert Munro, were the first officers of what was to become the Royal Company. The Company prospered, and under one of its subsequent Captains-General, the Earl of Cromartie, who was Principal Secretary of State for Scotland at that time, received a Royal Charter from Queen Anne in 1704. It endows the Royal Company 'perpetual access to all public butts, plains and pasturages legally allotted for shooting arrows'. In return they are required to render to the Sovereign, if asked, 'one pair of barbed arrows' every year.

Even today each of its members (there are around 400, of whom half are active) is required to be proficient with bow and arrow (though some of the more elderly members are archers in name only), and each June there is a contest in the grounds of the Palace of Holyroodhouse for The Queen's Prize, the most prestigious of many competitions held throughout the year. Archery continues to be the Royal Company's main activity. During the winter months shooting takes place in the Butts at Archer's Hall, Edinburgh, the Royal Company's headquarters since 1776, at a range of thirty yards, while in the summer The Queen allows them to use the grounds of the Palace of Holyroodhouse where the range is 180 yards.

As Gold Stick for Scotland the Captain-General of The Queen's Body Guard for Scotland, the Royal Company of Archers, is responsible for the personal safety of the Sovereign whenever she visits this part of her realm. Elsewhere in the United Kingdom that particular task falls to the two Gold Sticks of the Household, Major-General Lord Michael Fitzalan-Howard, a former Marshal of the Diplomatic Corps, and General Sir Desmond Fitzpatrick. The Royal Company is administered by a Council of eight members whose President, as Silver Stick for Scotland, assists Gold Stick whenever the Sovereign is in residence at the Palace of Holyroodhouse or making any official visit north of the border.

Only a Scot may belong to the Royal Company of Archers, and many famous Scots including Robbie Burns and Sir Walter Scott have served in its ranks. During its colourful history, a number of prominent Scottish families have been honoured by an invitation to join the Royal Company, and on several occasions father and son have served at the same time. When the late Lord Maclean was an officer, his son, now Sir Lachlan Maclean Bt of Duart, was Adjutant. The elder Maclean said he was unable to parade at the same time as his son, 'because he has cannibalised my uniform to make enough gold braid for his own'. The uniform is dark green with black facings and a very distinctive Balmoral bonnet with an eagle's feather. The long-bows, no longer made by the Royal Company's own full-time bowmaker, have to be paid for by the Archers themselves.

The Royal Company of Archers are seen at the Service of Installation for new Knights of the Thistle, the Sovereign's Personal Order of Chivalry in Scotland. This takes place in St Giles Cathedral in Edinburgh and is one of the most spectacular events in the Scottish calendar. The Archers march down the Royal Mile with all banners flying and in full ceremonial uniform.

As a personal bodyguard to the Sovereign since they were first appointed to the role by George IV, the Archers' most regular and public appearances are at the Royal Garden Parties held in the grounds of Holyroodhouse every July. They form avenues down which The Queen and the Duke of Edinburgh walk while guests are presented by the Captain-General and the President of the Council. They take their duties very seriously and can sometimes be rather brusque in their treatment of guests whom they think are getting too close to the Sovereign. As with all those charged with guarding The Queen, it is her welfare and her welfare only that matters, and on several occasions the Archers have been congratulated by the Duke of Edinburgh for the uncompromising manner in which they carry out their task.

THE HIGH CONSTABLES OF HOLYROODHOUSE

If the Yeomen of the Guard can claim to be the oldest military unit in the world, the High Constables of Holyroodhouse have an equally valid claim to be the oldest police force. Their origins can be traced back to 1130 when the Church owned the land on which the Palace of Holyroodhouse is built. (The ruins of the Abbey are still there, providing shelter for guests at Garden Parties when it rains.)

While the membership of the Royal Company of Archers comes from all over Scotland, the High Constables, whose duties complement those of the Archers, draw their members from among the leading citizens of Edinburgh itself. The Royal Company protects the person of the Sovereign, while the High Constables keep the peace within the precincts of the Palace and the Abbey Sanctuary. Until a little over a hundred years ago debtors could seek (and receive) sanctuary within the Palace of Holyroodhouse. The privilege was not rescinded until 1880.

The High Constables are on duty at all royal functions at the Palace, as well as on all ceremonial occasions even when no royalty is present. They wear distinctive blue uniforms and cockaded silk bonnets which were approved by King George V in 1914. They carry batons made of ebony, as their badge of office and a reminder of their original function.

When The Queen is in residence at Holyroodhouse, the High Constables add a touch of colour and dignity to the official dinners and receptions. And during the week when the Lord High Commissioner takes over as Her Majesty's representative at the annual conference of the Church of Scotland, one of the most prized invitations is to the High Constables' Mess, where the 'wee drams' have been known to reduce grown men to tears. The Lord High Commissioner, usually a member of one of Scotland's most distinguished families, is appointed by the Sovereign and during the week of his term of office resides at Holyroodhouse in her place. He is addressed as 'Your Grace' and receives bows and curtseys in exactly the same way as The Queen does when she is in residence.

All members of The Queen's bodyguards, whether a scion of the aristocracy with centuries of royal service behind him or the most recent recruit just retired from the army, have one common purpose: the welfare and safety of The Queen. They are aware of the historic background to the various bodies to which they belong and are justifiably proud of being part of the rich pageant of royal ceremonial. But in the terrorist-ridden days of the latter part of the twentieth century the threat of attack is never far away. If a Bodyguard sees any possible danger to his Sovereign he will react in as positive and urgent a manner as his predecessor would have centuries ago.

THE VALUES
UNCHANGED

IN AN AGE when materialism is accepted as the norm and rewards for efficiency and loyalty are measured mainly in terms of how much money can be made, it would be easy to sneer at the men and women who make up the Royal Household. They appear to come from another age; from a time when wages didn't matter and all that counted was service to the Crown. To work in the Royal Household wasn't just another job, it was a way of life. One was expected to remain at one's post as long as was required. The hours were long, the pay small, and many in the Household spent their entire working lives without even once seeing a member of the Royal Family. They didn't seem to mind. The very fact that they had a job for life and were performing a service, no matter how menial, for their Sovereign, was reward enough.

Obviously things have changed considerably since the days of Queen Victoria and Edward VII. The domestic staff are unionised; they work a five-day week, and even if they are still paid well below the market rate, other advantages such as free board and lodging help to make up for any loss in wages. Very few people are ever sacked. These days you have to commit a serious crime such as theft (or, almost worse, talk to the Press) to be dismissed. Minor peccadilloes such as drunkenness or getting into debt are tolerated so long as the person concerned is good at his or her job and does not bring disgrace on either the Royal Family or the Household. Even when there is no alternative to dismissal or resignation, The Queen and her family are

225

reluctant to sever ties with their servants, sometimes for many years. When on 19 July 1982 Commander Michael Trestrail was forced to resign his position as The Queen's personal bodyguard in the wake of newspaper revelations of his involvement in a homosexual scandal, he left the Palace in an atmosphere of goodwill from both the Royal Family and most of the Household. He had been brilliant at his job; he was popular with his colleagues and there was genuine regret that such a successful career had been brought to an abrupt halt.

Had it not been for the massive publicity surrounding the incident, he might well have remained. Human weaknesses are tolerated so long as the utmost discretion is maintained. On another occasion, a long-serving steward had been caught stealing from the Palace cellars. He was one of the most trusted of Her Majesty's servants and had even been made a member of the Royal Victorian Order for his services to The Queen. The Master of the Household knew that dismissal was inevitable, but other equally senior members of the Royal Household felt that allowances should be made because of his record as an outstanding domestic servant. The arguments went on for months before, eventually, the Lord Chamberlain of the day decided that an example must be made. The man left, but he was never prosecuted. The Queen was kept fully aware of the situation throughout the long negotiations but wisely allowed her Household to settle the dispute themselves.

In many ways the Royal Household is a throwback to another age. Several customs observed at Buckingham Palace have existed for generations. Old habits die hard. Different levels of servants still eat in separate dining rooms, each one as exclusive to those who are entitled to use it as any of London's older clubs. Certain things have changed of course; they had to. Ladies no longer wear hats at lunch in the Officials' Dining Room as was the rule at the start of The Queen's reign. But other customs are jealously guarded, such as the location of the rooms used by the various grades of staff. The Officials' Dining Room is separated by a servery from the much grander Stewards' Hall. Some years ago the Officials decided that they would like to take over the Stewards' Hall. It is a far superior room with a much nicer view, and as Officials are, in theory, senior to Stewards, they thought it would be more appropriate for their use. But as soon as the Stewards heard of the plan, their leader, the Palace Steward (Cyril Dickman at the time, now retired) went directly to The Queen to plead their case. Within hours the Officials were told, in no uncertain terms, to forget their ambitions. The Stewards kept their Hall and in doing so proved that the real power at Buckingham Palace is enjoyed by those who have the ear of The Queen.

Since the days when there was a vast Household and labour was cheap, a number of picturesque posts have disappeared. The Household no longer employs a Cobweb Cleaner or Spider Catcher as was the case a hundred years ago. In the kitchens, Pot Scourers and Scullery Maids have been replaced by automatic dish-washers and part-time workers who come in from their homes in Fulham and Streatham to make a little extra pocket money from the royal coffers. Neither is there a Master of the Revels to supervise entertainment at Court and the Master of The Queen's Music no longer conducts the Royal Band of Music, as he did from the reign of Edward IV in the fifteenth century until Prince Albert reorganised Queen Victoria's private band into a full orchestra in the middle of the nineteenth century, and Edward VII finally discontinued the practice of Palace Concerts. But there is still a Poet Laureate, Ted Hughes, who continues to draw an annual allowance of £27 in lieu of a 'Butt of Sack' – the payment to the first Poet Laureate, Ben Jonson, for whom the position was created by James I in 1617. And even though a number of posts are filled for single occasions such as a coronation, we no longer see a Royal Herb Strewer who, with her six maids, scattered sweet herbs and flowers before the Sovereign as he or she entered Westminster Abbey. Their last appearance was at the crowning of George IV in 1821.

Whereas in the early days of this century a junior footman or housemaid considered him or herself very lucky to be taken on by the Master of the Household – and was expected to show that gratitude constantly – the young men and women joining the Royal Household today are more independent and confident. They are more highly educated, healthier and better groomed; and they carry an air of assurance that contrasts vividly with the manner of their counterparts of fifty years ago.

Even twenty years ago a footman would never have dreamed of answering back to anyone senior, no matter how justified he might have felt. Today if a servant believes he is in the right, he is likely to stand his ground whatever the rank of the person admonishing him. The air of easy informality with which visitors to the Privy Purse Door are greeted is a welcome change from the stiff formality of former times. It helps to put the visitor at ease, without in any way detracting from the mystique of monarchy or the regality of the surroundings.

But not all the changes in the way the Royal Household operates are painless. Men who have served The Queen for years are leaving because they are unable, or unwilling, to come to terms with the new system. Within the corridors of Buckingham Palace it is secretly admitted that moves to streamline the Household and improve its efficiency have led to serious disagreements and a number of resignations.

The Lord Chamberlain, the Earl of Airlie, has taken a more positive role than any of his predecessors in reorganising the six departments under his control. He is a financial expert with a background in merchant banking, and he has brought into the Household another money man with a brief to 'make the Palace sweat'. As Director of Finance and Property Services, Michael Peat is charged with making the Royal Palaces pay their way. He has direct access to the Lord Chamberlain, and these two, together with John Parsons, the Deputy Keeper of the Privy Purse, have formed a small committee with the power to involve themselves in almost every aspect of the Household's finances. Inevitably, some Members of the Household see this as a 'triumvirate takeover' of the running of the Palace.

The Royal Mews is one department that has shown a marked reluctance to be involved in the new arrangements, arguing that one cannot run The Queen's Mews like a commercial garage. One example of the way in which the 'traditionalists' in the Mews defeated the 'time and motion' men of the Finance and Property Services Office came about in the early days of their attempts to streamline the Royal Mews. When it was discovered that every morning a horse-drawn brougham leaves the Mews to deliver mail between various Royal residences in London, the Director of Finance tried to stop the practice, arguing that it would be much more practical and economical to use a van. The Crown Equerry pointed out to The Queen that the brougham was used not only to deliver the mail but also to train the horses and coachmen before they were able to be used in ceremonial processions. No more was heard of the proposal to do away with the daily brougham.

No one doubts the sincerity of the Lord Chamberlain in his efforts to make the Royal Household more efficient – or indeed his right to do so. What troubles some of the most loyal courtiers is that profit seems to be a prime motive in the current innovations. They point out that modern business practices have already been applied in several of the Household departments – the Keeper of the Privy Purse being the most obvious example – with outstanding results. Companies dealing with the Royal Household now know that they must be competitive in their pricing, and important contracts are placed only after protracted negotiations to make sure The Queen gets the best deal possible. This is all to the good. It is vital for the Royal Household to be seen to be cost-conscious, particularly when it is handling millions of pounds of public money. The problem arises when profit becomes the overriding issue. It hasn't yet, and it is probably a long way from doing so, but some people in the Household believe the current management reviews could lead to a drastic change in the way in which the Palace operates, and fear that this can only mean an eventual reduction in the monarchy's style. If this were to happen the dignity of the Crown would be damaged, perhaps beyond repair; the Royal Family could be in danger of becoming just like all the other European royalty and would certainly not occupy the unique position it holds in the world today.

The Queen's Private Secretary, Sir Robert Fellowes, occupies the most influential position within the Royal Household. He maintains cordial relations with the Lord Chamberlain and his own previously successful career in the City enables him to see both sides of the argument. He knows how important it is to have an efficient, streamlined organisation as the monarchy approaches the twenty-first century, yet his instinctive feel for the conventional values of the Court will perhaps make him more cautious in seeking change. Sir Robert manages to disguise an inner toughness with the mildest of manners, but already, in the short time he has been The Queen's number one aide, he has shown a determination to be his own man that has surprised a number of his colleagues. He could well turn out to be one of the most successful Private Secretaries ever.

Whatever happens in the foreseeable future, the Royal Household will continue to be the unique organisation it is today: a blend of many disparate talents and personalities, a combination of privilege and protocol, snobbery and service, the occasional eccentricity and the overall dignity that characterises life at Court. Its members will exercise a remarkable capacity for hard work without ever appearing to do so. Below stairs will remain a world apart, and some of its staff will stay complacently out of touch with the realities of life beyond the Palace walls; while the secretariat, the men who organise the day-to-day running of the monarchy, will become ever closer to a totally professional meritocracy.

The Household is far from perfect. The Prince of Wales has been reported as claiming there are far too few black employees. He might easily say the same about women and Roman Catholics, though he has slightly improved the position with regard to females by appointing Belinda Harvey, a successful public relations expert, to be his Assistant Private Secretary. She is the first woman to reach this rank in the Waleses' Household and joins the Honourable Mrs Louloudis, Assistant Private Secretary to the Princess Royal, as the only two female Members of the Royal Household.

The whole business of race and sex discrimination in the Royal Household has been raised from time to time, and The Queen has been criticised for the fact that too few of her Household come from the ethnic minorities, or for not appointing women to positions of importance. The truth of the matter is that Her Majesty is probably the least racially conscious person living at Buckingham Palace. It simply would not occur to her to discriminate against non-white applicants for employment. Throughout her reign she has entertained men and women of all races, colours and creeds in her home and there has never been the slightest indication, even among her closest friends and confidantes, that she is prejudiced. It would make no difference to her whether a candidate was black, white, brown or yellow. If he or she was the right person for the job, The Queen would raise no objection. The difficulty would be in getting through the layers of top Household members, where old habits die hard and where tradition dictates that they seek colleagues among their own circle, very few of whom, it has to be admitted, are black. The argument that The Queen should set a positive example as Head of the Commonwealth, of which more than three-quarters of the population is not white, is merely another attempt to involve the Sovereign in a controversial issue – it makes good headlines. If she did go out of her way to appoint more blacks to her Household those same critics would immediately claim it was just another public relations exercise, so she cannot win either way.

Where women are concerned, it is a different matter. The Queen prefers to deal with men, as she has throughout her adult life, and she sees no reason for change. We are light years away from seeing a Lady Chamberlain as head of the Royal Household, or a Crown Equerry who likes to ride side-saddle.

However, the Palace is moving in the right direction, if rather slowly. Nor can it be accused of being over-manned. More people are employed in the White House Press Office alone than in the whole of Buckingham Palace.

If Queen Victoria were able to visit Buckingham Palace as it is today, she would see few physical changes from the Palace she knew – certainly in the State Apartments. On the surface the Court of Elizabeth II is as placid and unhurried as the Court of a hundred years ago. Underneath, the modern technology of the twentieth century has been adapted to cope with values that have remained unchanged for generations.

One thing of which Queen Victoria would be sure to approve is that under the leadership of her great-great-granddaughter, the 'Family Firm' is very much alive and well.

INDEX

Abel Smith, Henriette Alice, Lady 110
Abergavenny, Mary Patricia, Marchioness
    of 109
Accession Council 43
Adeane, Edward 13, 138
Adeane, Sir Michael (Lord Adeane) 13,
    136, 137–8, 139
Air Force Cross 76
Airlie, David Ogilvy, 13th Earl 1, 19–20,
    48, 50–1, 85, 228
Airlie, Fortune, Countess of 1, 57, 109
Alanbrooke, Alan Brooke, 1st Viscount
    34
Albert, Prince Consort 86–7, 133–4, 227
Alexandra, Princess 48, 108, 121, 154,
    192
Alice, Princess, Duchess of Gloucester
    105, 108, 121
Allison, Ronald 159–62, 164
Ancaster family 32
Andrew, Prince see York, Duke of
Anne, Queen 211, 221
Anne, Princess Royal: bodyguard 201–2;
    childhood 12, 26; driving 36, 111;
    engagement 159; Gatcombe 114;
    interviews 170; Ladies-in-Waiting
    108, 111, 112; offices 10, 46–7; Privy
    Council 43; tea-time 97; wedding
    160
Anson, Charles 47, 150, 167–9
Apothecaries 53, 83–4
Arbiter, Dickie 154
Ashmore, Sir Peter 89, 122
Assistant Comptroller of the Lord
    Chamberlain's Office 68, 94
Assistant Keeper of The Queen's Archives
    143
Assistant Press Secretaries 150, 153–4
Assistant Private Secretaries 39, 141, 150
Astell, Jane 169
Atholl, John Murray, 1st Duke of 221
Axe-Keeper and Butler 220

Baker, Sergeant-Major 'Snowy' 208
Balmoral Castle 81, 106, 121, 128, 130,
    196
Band of Gentlemen Spears 218
Banqueting House, Whitehall 197
Bargemaster and Watermen, Her
    Majesty's 55, 62

Baring, Lady Rose 108
Baronesses-in-Waiting 65
Barry, Stephen 172
Bath, Order of the 70, 74
Beard, Mr (Court Newsman) 151
Beaton, Chief Superintendent James 201
Beckwith-Smith, Anne 112
Berwick, David 92
Bigge, Sir Arthur (Lord Stamfordham)
    13, 138, 148
Black Rod see Gentleman Usher of the
    Black Rod
Blewitt, Julia, Lady 3
Blewitt, Major Sir Shane 3, 115
Blunt, Sir Anthony 187
Board of Green Cloth 33, 86
Boleyn, Ann 198
Booth, Reverend William 128
Britannia (Royal Yacht) 4, 40, 44, 89,
    100, 113, 118
British Empire, Order of the 72–3, 75
Brougham, Henry Peter, Lord 178
Buckingham, John Sheffield, 1st Duke of
    9
Buckingham Palace 9–23, 45, 53, 78, 98,
    102, 196
Burnet, Sir Alastair 169–70
Burns, Robert 222

Callaghan, James (Lord Callaghan of
    Cardiff) 39, 50, 69, 167
Cambridge University Press 194
Canterbury, Archbishop of 44, 60, 79–80
Captain of the Honourable Corps of
    Gentlemen at Arms 219–20
Captain of the Yeomen of the Guard 209
Captains of the Royal Bodyguards 35
Carnarvon, Henry Herbert, 7th Earl of
    126–7
Carrington family 32
Cawston, Richard 158
Central Chancery of the Orders of
    Knighthood 55, 67
Ceremony of the Keys 218
Chamberlain see Lord Chamberlain
Chancellor of the Duchy of Lancaster 121
Changing of the Guard 45
Chapels Royal 78–9
Chaplains of the Chapels Royal 77
Chaplains to The Queen 77

Chapman, Victor 166
Charles I, King 66, 80, 85
Charles II, King 212
Charles, Prince of Wales: bodyguard 204;
  childhood 12, 26; equerry 118;
  Garter 69; income 118, 119, 121–2;
  marriage 111; offices 29; Press
  Adviser 154; Private Secretaries 13,
  17, 230; Privy Council 43; Royal
  Mews 182; State Papers 134;
  television appearances 158; Thistle 70;
  US visit 171
Charlotte, Queen 9
Charteris, Sir Martin (Lord Charteris of
  Amisfield) 13, 136, 138–9
Chefs 101–2
Chief Clerk to the Crown Equerry 176
Chief Clerk to the Master of the
  Household 17
Chief Housekeeper 103–4
Children of the Choirs of the Chapels
  Royal 80–1
Cholmondeley family 32
Churchill, Randolph 31
Churchill, Sir Winston 26, 32, 137, 150,
  168
Civil List 3, 17, 116–25, 138, 174, 198,
  201
Clarence House 131, 156, 193
Clarence, Thomas, Duke of 33
Clarendon, George Herbert Hyde, 6th
  Earl of 50, 51, 85
Clerk of the Cheque 219, 220
Clerk of the Closet 53, 77–8
Clerk of the Records 68
Cobbold, Cameron Fromanteel, Lord 50,
  51, 52, 84–5, 114–15
Colebrook, Heather 103
College of Arms 32, 69, 70
College of Chaplains 77
Collingwood Ltd 75
Colville, Commander Richard 155, 158
Committee of Royal Warrants of
  Appointments 54
Commonwealth 146
Companions of Honour, Order of the 73,
  75
Company of Barber Surgeons 82–3
Comptroller of the Household 35
Comptroller of the Lord Chamberlain's
  Office 5, 34, 39, 46, 56, 197
Comptroller of Stores 176
Constable of Windsor Castle 53
Cooper, A. C., Ltd 195
Corby, Tom 157
Cornwall, Duchy of 17, 29, 119, 120,
  121–2
Coronation Day 32–4, 66, 168, 176–7,
  213, 218
Coroner to The Queen's Household 53
Court Circular 144, 151–2

Court Newsman 150–2
Coutts 115, 126
Crawford, Geoffrey 153
Cromartie, George Mackenzie, 1st Earl of
  221
Cromer, Esmé, Countess of 109
Cromer, Rowland Thomas Baring, 2nd
  Earl of 51
Cromwell, Oliver 116
Crown Equerry 6, 16, 39, 45, 89,
  175–86, 192, 229
Crown Estate 116–17, 121
Crown Jewels 62–4, 197
Cunningham of Hyndhope, Viscount 33
Curator of the Print Room at Windsor
  188, 194

Dawes, Charles 56–7
Dawson, Dr Anthony 82
Dawson, John Leonard 83
de Bellaigue, Sir Geoffrey 7, 187, 190,
  194
de Bellaigue, Sheila, Lady 7, 188
Defence Services Secretary 143
de Pass, Mrs Robert 110
Deputy Governor of the Tower of
  London 63
Deputy Keeper of the Privy Purse 228
Deputy Keeper of the Royal Archives 193
Deputy Palace Steward 96
Deputy Press Secretary 150, 153
Deputy Private Secretaries 39, 141
Deputy Surveyor of The Queen's Works of
  Art 188, 190
Deputy Treasurer to The Queen 189
Diana, Princess of Wales: bodyguard 203,
  204; children 81; family 2, 185, 198;
  income 118, 119, 121;
  Ladies-in-Waiting 108; menus 37;
  offices 29; press coverage 157, 171;
  swimming 98; television appearances
  158; wedding 185
Dickman, Cyril 227
Diplomatic Corps 45, 53, 55–6
Director of Finance and Property Services
  125, 228
Director of the Royal Collection 7, 89,
  187, 189
Disraeli, Benjamin 135–6
Distinguished Flying Cross 76
Distinguished Service Order 73, 75
Doane, Mr (Court Newsman) 151
Domestic Chaplains 77, 78–9
Dugdale, Mrs John 110
Dumbrell, 'Dougie' 157

Earl Marshal 31, 32–3
Ecclesiastical Household 53, 54, 77–81
Edinburgh, Duke of see Philip, Prince
Edward the Confessor, King 33
Edward I, King 214

Edward III, King 69, 82, 121
Edward IV, King 65, 227
Edward VII, King: Derby winner 29;
 income tax 117; Order of Merit 70–1;
 Osborne 196; Palace Concerts 227;
 private secretaries 147; Yeomen of the
 Guard 208, 212–13
Edward VIII, King 25, 51, 136–7
Edward the Black Prince 121
Edward, Prince 26, 43, 47, 157
Eisenhower, Dwight D. 38
Elizabeth I, Queen 30, 209, 211, 214
Elizabeth, Queen Mother: children 24–5;
 Clarence House 131; dressing for
 dinner 98; equerry 118; Garter 69,
 70; interviews 173; Ladies-in-Waiting
 108; menus 37; paintings collection
 193; press relations 154, 156; Privy
 Council 43; Royal Mews 182; Thistle
 70
Elizabeth R (book) 173
Elizabeth R (film) 170
Elton, Richenda, Lady 110
English Heritage 196
Epiphany Service 213–14
Equerries 176
Equerry-in-Waiting 55, 95–6
Everett, Oliver 103, 143, 190
Exeter, William Cecil, 8th Marquess of
 128

Fagan, Michael 87–8, 202
Fardy, Henry de 82, 83
Farnham, Diana Marion, Lady 109
Farrer & Company 126
Farrer, Sir Matthew 126
Feilden, Rowena 112
Fellowes, Lady Jane (née Spencer) 2, 141
Fellowes, Sir Robert: career 2–3, 136,
 141, 167, 229–30; Gorbachev visit
 147; income 17; informality 19;
 meetings 39; Order of Bath 70;
 Queen's appointments 48
Fellowes, Sir William 2
Finance and Property Services Office 228
Financial Controller of the Royal Palaces
 Presentation Fund 189
Fitzalan-Howard, Major-General Lord
 Michael 222
Fitzpatrick, General Sir Desmond 222
Forbes, Grania 157
Fortescue, Sir John 103
Francis I, King of France 198
Fraser, Flora 44
Friary Court Studio 192–3
Frogmore House, Windsor 189
Furniture Restoration Workshop 190–1

Garden Party Office 58–9
Garrard's of London 63, 75
Garter, Order of the 69–70, 74

Garter Service 215–16
Gatcombe Park 114, 201, 202–3
Gentleman Usher of the Black Rod 66
Gentleman Usher of the Sword of State
 54, 66
Gentlemen at Arms see Honourable Corps
Gentlemen Ushers 54, 65–6
George Cross 75
George II, King 79, 206, 221
George III, King 9, 115–16, 120, 134,
 150–1, 212
George IV, King 9, 134–5, 182, 223
George V, King: approval of Lascelles
 137; CH 73; Court dress 56–7;
 dressing for dinner 98; gratuities
 forbidden 99; High Constables'
 uniform 224; income tax 117; Lord
 Chamberlain 51; Maundy Service 215;
 Page of Honour 138; Press Secretary
 150; Private Secretary 13, 148;
 succession 25
George VI, King 24–5, 50, 85, 117,
 137–8, 148, 150
Gibbs, Lieutenant-Colonel Peter 46–7
Gielgud, Sir John 73
Gilbart-Denham, Lieutenant-Colonel
 Seymour 5–6, 45
Gloucester, Brigitte, Duchess of 108, 156
Gloucester, Prince Richard, Duke of 121,
 156
Gloucester, Prince William, Duke of
 105–6
Gold Stick for Scotland 222
Gold Sticks of the Household 222
Gorbachev, Mikhail 147
Gow, General Sir Michael 5
Grace and Favour homes 131
Grafton, Ann, Duchess of 108–9
Graves, Keith 165
Great Officers of State 31–5
Greening, Monica, Lady 4
Greening, Rear-Admiral Sir Paul 4, 46,
 87–90
Grooms-in-Waiting 54
Guards of Honour 206–24

Hailsham, Quintin Hogg, Lord 69
Hampton Court Palace 79, 182, 196–8
Harbinger 219
Hardy-Roberts, Sir Geoffrey 37–8
Harvey, Belinda 230
Haslam, John 150, 163, 166
Hassan, King of Morocco 165
Hawkins, Anne see Wall
Head Chef see Royal Chef
Head Coachman 177
Healey, Denis 73
Henry I, King 32
Henry III, King 82
Henry IV, King 120
Henry V, King 82, 120

Henry VII, King 52, 206, 214
Henry VIII, King 61, 79, 198, 209,
  217–19
Hereditary Grand Almoner 128
Heseltine, Sir William 136, 140–1, 152,
  158, 167
High Constables of Holyroodhouse
  223–4
Highgrove House 201, 202–3
Historic Palaces Agency 196, 197–8
Hobbes, William 82
Holderness-Roddam, Jane 112
Holyroodhouse, Palace of 46, 53, 182,
  189, 196–7, 199, 222–4
Home of the Hirsel, Alexander, Lord 39,
  70
Honourable Corps of Gentlemen at Arms
  35, 54, 218–21
Household Statutes 219
Hughes, Ted 227
Hussey, Marmaduke 111
Hussey, Lady Susan 110, 111

Imperial Service Order 74, 75
Information and Correspondence Section
  144, 152
Information Officers 155
Inland Revenue 117
Innes, Celia 112
Insignia Clerk 68

James I, King 209, 227
James II, King 215
Janvrin, Robin 141, 164, 166–7
Jarred, Anthony 37, 91
Joan, the Fair Maid of Kent 69
John of Arderne 82
Johnston, Sir John 54
Jones, Ronnie Gomer 157
Jonson, Ben 227

Kaunda, Kenneth 27
Keeper of the Palace of Westminster 32
Keeper of the Privy Purse 3, 113–32;
  Household bills 89, 104; Members'
  expenses 15; modern business practices
  229; Royal Palaces Presentation Fund
  189; staff 28, 39
Keeper of The Queen's Archives 143
Keeper of The Queen's Swans 55, 61
Kensington Palace 156, 197
Kent, Katharine, Duchess of 108, 154,
  156
Kent, Prince Edward George, Duke of
  69, 121, 154, 156
Kew Palace 197
Knight, John 159

Ladies-in-Waiting 107–12
Ladies of the Bedchamber 109
Lancaster, Duchy of 120–1

Land Agent at Sandringham 130
Lascelles, Sir Alan ('Tommy') 136–7, 148
Laski, Harold 148
Lee Kwan Yew 140
Leech, Major J. C. 58
Legge-Bourke, Shân 112
Librarian at Windsor Castle see Queen's
  Librarian
Lieutenant of the Honourable Corps of
  Gentlemen at Arms 219–20
Llewelyn-Davies, Baroness 220
Lloyd, Christopher 188
Lloyd George, David 117
London Gazette 68
Longford, Elizabeth, Countess of 173
Lord Chamberlain 1–2, 50–85, 229;
  form of address 19–20; Great Officer
  of State 31–2, 34; Office 29, 86–7,
  123; racing interests 182
Lord Chamberlain's Committee 54
Lord Chancellor 31–2, 34, 35, 44
Lord Great Chamberlain 31–2, 66
Lord High Almoner 127–8, 217
Lord High Commissioner 224
Lord High Constable 31, 34
Lord High Steward 31, 33
Lord Lyon King of Arms 70
Lord President of the Council 31–2, 34,
  35, 43–4
Lord Privy Seal 31–2, 34, 35
Lord Steward 33, 59–60, 86–7
Lords-in-Waiting 54, 64–6
Louloudis, Honourable Mrs 230
Lovell, Barrie 92
Ludlow, Robin 159
Lyons, J. and Company 37, 88

McDonald, Margaret 'Bobo' 19, 20, 142
MacDonald, Ramsay 50–1
Mackie, Philip 154
Maclean, Sir Charles (Lord Maclean):
  Chief Scout of Commonwealth 52,
  140; Lord Chamberlain 50, 52, 84;
  retirement 1, 76, 204; Royal Company
  of Archers 222; State Banquet
  etiquette 60; Swan Upping 62;
  wedding timetable 185
Maclean, Inspector John 204
Maclean, Sir Lachlan 222
McMahon, Colonel 134–5
Major, John 26
Mann, Lionel 37, 101
Mann, Very Reverend Michael 80
Margaret, Princess 25, 37, 98, 108, 136,
  156, 173
Marlborough House 146, 190–1
Marshal of the Diplomatic Corps 53,
  55–6, 109, 178, 222
Mary, Queen 24–5, 56–7, 98, 144
Mary II, Queen 26–7, 116
Master of the Horse 34, 175

Master of the Household 4, 86–106;
  Court Circular 152; Department
  footmen 11; meetings 39; menus 37,
  46; staff problems 226; staff
  recruitment 28–9; State Visits 46;
  wage bill 123; wine cellars 124
Master of The Queen's Music 55, 227
Maudsley, Piers 128–9
Maudsley, Sir Rennie 122, 128–9
Maundy Service 127–8, 197, 214–15
May, Thomas 85
Medical Household 53, 54, 81–4
Members of the Household 17, 18–19
Menzies, Sir Robert 141
Messenger Brougham 177–8
Messenger Sergeant-Majors 209
Michael of Kent, Prince 154
Michael of Kent, Princess 108, 154
Military Cross 76
Military Knights of Windsor 129, 215
Millar, Sir Oliver 187, 194
Miller, Sir John 16, 184, 185
Mistress of the Robes 34, 108
Moir, Jim 169
Monk, Roger 211
Moore, Sir Philip (Lord Moore of
  Wolvercote) 2, 13, 38, 136, 139–40,
  160, 172
Moore, General Sir Rodney 143
Morrison, Hon. Mary 110
Morrogh-Bernard, Major John 3
Morstead, Thomas 82
Munro, Robert 221

Nash, John 9, 182
Neville, Lord Rupert 17
Nicholson, David 36
Nightingale, Florence 71
Nkrumah, Kwame 139
Norfolk family 32
North, H. C. 151
Nunnerly, Mrs William 112

Office of the Lord Chamberlain see Lord
  Chamberlain
Office of Woods and Forests 86–7
Officials 17–19
Ogilvy, Sir Angus 48
Order of Merit 70–1, 74
Orders of Chivalry 67–8, 69
Organist, Choirmaster and Composer 53,
  80
Osborne House 196

Page, Her Majesty's 48
Page of the Backstairs 21, 93
Pages of Honour 128
Pages of the Chambers 93, 96–7
Pages of the Presence 21, 88, 93, 96
Paget, Sir Julian 65
Palace Livery Room 92

Palace Steward 18, 37, 88, 91–2, 100–1,
  227
Parsons, John 228
Peat Marwick McLintock 125, 187, 189
Peat, Michael 125, 228
Phaidon Press 194
Philip, Prince, Duke of Edinburgh:
  bodyguard 203; carriage driving 16,
  182, 185; consort role 133, 134; daily
  routine 38, 49; Garter 69, 70;
  interviews 170; marriage 26;
  newspaper tastes 11; Private Secretary
  17; Privy Council 43; Queen's
  appointments 50; Royal Company of
  Archers 223; spiritual guidance 80;
  State Opening of Parliament 60;
  Thistle 70; valets 92
Phillips, A. 151
Phillips, Captain Mark 114, 159
Phillips, W. 151
Physician to The Queen 82
Pinker, Sir George 81
Piper, John 193
Poet Laureate 55, 227
Ponsonby, Sir Henry 135–6
Poor Knights 129
Powell, Charles 71
Press Adviser 154
Press Association Court Correspondent
  156–7
Press Office 28, 49, 144, 149–74
Press Secretary 39, 49, 149–50, 152–3
Priests in Ordinary 53
Prime Minister 26, 44
Prime Minister's Private Secretary 142–3
Prior, F. J. 150
Private Secretary 2–3, 133–48; daily
  routine 38–9, 48–9, 60; income 15,
  17; offices 12–13; role 89; staff 28;
  wage bill of department 123
Privy Council 42–5
Privy Purse see Keeper

Queen's Archives 143, 193, 214
Queen's Body Guard of the Yeomen of the
  Guard 215
Queen's Bounty for Triplets 129
Queen's Box, Royal Albert Hall 127, 128
Queen's Commendations for Brave
  Conduct and for Valuable Service in the
  Air 75
Queen's Cottage at Kew 197
Queen's Flight 100, 113, 118
Queen's Gallantry Medal 75
Queen's Gallery 130, 188, 189, 190, 199
Queen's Librarian 103, 143, 187, 190,
  193
Queen's Pictures, The 194

Ralegh, Sir Walter 209
Ramphal, Sir 'Sonny' 27

Ramsey, Captain Alexander 44
Registrar 188
Resident Factor at Balmoral 130
Richard II, King 120
Richard III, King 61, 206
Riddell, Sir John 17, 48
Ridley, Matthew White Ridley, 4th
    Viscount 33
Roberts, Hugh 188
Roberts, Jane 188
Ross, Lieutenant-Colonel Malcolm 5, 46
Ross, Susie 5
Rothesay, Duke of 70
Royal Almonry 127–8
Royal Archives 143, 193, 214
Royal Ascot 178
Royal Bodyguards 35, 206, 218, 221
Royal Chef 37, 88, 101–2
Royal Collection 187–99
Royal Company of Archers 54, 221–3
Royal Equerries 118
Royal Family film 158
Royal Garden Party 88
Royal Gardens 131
Royal Household Social Club 21
Royal Household Staff 18, 19
Royal Library 55, 190, 193–4
Royal Mausoleum 127
Royal Mews 118, 123–4, 131, 175–86,
    189, 228–9
Royal Mint 75
Royal Palaces 55, 119, 125, 196
Royal Palaces Exhibitions Committee 188
Royal Palaces Presentation Fund 130,
    189
Royal Service 172
Royal Standard 10, 24
Royal Train 100, 118–19
Royal Trustees 122–3
Royal Victorian Chain 76
Royal Victorian Order 71–2, 74, 129,
    226
Royal Warrants 54, 115
Royal Yacht *see Britannia*
Royalty Protection Department 183,
    200–5

St James's Palace 29, 45, 79
St Michael and St George, Order of 71,
    74
Sandringham 79, 106, 121, 130, 196
Savoy Hotel 38, 121
Scarbrough, Roger Lumley, 11th Earl of
    50, 51
Scotland, Church of 81
Scott, Sir Kenneth 141, 167
Scott, Sir Walter 222
Secretariat of the Commonwealth 146
Secretary *see* Private Secretary
Senior Yeoman 215
Sergeant Footman 93

Sergeant Surgeon 82
Sergeant Yeoman 100
Serjeants at Arms 55, 67
Seymour, Jane 198
Shea, Michael 126, 162, 163, 164–6
Silver Stick for Scotland 222
Simpson, Wallis 25
Smith, F. 'Royal' 156–7
Smith, Inspector Paul 204
Smuts, Jan 73
Somerleyton, Lord 34
Sovereign's Escort of the Household
    Cavalry 213
Spencer, 7th Earl 198
Spencer, 8th Earl 185
Spencer, Lady Jane *see* Fellowes
Spink & Son Ltd 75
Stamfordham *see* Bigge
Standard Bearer 219, 220
Stanley, Sir William 52
Stark, Koo 171
State Apartments 130
State Coaches 176, 184, 185, 213
State Invitations Assistant 58–9
Steel, Sir David 164
Sub-Almoner 128
Summers, Bill 63–4
Sunderland, Robert Spencer, 2nd Earl of
    198
Superintendent (Deputy Crown Equerry)
    176
Superintendent of Public Enterprises 189
Superintendent of the Royal Collection
    198
Surgeon Gynaecologist, Queen's 81
Surgeons to the Household 83
Surveyor of The Queen's Pictures 187,
    188, 190, 192
Surveyor of The Queen's Works of Art
    187
Swan Upping 60–2
Sword of State 66
Sycamore Laundry, Clapham 104

Taylor, Sir Herbert 134, 135
Temporary Lady Clerks 58, 59
Thatcher, Margaret 71, 167
Theatres Act (1968) 53–4
Thistle, Order of the 70, 74, 223
Thomas, Ian 41
Thyssen, Baron Heinrich von 198
Titman, Sir John 18
Todd-White, Rodney, Ltd 195
Tower of London 62–4, 79, 197,
    216–18
Townsend, Group Captain Peter 136
Toye, Kenning & Spencer Ltd 75
Travelling Yeoman 100
Treasurer of the Household 35, 123
Treasurer to The Queen 126
Trestrail, Commander Michael 226

Trudeau, Pierre 73
Turk family 61–2
Turk, F. J. 61
Twining, R. & Company 38

Valois, Dame Ninette de 73
Vice Chamberlain of the Household
 26–7, 35, 39, 60
Vice-Marshal of the Diplomatic Corps 55
Victoria Cross 76, 219
Victoria, Queen: coronation 34; Court
 Newsman 151; divorcee ban 57;
 Gentlemen at Arms 219, 221; income
 tax 117; Osborne 196; Private
 Secretary 13, 133–4, 145; reign 30;
 relationship with Albert 87, 133–4;
 Royal Victorian Order 71

Waldegrave, William 111
Wall, Mrs Michael (*née* Hawkins) 107,
 155, 162
Wallace, Caroline 112
Wallace, Major Malcolm 112
Wellington, Arthur Wellesley, 1st Duke
 of 217
West, Colonel George 5
White Staff Officers 35
William I, King 214, 216
William III, King 116
William IV, King 129

William, Prince 111
Wilson, Harold (Lord Wilson of
 Rievaulx) 50, 69, 76–7
Windsor Castle 45, 53, 78–80, 83, 103,
 182, 189, 196–7
Windsor, Lady Helen 157
Women of the Bedchamber 109–10
Wood, Yeoman Allan 213
Wood, Sir Russell 172
Woodroffe, Mrs John 108
Wulff, Louis 157

Yeoman Bed Goer 206–7
Yeoman Bed Hanger 206–7
Yeoman of the Glass and China Pantry
 21, 94
Yeoman of the Laundry 214
Yeomen of the Guard 35, 54, 192,
 206–16
Yeomen Warders 208, 216–18
York, Archbishop of 44
York, Sarah, Duchess of: children 81;
 helicopter lessons 165; house 113;
 press relations 158; separation 167
York, Prince Andrew, Duke of: birth 26;
 equerry 118; house 113; Koo Stark
 171; marriage 111; press relations
 158, 171; Privy Council 43; separation
 167; staff 47
York House 156

BUCKINGHAM PALACE

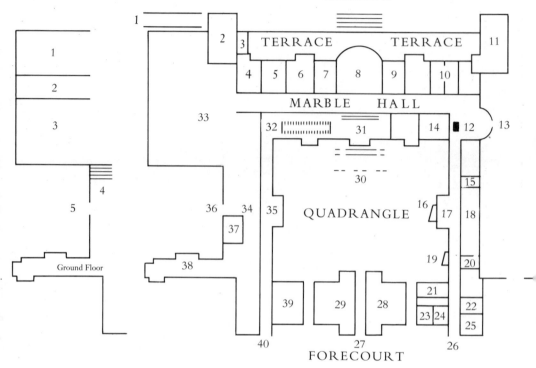

GARDENS

TERRACE   TERRACE

MARBLE   HALL

QUADRANGLE

Ground Floor

FORECOURT

PLAN OF
THE MEZZANINE FLOOR

1 Steward's Hall
2 Servery
3 Officials' Dining Room
4 Staircase
5 Ambassador's Entrance

PLAN OF
THE GROUND FLOOR

1 Public Entrance Corridor to Street
2 Queen's Gallery
3 Chapel
4 Queen's Cinema
5 Household Breakfast Room
6 Household Dining Room
7 55 Room
8 Bow Room
9 44 Room
10 Belgian Suite
11 Swimming Pool
12 Queen's Lift
13 Queen's Entrance
14 Lord Chamberlain's Department
15 Comptroller, Lord Chamberlain's Office
16 King's Door
17 Privy Purse Corridor
18 Privy Purse Offices
19 Quadrangle Entrance
20 Queen's Private Secretary

21 Press Office
22 Press Secretary
23 Deputy Press Secretary
24 Doorkeeper
25 Waiting Room
26 Privy Purse Entrance
27 Principal Entrance
28 Housekeeper's Flat
29 Superintendent's Flat
30 Grand Entrance
31 Grand Hall
32 Grand Staircase
33 Kitchens
34 Household Offices
35 Lower Corridor
36 Ambassador's Entrance
37 Stamp Rooms
38 Post Office
39 Pay Office
40 Visitors' Entrance